On the Road with

HILLARY

On the Road with
HILLARY

~

*A Behind-the-Scenes Look at
the Journey from Arkansas
to the U.S. Senate*

PATRICK S. HALLEY

VIKING

VIKING

Published by the Penguin Group

Penguin Putnam Inc., 375 Hudson Street, New York, New York 10014, U.S.A.

Penguin Books Ltd, 80 Strand, London WC2R 0RL, England

Penguin Books Australia Ltd, 250 Camberwell Road, Camberwell,
  Victoria 3124, Australia

Penguin Books Canada Ltd, 10 Alcorn Avenue,
  Toronto, Ontario, Canada M4V 3B2

Penguin Books India (P) Ltd, 11 Community Centre, Panchsheel Park,
  New Delhi - 110 017, India

Penguin Books (N.Z.) Ltd, Cnr Rosedale and Airborne Roads, Albany,
  Auckland, New Zealand

Penguin Books (South Africa) (Pty) Ltd, 24 Sturdee Avenue,
  Rosebank, Johannesburg 2196, South Africa

Penguin Books Ltd, Registered Offices:
Harmondsworth, Middlesex, England

First published in 2002 by Viking Penguin,
a member of Penguin Putnam Inc.

10 9 8 7 6 5 4 3 2 1

Photographs courtesy of the author unless otherwise credited.

ISBN: 0-670-03111-9

CIP data available

This book is printed on acid-free paper. ∞

Printed in the United States of America
Set in Minion with Weiss
Designed by Carla Bolte

For my fellow Boston Boys:
Steve Graham, Jack Murray, Sharon Kennedy, Paula (Thomasson) Scott,
and Lawry Payne (may he rest in peace).

ACKNOWLEDGMENTS

FIRST AND FOREMOST I WISH TO THANK SEBASTIAN STUART, BOOK doctor extraordinaire, writing tutor, mentor, and friend. His inexhaustible energy, skilled editing, and passion for politics turned an unwieldy and winding manuscript into the finished product before you today.

I also extend my gratitude to Candy Hanson, the first person to convince me the story and my presentation of it were worthwhile. Her time and effort in reading and critiquing several drafts of the manuscript were above and beyond the call of duty. My thanks to Barbara Rifkind, who saw the value of this project from the start and whose skill as a literary agent made it possible; to Helen Rees for her guidance; and to Jane von Mehren and Jennifer Ehmann at Viking, who made the editing process a pleasure.

Any project of this magnitude is possible only because of support from a wide network of friends, and in that regard I have been truly blessed. John Ciardi and Jim Sahakian used their considerable legal skills to keep me on the straight and narrow. Mo Cunningham and Mary Devlin provided a roof over my head and wonderful friendship during the several years I spent flying all over the world. Kevin Saba offered sage counsel at every step of the process. Steve Graham, Jack Murray, Sharon Kennedy, Paula Scott, and Melissa Graham experienced it with me and then helped fill in the details. Stephen McCauley lent his talented and practiced literary eye, and Jim King, the godfather of all advance people, convinced me that I should work for Hillary.

Finally, I thank Hillary Rodham Clinton for the opportunity to share her time as first lady and for the incredible sense of humor it took to put up with me for nine years.

CONTENTS

On the Road with
HILLARY

1

WHO?

September 1992

"HOW'D YOU LIKE TO GO TO NEW YORK AND DO A POLITICAL TRIP?"
Steve Graham asked over the phone. Steve is one of my best friends, a fellow Bostonian and a compatriot of the political wars.

"For who?"

"Hillary Clinton."

"Who?" I asked, incredulous.

"You know, Hillary Rodham Clinton, the woman married to Bill Clinton. You've heard of her, haven't you?"

"Of course I've heard of her, I just don't believe you think I'd want to get near her, much less do a trip for her."

The media attention Governor Clinton's wife had been getting was anything but flattering. Thanks in part to a couple of her own missteps, she had been cast as a prima donna, a militant feminist, and a political opportunist. She was developing a reputation for being shrill and unfriendly. I'd also heard war stories about her relations with her staff: that she sometimes showed up at events and then didn't go in if the arrangements displeased her; that once she fired staffers on the spot for no apparent reason. Plus she was the *wife* of the candidate, in political parlance a "secondary," and *I* worked only for "principals"—that is, candidates.

"Listen, Pat, I'm committed to helping out. You in or out?" Steve persisted.

"Steve, I have a great job and a nice apartment on Beacon Hill. I'm way too busy with my life to go chasing around after the wife of some guy running for President."

After I hung up, I tried to get back to work. As chief of operations for the Massachusetts attorney general I helped run the state's top law enforcement agency. A serious pile of paperwork sat there staring at me, but I found myself unable to concentrate. I couldn't get Steve's offer out of my head. This was a heady time for Democrats. After twelve years in the presidential wilderness and fielding losing candidates like Walter Mondale and Mike Dukakis, it looked as if we might finally have a winner in Bill Clinton. He was smart as hell, had charisma to burn and an empathy for people's problems that seemed genuine. His opponent, President George Bush, was so out of touch with real life that he didn't know what a supermarket price scanner was.

I hadn't been off the campaign trail for very long. I'd taken a leave of absence from work the winter before to run the primary campaigns in South Dakota and Hawaii for Paul Tsongas, a former United States senator from Massachusetts and a personal friend. But Paul bowed out after being trounced on Super Tuesday, and since then I'd settled more or less contentedly into my routine.

Steve's call upset my equilibrium. I stood up from my desk. Did I really want to sit on the sidelines and miss the most exciting presidential campaign in decades? Already my heart was pounding faster in my chest. Visions of filling a hall with screaming partisans, of setting up the perfect photo op, of running on an hour's sleep and cold pizza danced through my head. I was a political junkie, and Steve had just waved a fix—in the form of Hillary Rodham Clinton—in front of my face.

My addiction to politics started at an early age. Maybe it was something in the drinking water where I grew up. There's a small town in the Dominican Republic, San Pedro de Macorís, that has produced more than a dozen big-league shortstops. My hometown of Hudson, Massachusetts, is a lot like that but it's politicians, not shortstops, we export.

Hudson was at the time a sleepy town of about eight thousand people forty miles west of Boston. I grew up in a rambling old house my grandfather built and was known in town as Ferne Harrington's boy, notwithstanding the fact my mother's name was now Ferne Halley. My father was considered an interloper, having lived in Hudson for only twenty years. Dad worked in the La Pointe Machine and Tool factory at the bottom of the hill and walked to work every morning in his company-issue blue uniform.

I was a senior in high school when I got involved in my first campaign, helping out a former hockey teammate, Chuck Anastas, who was making a run for the town school committee. Eighteen-year-olds had just been granted the right to vote and Chuck decided to take on a forty-five-year-old incumbent. College protests against the war in Vietnam were inspiring a lot of people our age; we felt that we could change the world, that political activism mattered. Maybe electing some kid to the school committee in a small town wouldn't make that much difference in the grand scheme of things, but the raw sense of power we got from competing with the grown-ups was an eye-opener. I learned that if you want to change things, you've got to take action personally and that win or lose, people listen to what you've got to say when you participate in the political process.

Chuck's campaign manager was another eighteen-year-old named Bob Durand, and at Durand's direction I organized a large group of kids from school to go door to door collecting signatures, putting up lawn signs, and canvasing for votes. It was a lot of hard work but exhilarating.

Using persuasion both gentle and otherwise, I whipped my troops into shape, and we swept to victory on election day. I'll never forget the thrill I felt on election night as a group of us stood clustered in the dusty lobby of the old Hudson Armory listening to the vote totals being read aloud. Victory was ours! Anastas had won, and a small but passionate band of political activists had been born.

Chuck Anastas was at the time the youngest person ever elected to a municipal office in the United States, and he got a lot of press coverage. The stories mentioned his loyal band of followers, and we soon got a call from a young guy who was running for the state senate from our district. His name was Chet Atkins, and he was the scion of a wealthy family who was willing to spend a considerable amount of his own money to get elected. We met with Atkins and sounded him out on the issues. Satisfied he was in tune with the things we felt strongly about—such as opposition to the death penalty and the Vietnam War and support of abortion rights—we joined forces with his campaign.

Working from a beat-up old storefront office on Hudson's Main Street, we set about enlisting young volunteers. The thrill of our earlier victory had been infectious, and we capitalized on that energy to convince kids to give up part of their summer to help out. A lot of our volunteers were good-looking girls, whose presence didn't hurt recruiting among the boys, and after we'd snared the captain of the football team, the last of the female holdouts began showing up at headquarters. We hit a critical mass, and working on the campaign became the in thing to do. I guess you could say the Atkins campaign ran on idealism and hormones.

When our territory suffered an infestation of our opponent's lawn signs, we took umbrage, and one night Bob Durand and I decided to take matters into our own hands. We waited until well after dark and then went around town in a rickety red pickup truck, plucking the signs from front yards. We were making great progress and had the truck just about full of enemy signs when the flashing blue lights of a police cruiser appeared behind us.

"Uh-oh. We're in big trouble," Durand croaked.

"Just let me do the talking," I said as the officer got out of his cruiser and approached our truck.

"We got a call complaining about you," the cop said.

"Oh, I'm sorry, Officer," I replied. "I know it's a little late, but we promised we'd get all these signs put up tonight. I guess we'll have to knock off for the evening if we're making too much noise."

"Yeah. You boys go on home now. You can put up the rest of these signs tomorrow."

Durand just looked at me and shook his head.

Atkins won his race and shortly thereafter hired both Durand and me to work in his legislative office at the State House. At the age of seventeen I was on the state senate payroll. My initial duties included running errands and answering the phone, but I quickly progressed to helping constituents and then to writing speeches, drafting legislation, dealing with the media, and handling Atkins's reelection. I knew that politics was where I wanted to spend my life. I just wasn't sure what role I wanted to play.

A year and a half later I read a book titled *The Advance Man* by Jerry Bruno and Jeff Greenfield. It was the story of a working-class guy from Kenosha, Wisconsin, who had gone from driving a forklift at an American Motors plant to doing something called advance for President John F. Kennedy.

The book took me behind the scenes of big-time American politics: choosing events; getting them organized down to the smallest detail; making sure everything runs smoothly when the candidate takes the stage and the cameras roll. It was a sleeves-rolled-up bare-knuckles sort of world where you lived or died on your wits, where millions witnessed your triumphs and the slightest mistake could make national headlines, a world chock-full of adrenaline, fear, maniacal attention to detail, and over-the-top exhilaration.

I devoured Bruno's stories of screaming crowds, speeding motorcades, foreign travel, and the pomp and circumstance of the White House. It was a life as distant to me as that of a Hollywood movie star, but every bit as glamorous.

By the time I finished the book I had a new goal in life. But I was an inexperienced kid and not about to be hired by any national campaign. So I waited for an opening.

In 1978 Atkins was elected chairman of the state Democratic party, and he asked me to run the party for him on a day-to-day basis as executive director. I was twenty-four.

On the national level, Georgia Governor Jimmy Carter had been elected president in 1976, but his term had been marred by a poor economy and the Iran hostage standoff. He looked vulnerable in the upcoming 1980 election, and in the spring of 1979 there was rampant speculation that Ted Kennedy was going to challenge him for the Democratic nomination. My office was buzzing with excitement, fielding calls from around the country from people who wanted to help out. I saw my opportunity, and when Kennedy finally committed himself to taking the plunge, I attached myself to the advance team responsible for organizing his announcement. This was my first time in the big leagues, and I was a human sponge.

I quickly learned that campaigns for national office are organized into five divisions: (1) Administration includes the campaign manager, strategists, polling, issues research, advertising, and speechwriting; (2) Finance is responsible for raising and accounting for the money; (3) Media deals with the press; (4) Field Operations, usually the largest group, consists of the organizers and volunteers who put up signs, collect signatures, drop off literature, and canvass voters by telephone or on foot; and (5) Scheduling and Advance allocates the candidate's time, makes sure events go smoothly, builds crowds, and decides which sites will play best in the national media.

The last division was where I'd longed to be for six years. Now I was.

Within this society of national campaigns there are different species of political animals, each with its own traits and distinct culture. And just like out in the natural world, sometimes one species wants to devour another. The creatures most likely to be at each other's throats are the field staff and the advance contingent.

Field staff people, who have titles like state director or political director, take up residence in a state for the duration of the campaign. They tend to be methodical, workaholic, organizational types. Since presidential campaigns are really fifty-one statewide elections held simultaneously, each staff will have a specific strategy for winning its state.

Advance staffers are constantly on the move, living out of suitcases. The job attracts mavericks, hyper, creative, seat-of-the-pants types, who roar into town on all cylinders and expect everyone to get out of their way. Sometimes our mission conflicts with the field staffers' priorities. They're thinking locally; we're focused nationally. For example, they may think a senior citizen event will help boost the candidate's chances in their state, while the message of the day from the national campaign is the environment. The state director may suggest two events, one for each message. But that would mean that nationally the senior message was stepping on the environmental message. Sorry, gang, no senior event. Then, of course, egos get involved. In more than one campaign I've been involved in, the Field and Advance rift has become serious enough to damage the candidate's chances.

Kennedy's announcement took place at Boston's historic Faneuil Hall in late November 1979, and it attracted a huge crowd. I was fascinated by the level of detail; for example, the seating arrangements for the Kennedy family and important guests were negotiated for hours. I did what I could to help out, mostly running errands and helping direct the crowd. The announcement went well, and Kennedy's candidacy was generating a lot of excitement among Democrats, who perceived President Carter as being vulnerable to a challenge from California Governor Ronald Reagan, the presumptive Republican nominee.

With the announcement behind it, the Kennedy for president show hit the road. First stop: Iowa. I arranged with Chet Atkins for a leave of absence and prepared to head out to the land of corn and caucuses.

Before I left town, I checked with two older political operatives who had done presidential advance to see what tips they could give me. Frank Quirk was a grizzled veteran who worked in Atkins's state senate office.

"Frank, I'm going to take the plunge and sign on with Kennedy as an advance man. What do I need to know before I get started?"

"Paddy, here are the two most important things: First, never let them issue you a one-way ticket, unless you fancy being stranded in Timbuktu. Second, leave your credit cards at home, and never, *ever* pay for anything for the campaign. You'll go broke in a hurry, and you'll never in a million years get the money back."

The other guy I called was a former Kennedy advance man named Jim King, widely regarded as the best in the business. "All right, Pat," he told me, "I'll give you three things to think about. Most important, if you say you're going to do something, do it. Your word has to be your bond. No matter what it is, close the deal. That's the basis for your whole reputation. Next, always deal with primary source information. Don't let someone tell you the mayor has agreed to introduce the senator. Speak to the mayor yourself. Third, you're not truly an advance man until things get screwed up and you fix them. On the spot. A lot of people can plan a flawless event, maybe even pull it off. It takes an advance man to salvage a situation when things turn ugly."

I had a lot to think about on the flight to Iowa City.

Kennedy was going to be speaking in an auditorium at the University of Iowa with fixed seating for close to five thousand people. My assignment was to build the crowd. Those seats were bright red, and every one that went unfilled would look like a missing tooth to the press cameras.

I worked like a demon for twenty hours a day. One lesson you learn right away is that you're being paid to organize, not to do things on your own. For example, you never put up posters or distribute flyers yourself. The time it would take you to hand out fifty leaflets could be spent lining up ten people to hand out fifty each. The night before the event I thought things were going pretty well. I was ragged, my back was killing me, and I finally made it to bed at 3:00 A.M. I can't say I got much sleep; visions of empty seats kept dancing through my head. I had to fill that auditorium or my career as an advance man was over before it started.

The next morning I got out of bed to find the temperature at twenty below, not exactly ideal weather for bringing out a crowd. I went into the bathroom and threw up.

I joined the rest of the advance team and we drove over to the site, and as we approached, I saw a line of people four wide snaking all the way down the block and around the corner. My very first job, and I had delivered. I felt a surge of elation I remember to this day.

After a series of events in Iowa, I took a brief break for Christmas. One thing my friends noticed was that my time on the road had taken a toll on my attention span and patience level. I could carry on a conversation for only so long before I got fidgety and restless and wanted to move on to something else. In restaurants I wanted my food delivered to the table pronto, and I wasn't shy about letting people know it. I realized that this agitation was a by-product of the stress I'd been under, but I also realized that I liked the pumped-up, running-on-overdrive feeling. I had found my drug of choice.

Shortly after Christmas I was summoned to Langley, Virginia, for the Kennedy campaign's version of boot camp, Advance School. There were about a hundred hopefuls in my class, and we were warned that only half of us would make the cut. The course was rigorous and included a detailed explanation and analysis of advance work, as well as a simulation of life on the road that included sleep deprivation and being screamed at by instructors playing angry vendors and harried politicians. But I made it through. I was now officially a Kennedy advance man, just like my hero Jerry Bruno.

I did a few more events before the campaign started to unravel. President Carter got off to a late start, but the combination of a number of gaffes by Kennedy and a strong campaign by Carter soon had us on the ropes. The money dried up, and it became increasingly difficult to line up support.

I headed home, leaving the failing Kennedy campaign behind. I was now twenty-six, older and maybe a little wiser. I took a job in the private sector, working for a market research firm. After the excitement of the campaign it seemed like doing time in jail. Two long years later, I jumped at the chance to help a friend, Scott Harshbarger, who was running for district attorney of Middlesex County, just outside Boston. When Scott got elected, he asked me to help run the DA's office. I didn't have a background in law enforcement and wasn't sure it would interest me, so I told him I'd test-drive the job for ninety days. I ended up being chief of operations for the full eight years he was district attorney.

One advantage of the job was that it allowed me to take brief sabbaticals to help out on campaigns. In 1988 another Massachusetts Democrat emerged as a candidate for president, and I was asked to run South Dakota for Governor Mike Dukakis. I moved to Sioux Falls.

South Dakota is a large state, and I'd fly from one end to the other to avoid the long drives. To save money, I'd hitch a ride whenever possible with Senator Tom Daschle, who was a pilot and flew a chartered plane. I'd sit next to him, trying to disguise my anxiety, peppering him with questions about the state's politics.

Daschle was a great guy who really cared about his state and its people. Every summer he drove across South Dakota by himself, visiting all fifty-four counties, stopping at cafés and grain elevators to stay in touch and hear people out. On one of our long flights I asked him how many of his constituents he'd met personally. He was intrigued by the question and thought about it for a minute before answering. "There's a two-part answer to that question. The first part is: probably more than any other member of the Senate. The second part is: not enough."

Dukakis came out for a farm states rally, an old-fashioned barnburner of an event held at the county fairgrounds in Sioux Falls. We were trying to build a massive crowd and did everything we could think of to attract people, including offering free pony rides and hot dogs. The day before the rally I got a call in my office.

"This is Attorney General Roger Tellinghuisen. I think this rally you're going to hold tomorrow is illegal."

"Who is this, really?" I asked, incredulous.

"Giving away hot dogs and pony rides is voter bribery, and if you do it, I'll have you arrested."

"Did you go to law school?"

"Of course I went to law school! I'm the attorney general of the state. And I'm telling you I'm going to throw you in jail!"

"Listen, pal, this is just some cheap trick, and I'm not going to fall for it. Go ahead and arrest me. I'll sue you to the Black Hills and back. You got that?" I slammed down the phone and yelled to my secretary, "Get my lawyers in here!"

The attorneys soon arrived and advised me to cancel the rally. I couldn't believe it. I knew that both federal and Massachusetts statutes didn't preclude giving away hot dogs or pony rides, but this was South Dakota. A colleague from the Middlesex DA's office, Jim Sahakian, had come out to South Dakota to volunteer on the campaign. Jim was a wizard at legal research. I told him: "Jim, get over to the library and see if there's some bizarre state statute here that would make this illegal. If not, I'm going to have some fun."

Sahakian scurried out of the office with a legal pad under his arm. The media began arriving in force and were massing in the front room. I stalled them. My local barristers were still singing like a Greek chorus, trying to get me to fold the tent. Within an hour Jim was back from the library, breathless. Through the window of my office he flashed me the baseball umpire's safe sign.

I went out to greet the media horde, stepped up to the microphones, looked right into the television cameras, and made my statement: "Just because we're giving away free hot dogs and free pony rides at our rally tomorrow, the attorney general says he's going to arrest me. That's the rally at the county fairgrounds, exit seventy-nine off the interstate, and it starts at noon. There's plenty of free parking, and did I mention the hot dogs and the pony rides are free too?"

"Aren't you afraid of being arrested?" asked a reporter.

"Arrested? Are you kidding me? This is the most blatant attempt at political intimidation I've ever seen. I won't stand for it." I held my wrists out in front of me. "I've got something to say to the attorney general. You want to arrest me for giving away free hot dogs and pony rides at our rally at the state fairgrounds tomorrow at noon? Well, here are my hands. Go ahead and put the cuffs on. Because if you do, I'll sue. And when I'm done suing, I'll own your house and the statehouse too."

There was a moment of stunned silence from the press corps.

"Wow!" someone said. "Can we use that?"

"You bet," I answered.

When the cameras were turned off, I looked across the room and saw Jim Sahakian looking green around the gills.

"What's the matter? You gave me the safe sign."

"Yeah. But I didn't know you were planning to dope slap the attorney general in front of the media. I hope you like jail food."

The headline on the front page of the next day's *Sioux Falls Argus Leader* was: CHARGES OF VOTER BRIBERY, accompanied by a picture of me. Not a bad picture either.

The rally was a screaming success, drawing ten thousand people, at the time the single largest crowd ever assembled for a political event in South Dakota. I did take the precaution of rounding up five thousand dollars cash, which I gave to Sahakian to hold as bail money, just in case. But there was no sign of Tellinghuisen or his state troopers. I had called his bluff. In fact, a political columnist from the *Rapid City Journal,* making great fun of the state's top law enforcer, termed our skirmish the Weenie War, and Tellinghuisen wisely cut his losses and dropped the matter.

Dukakis got more than forty-one million votes that fall, more than any Democratic candidate since the Johnson landslide of 1964. Still, he lost to Vice President Bush by just over seven million votes. We came close, within a few thousand, but failed to carry South Dakota, and I went back to Boston and spent two more years at my job in the DA's office.

In 1990, after eight years as district attorney, Scott Harshbarger decided to run for state attorney general. I was the political director of his campaign, and after a tough fight to secure the Democratic nomination, he won a relatively easy race in the general election.

I made the move across the Charles River from the Middlesex County Courthouse in Cambridge to the attorney general's office in Boston, the state capital. That's where I was when that call came from my buddy Steve, asking me to help out with Hillary.

Steve Graham has been involved in politics all his adult life. He grew up in Dorchester, Boston's largest neighborhood, long a solid bastion of Irish Catholic Democrats, today a melting pot of every race and ethnicity. Steve's a big bear of a guy with penetrating blue eyes, the map of Ireland etched on his face, and a Boston accent so thick you can cut it with a knife. We first met, voice to voice, on the Kennedy presidential campaign in 1979.

I was stuck in some remote corner of Iowa and needed approval from headquarters for a plane ticket to fly to Chicago to do a rally. After I had gotten the runaround from several young staffers, my frustration reached the boiling point, and I screamed that I wanted to talk to someone who grew up in Boston. I almost reduced the unfortunate neophyte to tears, but a moment later a gruff, gravelly voice with a thick Dorchester accent came on the line. "Who the hell is this and what do you want?"

"Did you grow up in Boston?" I asked, just as gruff.

"Yeah. Dorchester. What's it to you?"

"My name is Pat Halley. I'm stuck in the nether reaches of Iowa, and I need a plane ticket to Chicago. All I've been getting is a bunch of bureaucratic double talk from the kids you've got handling travel. Either issue me a damn ticket to Chicago or send me home to Boston so I can get on with my life."

I heard a deep chuckle, and within ten minutes I had my ticket. First class no less.

"And listen," he said before hanging up, "next time you're in Boston, come in and see me."

Steve and I have been coconspirators ever since. All told, we've won a lot more than we've lost, and people often seek us out when they need last-minute political help.

―――――――――

The night after Steve's call was a restless one for me. I was definitely tempted, but did I really want all the stress, all the upheaval, all the hangovers? The term "political junkie" is not entire facetious. The mere mention of a campaign has been enough to make people quit their jobs, ignore their families, and start spending all their waking hours in drafty storefront offices in the hopes of electing some friend mayor or member of Congress. I've seen grown men and women act like the Dalmatian at a firehouse as it forlornly watches the fire engine pull out. The very thought that the truck will roll without it—or that the voters might actually make up their minds without their involvement—is enough to start them howling. It's not necessarily a strong ideological commitment, or even a paycheck, that lures these political professionals back into the fray. It's the heat of battle, the camaraderie of fellow campaigners, and the chance to experience that fleeting narcotic euphoria—winning.

But I had genuine misgivings about Hillary Clinton.

As soon as I sat down at my desk the next morning, I got a call from Jim King, the venerated Kennedy operative. "Pat, I'm going to get right to the point. You should do whatever you can to help Hillary Clinton."

"Did Steve Graham put you up to this call?"

"What does that matter? You know I never pass up an opportunity to have a chat with you. The point is I've been around a lot of these, and we've got a *chance* this time. And we've got a chance with somebody *really good,* Pat. These Clintons are the real thing. Don't believe all that nonsense in the media. Hillary Clinton is a fine human being. She's one of us. Her only problem is that she's saddled with an advance staff still in short pants. She needs the likes of you and Steve," Jim said, his voice filled with passion. Then, sensing from my silence that he had made the sale, he switched gears, and his voice turned to honey. "Now look, Patrick, it's only one trip, just a couple of days down in New York, then it's back home for you."

Jim King knew my breed. That one short trip proved to be enough to get me to quit my job, sell my house, and run away to join the circus.

2

COOKIE MONSTER

September–October 1992

AS STEVE GRAHAM AND I CLIMBED ONTO THE SMALL COMMUTER PLANE that was to take us to our first meeting with Hillary Clinton, I was feeling equal parts exhilaration and trepidation. I was back in the big leagues and Clinton was definitely the most formidable candidate to hit the American scene since Ronald Reagan, but there was always the fear that at any moment the other shoe could drop. Clinton and scandal seemed to go hand in hand. There had already been Gennifer Flowers, pot smoking, and accusations of draft dodging. Each revelation knocked him off stride and took time to address. We couldn't afford any new scandals this late in the game. There were only thirty-three days remaining before the election.

As we flew over the hills and valleys of southeastern Massachusetts at sunset, I could detect the first blush of autumn colors in the foliage and spotted a football team on a practice field far below. I was looking forward to meeting Hillary Rodham Clinton, so I could judge for myself if Jim King was right. I knew she was a successful attorney and active in a number of public causes. Her bio said she had been chosen one of America's top hundred lawyers the previous year. Until very recently she had been little known outside Arkansas. Then in March, after being pestered by reporters about her career and the prominent role she was playing in the campaign, she snapped, "I suppose I could have stayed home and baked cookies." Instantly she was a feminist hero, conservative pariah, and media star. These days lots of people were showing up to catch a glimpse of her.

Steve and I used the time on the plane to discuss the few details we knew about the trip. We had two days before Hillary arrived. She was coming to White Plains after an overnight stay in New York City. She was to arrive by train sometime late in the morning, stay a couple of hours to do the event we were putting together, then proceed by train to New Haven to give a speech at Yale. Our goal was to find a forum that would generate as much local media coverage as possible. This close to the election, the voters were really starting to focus, and it was more important than ever to get every event just right. The people at campaign headquarters in Little Rock weren't sure what kind of event they wanted, so they asked us to look around and make recommendations. I began to jot down a list of the things we'd need to do to get started, such as meet our local political contacts, get a list of the local media, and find enough volunteers.

We were billeted at a budget hotel, and for the chain's sake I hoped it was one of its worst. The seedy, dimly lit lobby had a gaggle of hookers seated on plastic couches behind a screen of dusty plastic plants. I shot Steve a glance. "Charming spot," I said, beginning to wonder just what the hell he'd gotten me into.

"Look, would you rather be in a fancy hotel working for the Republicans?" Steve shot back.

"It would probably pay better," I answered.

We moved our base of operations to the Rye Hilton, which had real trees and no hookers, and set to work.

Word had come down that Hillary wanted to do an "elderly event." In political parlance, all classes of people are reduced to event prefaces. You have black events, Jewish events, Polish events, women events, and so forth. Helps us focus. Since Hillary had Secret Service protection, we had to decide on a location quickly so the agents could make security checks. After a few site visits, we picked a senior citizen center in the nearby town of Port Chester. It was called the castle because of its turreted architecture, and it had the advantage of being across the street from the train station. We began working on the hundreds of small details that must be seamlessly planned and executed for a trip to work well.

When you see a political event on television, you probably don't realize how much thought and effort are poured into picking the site and making sure the principal looks good so that the event goes off without a hitch. For Hillary's relatively simple hour and a half visit to Port Chester to succeed, three of us had to work full-time for the next two days; when you figure in all the hours put in by town officials, the Secret Service, railroad employees, police, and volunteers, hundreds of person-hours would be expended before she even stepped off the train.

At the beginning of each workday, advance teams get together for a countdown meeting to discuss the trip. Everyone involved—staff, Secret Service, police, and volunteers—shares his or her information. We run through the schedule minute by minute to make sure nothing's been overlooked. Each team member gives a detailed report on his or her bailiwick—for example, what time the volunteers are arriving, which door they'll use, and where they'll be briefed. This level of detail is essential since you may find that the Secret Service will have a door locked for a bomb sweep or that someone else will be using the room you wanted. At the end of the workday, often close to midnight, the advance team meets again, this time alone, to recap the day and fine-tune plans for the morrow.

When Hillary's train pulled into Port Chester, a huge crowd was gathered at the station. We had filled the parking lot with schoolchildren waving small American flags, senior citizens, the local Democratic Committee, and everyone else we could round up. A Dixieland jazz band was belting out a tune, and Port Chester's entire Board of Trustees, including the Republican mayor, was on hand to present her with a key to the city.

Even though the castle was just across the street from the station, the Secret Service insisted on driving Hillary. I was waiting at the curb when her limousine pulled up.

There's always that moment when your specific portion of a candidate's trip begins. Suddenly all the focus is on you. It's your time to sink or swim, and the pressure can be overwhelming. Things were even more heightened this time because it was my first look at Hillary. Would she be the monster of campaign rumors or the warm, witty figure Jim King described?

Hillary stepped out of the car. The first thing I noticed were her bright blue eyes. She was wearing a green business suit, and I remember thinking she was a lot more attractive in person than in photographs. And there was no missing her charisma, her presence. This was a woman who commanded your attention without trying. She seemed very focused and eager to get on with the event.

"Good morning, Mrs. Clinton, I'm Patrick Halley."

"It's a pleasure to meet you," she said with a smile. If she felt any apprehension about the event, it didn't show. There was certainly no sign of an ogre, and she didn't even come close to demanding my head.

That late in any national campaign, the presidential and vice presidential candidates and their wives are like rock stars. Their faces are on television every night; they're surrounded by cadres of Secret Service agents and high-strung aides; crowds reach out to touch them. Some people have trouble living under that kind of pressure. I've seen principals become vain or churlish and occasionally even shy, drawing inward and shrinking before your eyes.

I could sense immediately that Hillary was a natural for the role. She exuded strength and confidence, clarity and purpose, yet somehow they all were tempered by a palpable sense of humanity. Her smile that day was unforced, warm, and sincere. It conveyed both friendship and appreciation. I knew instantly that Jim King was right: This woman was the real thing.

Her entourage consisted of five well-dressed, bright-eyed, intense females in their early twenties. Each had a specific responsibility, such as dealing with the traveling press or providing issue briefings, and they went about their duties with professional dispatch. I was very impressed.

I escorted Hillary into the building, and she took the stage to rousing applause. She spoke for a few minutes about why her husband should be elected president and what the folks in the hall could do to help the campaign. It was a standard stump speech, but she clearly connected with the crowd and won them over.

After the speech Hillary went to a holding room we had set aside and paused to catch her breath and drink a cup of tea. We had to get her back to the station on time or she'd miss the train to New Haven, and when she didn't emerge for several minutes, we began to worry. I decided to go in.

Hillary was finishing her tea as I explained our time pressures. As the staff began to pack up, Hillary grabbed a couple of pieces of the fruit we had laid out and stuffed them into her bag.

"Hey, what are you doing?" I demanded.

Hillary turned and fixed me with a bemused stare.

"That fruit is to be eaten here. You can't take it home with you unless you're at least sixty-five," I said.

The staff people stared at me in horror. There was an awkward moment of silence as they waited to see how Hillary would respond. She burst out laughing. "Can't you make an exception this one time?" she asked.

"Well, I suppose I can let you get away with it this once, since this is our first event together, but don't make a habit of it!"

I have no idea why I do things like that, poking fun at serious people in stressful situations, the urge just strikes me, and off I go. In this case, it really helped break the ice with Hillary and provided everyone with a welcome laugh in the middle of a stress-filled afternoon. Then I had them up and on their way out the door. My first advance for Hillary had come off without a hitch.

I left Port Chester with a very favorable impression of Hillary Clinton. Our encounter had been brief, but there was something about her that I connected with on a gut level. Love at first sight? Not that, but perhaps the political equivalent. She had a certain electricity about her, a star power that rivaled her husband's, and a sincerity and lack of cynicism that are all too rare in politicians. Besides, within a span of ten minutes I heard her both deliver a powerful speech and let out a genuine belly laugh. This was my kind of woman.

Having fulfilled my promise to Jim King to meet Hillary once, I was free and clear if I wanted to call it quits. But getting me off the campaign trail at that point would have been like trying to talk a dog off a meat wagon. I needed another fix, and when the phone rang three days later, I was off again, this time to Denver.

The campaign had planned a very busy day for Hillary, with two fund-raisers and a message event. Message events are events meant to make it into the media. Often they're the only thing on the schedule, but not in this case. The main reason Hillary was going to Denver was to raise money. Swanee Hunt, a Democratic activist and oil heiress from one of the richest families in the country, had put together a "million-dollar luncheon" aimed primarily at women.

Naturally you'd much rather have the picture on the front page of the *Denver Post* show your principal meeting with nurses than hobnobbing with rich folks at a fancy hotel. Fund-raising is a necessary part of the political process, but as we were to learn in the second Clinton campaign, people don't want to see it happen. Since you can't keep it secret, the way to minimize the impact is to give the media something else to focus on. My job was to find that something else, a political event that showcased Hillary's concern for issues that were important to the voters. In this case, I chose a message centered on health care services to minority communities.

I explored a couple of site options but ruled them out because I didn't think we could make a decent picture. Pictures on a campaign trip need to pass what I call the couch test. Someone seated on the couch watching television back home in Tampa or Tacoma should be able to tell where you are, what you're doing, and why it's relevant to his or her life. Pictures that require explanation don't cut it. Ours is a very visual business, and it's driven by the television set, the most powerful weapon in politics. As a result, no politician worth her salt ever stands behind a podium and talks about the need to stimulate economic development. She goes to the gate of the closed factory and addresses a crowd of union workers who have lost their jobs. You use the visual imagery to tell the story and get the point across.

A good rule of thumb is that the media are going to highlight the most interesting picture you provide for them. Those pictures of politicians standing at podiums yawning or caught in unflattering expressions are there for a reason. The photo editor is sending a message to a politician's advance staff: "See, if you don't give us something interesting, we'll catch your principal at an odd moment and make him look foolish." This game of manipulation is nothing new. President Franklin Roosevelt, confined to a wheelchair after contracting polio, would be brought into a room and placed at a table before the media or the public was allowed in. Very few pictures exist of him in his chair.

To make a good picture, not only do you need the site and the subject, but you also need to make it technically feasible for the press to get the picture. The distance, angle, light, and depth all have to work. In the advance business that means allowing sufficient space for the pool of photographers, building platforms for them to stand on, and providing television-quality lighting. In addition to your main photograph, you should provide another perspective, called a cutaway, to give the event depth. A good television report will change scenes and perspectives often to keep the viewers' interest. A photographer tries at all costs to avoid a single angle of one person talking. The "talking head" shot is considered the most boring thing he or she can produce.

Then there's the B-roll to consider. This is the videotape of the event that plays silently while the reporter or anchorperson talks. An advance person has to make sure camera people get some decent B-roll shots to add depth and interest. For instance, a story about a visit to a hospital might include a shot of the outside of the building, a nurse drawing blood, or a researcher looking into a microscope, all without natural sound, to set the scene for viewers.

A visit to one of Denver's largest hospitals looked promising. I met with the public relations director, who showed me around and explained the many services provided to the minority community. The family planning and prenatal care clinic looked interesting, and I grilled the PR person in depth about it. The program was right on message, and there were plenty of ways to make good pictures. I was about to call Little Rock to recommend that Hillary visit when I asked what is normally an innocuous question. "Is there anything new at the hospital? Anything that's gotten you into the newspapers lately?"

"There has been one small issue. The doctor who runs the clinic was charged with raping one of his patients. He hasn't been arrested yet, though. Do you suppose that would be a problem for you?"

I certainly did. My search continued.

I hit pay dirt at University of Colorado Hospital, a teaching facility of the University of Colorado. It had a nationally recognized neonatal care facility. We could make some terrific pictures of Hillary with the premature babies, and then she could talk to the medical students about the need to reform health care in America. This was a nice two-for since the television people would get powerful visuals and the radio and newspaper people would get text and voice from her talk.

With the site selected the hard work began. Who would greet Hillary when she arrived? Who would conduct the tour? How could we limit the number of people so that we got a "clean" picture of her and the babies, not a shot of her and twelve eager hospital administrators crowded around a bewildered newborn? Would our visit impose any health risks to the babies? What restrictions should we place on the photographers, such as making sure they didn't use lights that were too bright? Could we get photo releases from the parents of the babies? How could we assure that we filled the lecture hall with students? What steps could we take to be certain that protesters wouldn't interrupt our event? Any one of these hundreds of details, left unattended, could mean ruin, and that is why one of an advance staffer's most important qualities is being somewhat obsessive compulsive.

The day before the visit I learned that Tipper Gore, wife of vice presidential nominee Al Gore, would be accompanying Hillary. All our plans had to be adjusted to make sure Tipper wasn't shunted off to the side. I soon learned the Clintons and the Gores really did get along well; their harmonious relationship wasn't merely a public relations creation. The Gore staffers were helpful and cooperative, not always the case with folks in the second tier. We quickly integrated Tipper into our plans, making sure the press would get plenty of shots of the two women together.

Our visit ended up being a tour of the neonatal clinic, where the press was as respectful and well behaved as I had ever seen it; a tour of the prenatal diagnostics center without the press; and an address to an auditorium full of nursing students in a building across the street. By structuring the visit this way, we were able to get the press people positioned in the neonatal unit and then leapfrog them to the auditorium while Hillary and Tipper visited the diagnostics unit. That meant Hillary and Tipper never had to spend any time waiting for the press to set up, something I soon learned was of paramount importance to Hillary.

Many politicians like to go to a holding room as soon as they reach an event, to catch their breaths and get one final briefing. Hillary liked to get out of the car and go right to work. Unlike many political figures, she actually read and understood her briefing material and didn't have to depend on a last-minute shirt-cuff tutorial. The few times I saw advance people make the mistake of scheduling a hold on arrival, Hillary was like a caged cat. She'd want to know why we were holding and how soon we could get started.

Tipper Gore proved to be delightful, with a quick sense of humor and a very pleasant personality. A lot of people in politics have trouble being the second banana, often relegated to the role of introducing the star. Tipper managed with grace and dignity. After I saw the wives of our candidates in action, my confidence in the campaign soared. Not only were Bill Clinton and Al Gore intelligent and articulate, but Hillary and Tipper were as well, giving the Democrats four powerful weapons.

The reception the two women got at the hospital was extraordinary. Students hung a large welcome banner across the main entrance, and not only did we fill the auditorium, but we had a big overflow crowd outside. When they left the building, Hillary and Tipper paused to address the crowd through a bullhorn I handed them. The next day the *Denver Post* ran a front-page color picture of the two, Hillary in green and Tipper in red, surrounded by the enthusiastic crowd. The colors and the contrasts made it a very appealing picture, and it ran in other markets as well.

When all was said and done, our media package for the day was heavy on message and had great pictures of the neonatal unit and the crowd. There was only minimal mention of the fund-raisers and no pictures of people writing checks. We had accomplished our mission.

From Denver it was on to Columbia, Missouri, for a get-out-the-vote rally at Stevens College the day after Columbus Day. With less than three weeks to go before the election it was important to energize the Democratic base, and we planned to do a series of these events on college campuses, in minority neighborhoods, and at union halls. The idea was to get the troops charged up so they would help us drag every possible voter to the polls on election day. The campaign was going very well, and Clinton's lead was holding. The excitement was building to fever level, and it was reflected in the size and enthusiasm of our crowds.

Our handlers in Little Rock asked me to be the lead for this event and sent me a team of three, including another Bostonian, Jack Murray. Jack was tall, friendly, and efficient, with soft eyes and an easy smile. The only problem was that Jack couldn't say no. If you didn't keep a close eye on him, there would be a hundred people lined up to shake hands with Hillary. This may seem like a small thing taken in isolation, but when you looked at a typical day's schedule for Hillary and saw that she was doing four or five events, often in four or five different states, having a dozen extra people for her to shake hands with at each stop added significantly to her workload.

My biggest concern was building the crowd for the rally. The auditorium held eight hundred people, not a huge number, but I would count each empty seat as a glaring failure. It comes back to what we call the reality factor of news coverage. Basically it means that reality doesn't matter, but that what gets reported *does*. It doesn't matter how many people actually show up; if the media report that the crowd size was "disappointing" or show the deadly sight of empty seats, you have a failure. By the same token, if your crowd is described as "large and enthusiastic," it doesn't matter if it was made up of ten people dragged in off the street at the last minute. Success! The reporters working the event tend to keep one another honest since no one wants to have to explain to his editor why his account was different.

This is why good advance people will always choose a site small enough to fill. If you reasonably believe you can draw a crowd of a thousand, you look for a site that can hold seven hundred. You always want that margin of error. If you get the full thousand, you've got a jam-packed event with the coveted overflow that never fails to attract the media's attention.

To fill our eight-hundred-seat auditorium, we printed twenty thousand flyers and two hundred posters and recruited about seventy-five volunteers to pass them out and make telephone calls. We spread out and blanketed the Stevens campus, the University of Missouri campus, and the downtown area. We also called every student organization we could find and asked it to get out the word. As an inducement we offered preferred seating to the organizations' leaders. We taped radio spots advertising the rally and bought time on all the local stations.

One detail that I'd never encountered with male politicians was color coordination. At this event there would be three women on the stage: Hillary; Dr. Patsy Sampson, the college president; and the leader of the student government association. The latter approached me as we were setting up the hall.

"Mr. Halley, may I ask you one question?"

"Shoot."

"What color dress is Hillary Clinton going to be wearing?" she asked.

"I have no idea," I replied, wondering if this was some sort of joke. "Why do you ask?"

"Well, I just spoke to President Sampson, and she's planning on wearing a green business suit. Strangely enough, I was too. So I thought I'd better see what Mrs. Clinton's going to have on, so we don't all show up in the same color."

"Since green is Hillary's favorite color, I'd say there's a better than even shot she'll be wearing it."

"In that case, I'll find another outfit. Thanks."

It would never have occurred to me that this would be a problem. After all, what's the big deal if three guys appear in blue suits with white shirts? But clearly, at least to some women, this would be a fashion faux pas. I made a note to add dress color coordination to my list of things to cover for each event.

We filled that auditorium, and Hillary, as I was coming to expect, held the crowd's rapt attention. Like all political figures at this stage of a campaign, she delivered a set stump speech, but where she differed was in her ability to weave in two or three key local points seamlessly and make the crowd really invest in what she had to say. No matter how tired she was or how mercilessly the scheduling people had moved her around the country, she always found the energy to deliver a virtuoso performance.

By the time we got Hillary back to the airport and onto her plane, there wasn't much time left before our own flights. After a successful—or, God forbid, unsuccessful—event the adrenaline is really pumping, and there's a tradition of having a wheels-up party to take some of the edge off. This is so named because when your principal's plane takes off and the wheels go up, someone else becomes responsible for his or her well-being. It's a tremendous load off your shoulders, and it's amazing how glad you are to see her go, considering that a couple of hours earlier you couldn't wait for her to arrive.

We were disappointed to learn that the Columbus Airport didn't have a cocktail lounge and were about to give up all hope of our party when one of the Secret Service agents remembered we had passed a roadside store that sold beer. We hopped into the motorcade again and, with the agent leading the way with lights flashing and siren blaring, made it to the little store in no time. Goodness knows what the local folks thought when a half dozen people in business suits came screaming into their establishment and made a beeline for the beer cooler. They were probably even more shocked when we sat in the dirt parking lot next to a tractor trailer load of live chickens and toasted one another before roaring off in a cloud of dust to the wail of sirens.

Working for the Clinton campaign was like something out of *Charlie's Angels,* in which the three crime-fighting babes never saw their boss. None of us had ever been to Little Rock, and we had never met the people who called and assigned us our work. A mysterious voice over the telephone would say, "Go to Columbus and await further instructions," and off we'd go. The only muckety-muck from the campaign we had any regular contact with, or had even met, was Hillary.

The way the system worked was that Hillary's scheduler, Patti Solis, allocated Hillary's time. Patti would alert the advance office that a team was needed in this or that locale. The advance office would consult its roster of available people and marshal a team. The team would coordinate everything with Little Rock through the scheduling desk, which then closed the circle by reporting back to Patti Solis.

Hillary's "Boston Boys"—Steve, Jack Murray, Lawry Payne, Sharon Kennedy, and I, with Paula Thomasson as an honorary Bostonian—were different from the rest of the pool of more than four hundred advance people. We had been recruited rather than applied, we were considerably older and more experienced, we had never been to any of the campaign's training schools, and we worked exclusively for Hillary. We'd all come to the campaign at different times and under different circumstances, but we quickly bonded into a cohesive unit, trusting one another implicitly, building on one another's strengths, and collectively overcoming any weaknesses.

Steve and I had now been close friends for more than a dozen years. Some people said we were so different that it was hard to imagine us as buddies, but in fact, our personalities complemented each other quite nicely. Steve is an idea factory. He has a vast and vivid imagination and can conjure some of the most incredible political events you'd ever hope to see. But like a lot of creative people, he gets bored easily and doesn't relish the nitty-gritty work needed to turn an idea into reality. That's where I come in. If someone describes an event to me, I can figure out a way to make it happen, down to the minutest of details. Also, while Steve is somewhat laissez-faire about managing people, I tend to be direct and demanding. We both have a deep commitment to molding our people into a team and somehow never had a conflict deciding which one of us would be the alpha male at any given time. We just passed it back and forth, no ego involved.

Lawry Payne was a political junkie and a successful businessman. A graduate of Harvard and Harvard Business School, he owned a chain of frozen yogurt stores in Greater Boston and regularly left them in the hands of his brother-in-law while he indulged his passion for the campaign trail. Tall, with wire-rimmed glasses, a shock of curly black hair, and a trimmed mustache, he looked a little like a young Groucho Marx. He was meticulous in every aspect of his being, always dressed in custom-made suits and shirts, not a hair out of place. Lawry had two distinct personalities: his campaign mode, which was uptight, overbearing, and maniacal about the tiniest detail, and his off-duty mode, which was easygoing, fun-loving, and generous. Lawry absolutely loved doing advance, even though the pressure made him crazy.

Sharon Kennedy, in her mid-twenties, was a small-town girl from western Massachusetts, the former manager of a clothing store, new to big-time politics. She was a natural, smart and hardworking. She had a vivacious personality that reminded us all of Mary Tyler Moore in *The Dick Van Dyke Show*. In fact, Sharon even looked like a young Mary Tyler Moore. She always wore a turtleneck and was known to express her displeasure with an exasperated, utterly charming "Oh darn!" She was a perfectionist in everything she did, and we took to referring to her as high maintenance. Sharon had signed on with Hillary first.

Jack Murray had grown up in Boston's working-class Hyde Park neighborhood and cut his political teeth in Boston mayoralty races, a very fast track. He was in his early forties, over six feet tall, trim, with a pensive personality and a hint of vulnerability that was very attractive to women. Just about every woman he met wanted to be either his mother or his lover. Every guy wanted to have a beer and talk sports. He collected people the way some folks collect stamps and had a broad range of friends salted all over the world. His easygoing personality was a great complement to my sometimes rough edges.

Paula Thomasson, our honorary Bostonian, was a native of Pine Bluff, Arkansas. She had been sent to scope us out by the people at the Little Rock headquarters, who weren't sure what they had on their hands with the Boston Boys. Paula was an attractive woman in her early twenties, with light brown hair and caramel-colored eyes, and her southern accent and folksy mannerisms belied her extensive education, which included a year studying at Cambridge University. She was fond of jeans and cowboy boots and absolutely hated getting up before noon. But once we got her rolling she had enough energy to light up a small city. Paula was part of the same Arkansas clan as Harry Thomason (despite the different spelling of their names). Harry and his wife, Linda Bloodworth-Thomason, were television producers and old friends of the Clintons. They had produced *A Man from Hope,* the brilliantly effective short film shown at the Democratic Convention that had introduced Bill Clinton to the American people. Paula knew both Clintons well and had been on the campaign since the beginning. She was fed up with the inexperienced kids who'd been messing up Hillary's events and, once she realized we knew what we were doing, quickly became a great friend and ally.

So there we were, the Boston Boys, out there on our own, racing around the country working our tails off to help the Democrats capture the White House. And I do mean on our own. The Clintons are brilliant political animals, and when they saw we knew our stuff, they left us alone to do it. Still, looking back, I find it remarkable that we played such a significant role in Hillary's part of the campaign without ever having met our putative supervisors.

The scheduling desks, through which all information was supposed to flow, had a hard time adjusting to our style of operating. Hillaryland had three desks: Julie Hopper, Sara Grote, and Lucy Naphin. These three hardworking women put in ungodly hours and managed to bring consistency and professionalism to Hillary's advance teams. Their methods worked wonders when they were playing twenty questions with twenty-three-year-olds working on their first presidential campaign, but they came up a little short trying to put the leash on us. Our feeling was that we knew best what would and wouldn't work on our trips. We were on the ground, our information was fresh, and our instincts were finely honed. Anyway, no matter who made the decisions, we would be the ones to take the blame if anything went wrong.

Despite the friction between the Boston Boys and the scheduling desks, we survived because we produced. Our events got big crowds and favorable publicity and left Hillary happy. No one in Little Rock was going to mess with success, even if we drove them crazy accomplishing it.

My next assignment from the great unseens was to meet Steve Graham and his team in Dallas and help put together a visit to an early-voting program. Texas was one of a handful of states that were allowing people to vote before election day at community centers and other locations around the state. There were just nineteen days remaining until the election, and the state was about to kick off the program. Since a higher proportion of Democrats are working people who might not be able to get to the polls on election day, this was an important program for us to highlight.

The cabbie who drove me in from the airport was listening to the vice presidential debate on the radio. It was Vice President Dan Quayle, Al Gore, and Admiral James Stockdale, Ross Perot's running mate. Both the driver and I roared with laughter when Stockdale uttered his now-famous rhetorical question "Who am I and why am I here?"

Steve had chosen a community center in an African-American neighborhood. Hillary was going to address a small rally in the gym, then stand outside a nearby polling place shaking hands with the voters as they filed in, asking them to support her husband. When I arrived, I was surprised to learn that Steve and the Secret Service had been having a hard time getting cooperation from the Dallas Police Department. I should have thought that Dallas would be particularly sensitive to the security needs of political figures after the assassination of President Kennedy, but apparently they didn't view the visit of the Democratic nominee's wife as a reason for concern. When I asked the lead Secret Service agent about getting a truckload of barricades to use at the site, he wished me luck and told me he couldn't even get the police to provide a tail car for the motorcade. His counterpart from the police department, a captain who spoke with a good old boy Texas drawl, was just showing up for a meeting, so I confronted him directly. "Sir, I want a tail car for Mrs. Clinton's motorcade and a truckload of barricades for the site."

"I don't think that's going to be possible," he answered.

"In that case, I suggest the Dallas police just stay at home and we'll call Governor Ann Richards and have the Texas Rangers handle our motorcade and crowd control." Being from a law enforcement background, I knew such a threat would mean war.

"The Rangers have no business taking over an event in Dallas. In fact, they may lack the legal authority to do so," he said.

"Last time I checked they were the Texas Rangers, not the Texas *except Dallas* Rangers. They can damn well take jurisdiction away from your sorry little department if they have a mind to."

He glared at me. I whistled a little Irish tune. He glared some more. I smiled at him.

"All right, you can have your tail car. And I'll see what I can do about the barricades."

The first part of the event, the rally, was pretty straightforward and happened as planned. The second part, where Hillary was going to stand outside the polling place and greet arriving voters, was a little more complicated. There's a law in Texas controlling how close to a polling place politics can be conducted. Some of the local media questioned Hillary about whether or not she was too close to the entrance.

She turned to Steve. "Steve, did you measure to make sure we're a legal distance from the door to the polling place?"

"Yes, ma'am," he replied. "The election warden and I measured it yesterday."

"Well, it doesn't look like fifty feet to me," she said. "What kind of ruler did you use?"

"A Democratic ruler."

"In that case I'd better move back a foot or two," Hillary said with a smile, defusing any potential controversy.

The more I worked with Hillary, the more impressed I was. Many politicians are remote and inattentive to detail. Others become overwhelmed by the rigors of campaign travel and either require extensive handholding or have nasty streaks they vent on their staffs. Hillary had none of these drawbacks. She was bright and articulate and unfailingly courteous to all of us. We marveled at what a quick study she was and how adroitly she picked up on even the subtlest political nuances.

I was trying to contain my optimism about the final two weeks of the campaign. Clinton's lead remained substantial, and it looked as if we had an excellent chance of beating President Bush. Ross Perot's support seemed to be coming largely from Bush voters. Things appeared good, but having been involved with many unsuccessful Democratic presidential campaigns in the past, I wasn't ready to put this one in the win column just yet.

One of the key elements of the Clinton strategy was to make the Republicans fight for the South, a region Mondale and Dukakis had pretty much written off. By forcing the Republicans to pour resources into such formerly safe states as Louisiana, Florida, and Georgia, Clinton was serving notice that he really was a new Democrat.

Five days after returning to Boston, Steve and I were dispatched to New Orleans, where we were joined by Sharon Kennedy. There were just ten days left in the campaign, the last sprint. Our instructions, as was often the case, were vague to the point of being mysterious. As the lead, Steve had the most information, and it wasn't much: Fly into town, check into the Fairmont Hotel, and put together an event targeting Roman Catholics. Our local contact was Kathy Vick, the secretary of the Democratic National Committee and a powerful player in local politics. The word was that she hated advance people and could make their lives difficult.

By recruiting some of us old hands from Boston, the Clinton campaign was trying to cool the conflicts between local political operatives and Hillary's advance staff. Both Steve and I had extensive experience in field operations, and Sharon, Jack Murray, Lawry Payne, and a half dozen other Boston political operatives now working for Hillary were older and had experience on both sides of the Field and Advance chasm. We were sensitive to local concerns and went out of our way to make sure we left the hometown organization in better shape than we found it. Part of this was just simple bedside manner; unlike some younger advance people, we didn't play the brash cowboy-riding-into-town role. Part of it came from our actual political skills. To limit the resentment that some field staffers felt about the financial disparity (we stayed in hotel rooms and had rental cars; they often lived on pull-out cots in supporters' basements and took buses to work), I'd always try to give them a peace offering of signs.

Lawn and rally signs are like currency in a political campaign. They cost anywhere from a dollar to three dollars apiece, and everybody wants them. Field organizers never can get their hands on enough to satisfy demand, and whatever they can get costs them dearly from their limited budget. But for the advance staff, signs are a breeze. The last thing the campaign wanted was a sea of opposition signs at an event, so one call to Little Rock begat an overnight sign delivery. I made it a practice of ordering five thousand more signs than I actually needed and leaving them with the state director. This proved to be more effective than wampum and no doubt accounted for my popularity among field staffs.

We unleashed a charm offensive on Kathy Vick. Steve invited her to join us at the Fairmont so we could get a political briefing before we set out to find an event. We spent the next several hours spinning tales about Boston politics and dropping names of friends we thought we might have in common. Kathy regaled us with tales of the Byzantine politics of Louisiana and New Orleans and by the end of the evening had taken us under her wing.

After Kathy left us, Steve, Sharon, and I headed to Bourbon Street to get a feel for the city. As we walked through the hurly-burly carnival of the French Quarter, drinking beer in "go-cups"—marvelous invention, those cups—we picked up a local newspaper. Steve noticed that the Boston College Eagles were going to be in town Saturday to play Tulane. I saw that wild look in his eyes and knew he'd had a brainstorm. What about a rally at the Superdome? Why not do a tailgate party before the game between these two Catholic schools and have Hillary serve as mistress of ceremonies? It sounded crazy at first, but the more we walked and the more beer we drank, the more sense it made. By the time we crawled back to our hotel well after midnight it seemed downright brilliant.

The reaction from Little Rock was a little more subdued. "Are you crazy? You want to do a rally *where*?" was about as much as Steve got out of them before they demanded we come up with another plan.

The Superdome, after all, seats sixty-five thousand people, and they initially thought we were going to try to fill it for a Hillary rally. The general rule of thumb is that a political crowd costs about $2 per head to build, and they sure weren't going to give us $130,000 for our event.

Steve, to his credit, kept at it. He enlisted Kathy Vick in his vision and got Boston Mayor Ray Flynn to agree to fly down and make a public bet with his New Orleans counterpart, Sidney Barthelemy, over who would win the game. The stakes: five gallons of Boston clam chowder against five gallons of New Orleans gumbo.

Ray Flynn was one of a dying breed, a big-city machine Democrat who could turn out the white ethnic vote. He was a former college basketball player with thinning dark hair and a complexion that gave ruddy testimony to his well-known fondness for the occasional libation. A devout Roman Catholic, he was later appointed ambassador to the Vatican. With abortion a big issue in the campaign and urban and suburban Catholics a key demographic group in many swing states, Flynn was spending a lot of time campaigning for Bill Clinton at Irish social clubs, Knights of Columbus meetings, and union halls. He urged his fellow Catholics to get beyond single-issue politics and put their economic security front and center when they walked into the voting booth.

Kathy suggested we line up the Olympia Brass Band, a world-famous marching jazz band that had appeared in the James Bond movie *Live and Let Die,* and make it a real Hurricane City blowout.

We refined our pitch to Little Rock and managed to get it approved, albeit reluctantly. We would hold a pregame tailgate party outside the Superdome and encourage people going to the game to attend. We managed to find a plaza between the parking garage and the main entrance to the stadium, which funneled everyone going to the game through our site, all but guaranteeing us a large crowd. Now we had to secure permission to use the site and set up all the technical aspects.

We arranged a meeting with the people who ran the Superdome, a state facility. We were greeted about as warmly as General Sherman during his march to the sea. The meeting took place in a large conference room in the stadium's corporate offices. A conference table long enough for a small plane to land on dominated the room. Seated around the table were about twenty people, representatives from various city and state departments and from the Superdome itself. Way, way down at the head of the table, resplendent under a minispotlight, sat Angelo Chetta—"Mr. Chetta" to all assembled—the Superdome's vice president for operations. Steve and I were directed to lonely seats all by ourselves at the far end of the table, and I thought we'd need a telescope to see what was happening at Mr. Chetta's end.

We quickly got down to business. The atmosphere might charitably be called less than enthusiastic, and each and every one of our requests presented a problem to someone at the table. The stadium's money guy kept spouting prices, and soon we were looking at a budget approaching a hundred grand for our little rally.

I passed Steve a note telling him to stall and, feigning nature's call, excused myself from the meeting. I managed to find a telephone and called Kathy Vick. "Kathy, this meeting with Chetta is *not* going well. All we're getting is the runaround," I said.

"Those morons. Listen, Pat, give me ten minutes. I have a friend in the statehouse who might be able to break that logjam up," Kathy said.

When I returned to the conference room, Steve was still butting his head. Electricity. Oh, you want electricity on your stage? Let's see, that will involve two union calls and will cost you at least another ten thousand dollars. And so it went as we pressed them on every little detail. After about ten minutes a small man entered the room, cleared his throat, and said: "Mr. Chetta, there's a phone call for you."

"Boy, can't you see I'm busy?" Chetta thundered. "The phone call will have to wait!"

"Uh, Mr. Chetta, the phone call is from the governor. He's waiting for you."

"Well, why didn't you just say that? Excuse me, gentlemen, I've got to go take a call from the governor," Chetta said as he swept from the room.

We all sat there silently staring at one another. After a couple of minutes Chetta came back in, sat down, and told three of the men that they should stay. "The rest of you boys go on about your business, and we'll let you know how all this turns out," he said, before turning to Steve and me and adding, "Why don't you fellows come on down to this end of the table and make yourselves at home?" When we were seated within the same zip code, he smiled warmly and said, "Now what can we do for y'all?"

The sky-high budget melted as quickly as April snow, and within a half hour we had the deal we wanted. Our rally cost just under two thousand dollars.

The day of the rally arrived. Kathy had succeeded in getting the Olympia Brass Band, and they marched up to the plaza like pied pipers, drawing a crowd behind them. Sharon had heard about something called second lining and said it would make a great picture if we could get

Hillary to do it. Kathy explained that to second-line with the band was a great local honor that involved marching at the head of the band, twirling a parasol, swinging your hips with abandon, smiling till it hurt, and generally acting like a southern belle on speed. Being from Boston, we'd never heard of this exotic custom, but we were assured the crowd would get a real thrill out of it.

Even though Hillary had lived in the South for quite some time, she was originally from Chicago and had never heard of second lining either. When Steve met her plane at the New Orleans airport and briefed her on what we wanted her to do, she said, "No, I will not twirl a parasol and shake my hips."

The wife of a local congressman overheard the exchange and weighed in with "Oh, darlin', he's talking about second lining. That's a great honor. Now you just grab that old parasol, follow the bandleader, and shake it for all you got. You won't be embarrassed, and the crowd will just go wild."

Pleased with the massive turnout and anxious to see how Hillary would handle the situation, I was waiting on the plaza. All New Orleans motorcades are done with great fanfare—many flashing lights and wailing sirens—and we could hear Hillary's approaching from a mile away. As her limousine pulled to a stop and Secret Service agents popped out of the car and rushed to get into position, I told the bandleader to be prepared to handle it either way. The door of the limousine opened, Hillary stepped out, and the bandleader tentatively proffered the parasol. Hillary grabbed it, they struck up the band, and off she went in front of several thousand people, twirling the parasol and shaking her hips as if she'd been practicing all her life.

The next day the headline in the *Times-Picayune* read HILLARY CLINTON SECOND LINES FOR VOTES AT THE SUPERDOME. The accompanying picture was a classic.

Hillary left immediately after the rally, and for our wheels-up party we had been given the president of Tulane's box at the Superdome. It came fully stocked with food and drink, and we set about having one hell of a good time for ourselves as we watched the football game. The Boston College Eagles won, 17 to 13, but I'm not sure Ray Flynn ever collected his five gallons of gumbo. After the game Kathy Vick, Mayor Flynn, Steve, Sharon, and I decided to move the party to Bourbon Street. Steve had gone ahead and was waiting for us at a popular nightspot. As we walked down the street, Ray Flynn spotted an Irish pub and decided he'd rather drink there. I told him and the rest of the folks to go on in and I'd collect Steve at the other bar.

When I got there, I found a long line outside. I walked right up to the door and spotted Steve seated at the bar. He was facing the other way, though, and didn't see me. I told the bouncer that I just wanted to retrieve my buddy. He was a thick-necked chap with rudimentary social skills. He growled that I would have to go wait at the end of the line. I tried again to explain that I didn't want to patronize his establishment, that I merely wanted to extract my friend. He again insisted I go wait in line. Impatience got the better of me, and I began to barge past him. He lunged at me. I turned slightly, grabbed his shirt, and used his forward momentum to my advantage, tripping him with my leg and sliding him to the ground. As I did, two of his large mates appeared and attempted to join the fray. Fortunately they came at me from opposite sides at exactly the same time, so that by simply getting out of the way, I caused them to crash into each other and thus was able to add them to the growing pile of bodies on the floor.

Now I'm not that big a fellow, these guys were huge, and it was only a matter of seconds until they organized themselves to pulverize me. They had just sprung up from the floor and were coming at me when a voice boomed out, "I'm the mayor of Boston. There'll be no fighting here." Ray Flynn had appeared like a guardian angel and kept me from leaving some teeth in the French Quarter. I was most grateful, and back in the far more civilized Irish pub, I bought him a pint of Guinness to prove it.

3

HAPPY DAYS ARE HERE AGAIN

October–November 1992

AFTER NEW ORLEANS MY ROLE IN THE CAMPAIGN CHANGED. FOR THE remaining ten days I was shipped from one event to the next to tighten things up for the team already in place. It was a grueling pace, and often I wasn't in a city for more than a day—a frenetic, pressure-packed day. There was no official title for what I did, but my friends called it the whip—because I'd whip things into shape or whip the hell out of anyone who got in the way. At this stage of any successful campaign the happy-faced ideologues are gone. The hard-nosed political professionals take over and make things happen. It's no longer about political theory or broad-based strategy; it's about the ruthlessly efficient execution of your plan. I wasn't there to share good feelings with the advance staff about the marvelous policy changes Clinton would bring to the White House; I was there to make sure Hillary's events worked. At any cost.

There's one big problem with being the whip: You get whipped yourself. There's no such thing as downtime, regular meals become a distant memory, and sleep is a luxury you can ill afford. Probably out of pity, the campaign agreed to fly me first class everywhere I went, and I took full advantage of the wider seats, getting most of my sleep at thirty thousand feet. Still, it was never enough, and I was operating in a state of permanent exhaustion. I should add that I was having the best time of my life.

Hillary was scheduled to do two events in Scranton and Wilkes-Barre,

Pennsylvania. The neighboring towns are located in the bucolic Pocono Mountains, where Hillary and her brothers had spent their childhood summers. The area was predominantly Roman Catholic and crucial to us if we were going to carry Pennsylvania. The team in place included Paula Thomasson; Amanda Deaver, the charming, efficient, and very Democratic daughter of Michael Deaver, formerly President Reagan's chief political adviser; and Lawry Payne, the lead, who called the shots.

Hillary's main event was a rally in Wilkes-Barre, and the team had already chosen the venue, the F. M. Kirby Center for the Performing Arts, a real barn that had eleven hundred seats downstairs and another five hundred in the balcony. (My use of the word "barn" has nothing to do with the function of the building; in the advance world lexicon it simply means a large hall that could prove difficult to fill.)

While Lackawanna County was considered a second home to the Rodham family, it was also a place where the radical antiabortion group Operation Rescue was very active, and the campaign had significant concerns that protesters were planning to disrupt Hillary's event. I was sent in because of my law enforcement background; I had a reputation as someone who could minimize the odds of trouble. By this stage of the campaign virtually every stop included some form of organized protest from the opposition; its goal was to step on our day's message and throw us into disarray. It's hard enough to put one of these complicated events together when everything is going well, but when you have a group of people purposely trying to mess you up, life can get terribly ugly really fast.

The best way to limit your vulnerability to protesters is to have a plan in place to deal with them. Like the people planning the event, those planning the protest can't do it in a vacuum, so the first element is intelligence. Don't give your enemy any inside information. That means watching your communications, making sure you know everyone at each meeting, limiting the distribution of internal documents, watching what you say on cell phones, and refraining from discussing the details of your event in bars and restaurants. Also, keep your eyes and ears open. Find out what the word is on the street. Send someone posing as a volunteer down to the opposition party's headquarters with the assignment to sniff out any protest plans. Try to get information about any telephone trees—where friends contact three friends, who in turn contact three more—that may be operating. Check with the local printers about signs or banners that may have been ordered, and see if any buses, bullhorns, and sound systems have been rented.

Next, review your event to make sure every reasonable effort has been made to limit the chance for a protest to be successful. At events where the Secret Service is protecting the principal, your interests and its are parallel, and the agents are very helpful. Limit the exposure of the principal; don't have her walking all over creation. Provide a secure buffer of space between the audience and the stage. Use barricades, ropes, and stanchions to shield the principal from any surge from the crowd. Handpick the people who will be up front, and give them admission tickets, so that if someone unwelcome infiltrates, you can revoke the ticket and expel him from the event. Don't put the stage in the direct sight line of a door or window; doing so expands the area from which a protest could be seen by the principal (and increases the physical danger).

Supporters are your biggest asset in limiting protests. Recruit a group of people to hold friendly signs, so that if protesters do make an appearance, they aren't the only ones outside your event. Use the sheer size of your crowd to intimidate dissenters. If a small group finds itself significantly outnumbered, it'll be far less likely to cause any problems.

Finally, be prepared to respond if a protest does occur. Have a plan in place, and make sure everyone involved knows how to react. I always recruited what I called an etiquette squad. Less genteel souls sometimes referred to them as goon squads, but I objected to the term and pointed out that my people always acted with dignity and restraint, and while they could certainly be intimidating if the occasion called for it, I was proud of the fact that not one of them had ever been arrested. The makeup of the etiquette squad differed from event to event, and I always found it was best to have folks who were indigenous. After all, you wouldn't want to send a team of broad-shouldered teamsters into an event at a women's college, and you wouldn't want to send in the women's field hockey team to maintain order at a labor rally. My etiquette squads were given a thorough briefing and assigned specific responsibilities. I'd sprinkle them throughout the crowd so that there was always someone able to respond quickly but that they wouldn't be too obvious, all standing around in one place, looking menacing. Some would be armed with posters, signs, and even sheets to cover up any unfriendly signs, and others would have some sort of noisemaker to mask screaming protesters. We never advocated physical confrontation and always insisted that the etiquette squad act within the boundaries of the law. Sadly, but inevitably, things sometimes got a little frisky, but my recruits knew how to handle themselves. The etiquette squad for the New Orleans event had come from the longshoremen's union, and I'd heard rumors that they had been very adamant about defending themselves when set upon by protesters at the fringes of the crowd. I'm sure both Emily Post and the Marquis of Queensbury would have approved.

The task ahead of us in Wilkes-Barre, then, was not only to fill the barn but also to make sure it didn't turn into an indoor antiabortion rally. Amanda was working with the people at the local Clinton-Gore headquarters on crowd building, Paula was drumming up all the free publicity she could, and Lawry was reaching out to the unions, the local Democratic party, and any other group he thought could bring in a few bodies.

Our accommodations at the Holiday Inn appeared adequate to me, but Lawry wasn't satisfied. I later learned that this was an annoying habit of his, moving from hotel to hotel during a trip, but I went along when he said he wanted us someplace both closer to the event and less expensive. Since I was busy running around town, I didn't pay all that much attention to his plans. By the time I finished work and met the rest of the team for a late dinner, it was about 10:30 P.M. It was a chilly meal. Paula and Amanda were furious about the new accommodations. It seems Lawry had found an inn made up of converted old railroad cars located on an abandoned industrial spur. Lawry described it as something out of *The Wild, Wild West;* Paula, through clenched teeth, voted for *Psycho.*

Paula was being generous. My "room" was located about a half mile from the main building, right under a noisy highway overpass. The railroad cars were placed side by side, and those that didn't have paying customers were commandeered by exactly the kind of people you would expect to find hanging out in a rail yard late at night. Most of the exterior lights were burned out, and there were ominous shadows everywhere. It was the only time in the campaign I walked back to my room with my six-inch Buck knife in my hand. The inside of my room looked like something out of a 1960s bachelor pad: shag carpet, mirrored ceiling, vibrating bed. The cockroaches were a creative touch. Paula was so upset the next morning, even after we had agreed to move back to a real hotel, that she took pictures of her room to show her father how badly the Yankee boys were treating her.

My major concern about the event was that it was going to take place in a fixed-seat auditorium. That gave us a lot less latitude than an outdoor venue, where protesters can be drowned out more easily. All it takes to create a disturbance indoors is for one person to stand up and start screaming. My etiquette squad for the event was recruited from an unusual source. There was a delegation from the British Labor party in town conducting a study on the American electoral system. They had volunteered to help at headquarters, and I thought they were a sturdy group that seemed to be up to the task.

The Secret Service didn't usually require people going to Hillary's events to go through magnetometers or bag searches, but the folks in Wilkes-Barre didn't know that. I had my Laborites dress in suits and ties, and we set up tables at each of the theater's entrances. Everyone coming in was asked very politely if we could look inside his or her bag. The Brits were extremely cordial and careful not to identify themselves as Secret Service agents, but people saw these well-dressed middle-aged folks who had radio wires coming from their ears and made their own assumptions. No one objected to our voluntary search, and we managed to turn up three knives and a smoke bomb. The knives probably wouldn't have posed any threat, but just who do you suppose totes a smoke bomb to a political event? The folks with the knives were asked to leave them in their cars, and the local police carted off the fellow with the smoke bomb for questioning.

Hillary's plane was delayed because of bad weather, and she was almost an hour late. Boston Mayor Ray Flynn had flown in to offer his support, which was particularly needed at the next event, at which Governor Casey was scheduled to appear. Flynn kept the crowd entertained, speaking off the cuff for about thirty minutes and then leading them in singing Irish songs. Hillary arrived to a boisterous welcome from a throat-weary crowd.

We left Wilkes-Barre by motorcade and headed to our showdown with

Governor Casey. Robert Casey, a Democrat, was a devout Catholic and staunchly prolife. He was openly critical of Bill Clinton's prochoice stance, and unless we did something to blunt his criticisms, our chances of winning this key battleground state could slip away. Casey was scheduled to speak at the Scranton event. The campaign was sending Hillary into the lion's den. It was a Lackawanna County Democratic Committee fundraiser, and Hillary asked me to stick close by in case any of Casey's people tried to embarrass her. I spent the ride on the telephone checking for trouble. Ray Flynn spent it regaling Hillary with the tale he had now titled "The Battle of New Orleans," boasting about what a great fighter I was, but how it had taken his eleventh-hour courage to save my skin. I thought I'd escaped without any notice of my little French Quarter dustup, and here he was babbling about it to Hillary!

Our much-anticipated showdown with Governor Casey never materialized. As soon as he saw us arrive, he quietly excused himself and left the function. Hillary was greeted like a returning native, and not a word was spoken about abortion. Ray Flynn was reduced to introducing himself as my bodyguard and repeating the saga of my New Orleans fisticuffs.

As the campaign made the clubhouse turn, with less than a week to go, Hillary was relying on me more and more to make sure her events were successful. Little did I realize how much our bond would be put to the test at a monster rally in the small college town of Athens, Ohio.

The day after the Scranton and Wilkes-Barre events I arrived at the Columbus airport and was met by a campaign volunteer, a Little Rock architect I'd worked with a couple of times before. He drove, and since it was about an hour and a half to Athens, I tried to get some badly needed sleep. All I knew about the event was it was supposed to be huge. Steve Graham was the lead, and he was determined to build the largest crowd Hillary had ever had. I slept for about half an hour, and when I opened my eyes, we were deep in farm country.

"Where the hell are you going?" I asked.

"Athens," the architect answered.

"Well, this can't be the right way to get there. There's nothing but cows out here, and we're supposed to be doing a monster rally!"

He swore we were heading in the right direction. I closed my eyes to try to get some more rest. It was a fitful sleep.

Those of us on the advance teams knew we had a shot at winning this thing, but as odd as it may seem, in some ways we were out of the loop. After all, we were down in the engine room keeping the bastard greased and running, and we didn't know what the weather looked like up on deck. I was on my fourth wind, exhausted but focused like a laser. In fact, my focus was so intense I was scaring people. If I told someone the press riser needed to be moved, I didn't want to spend ten minutes discussing it, I wanted it moved. *Immediately.* People got the point. I was heading to Athens to tighten things up and make sure protesters didn't ruin the event, and that was exactly what I was going to do.

I arrived in town around noon and found Steve and the rest of the team. Sharon Kennedy was the press lead, Jack Murray was doing the site, and a young guy named David Beaubaire was our crowd builder. Athens, a college town, is home to Ohio University and has a population of nearly sixty thousand people, but it sits in the middle of nowhere. The nearest airport is a small regional affair more than an hour away in Parkersburg, West Virginia. The rally was going to be held on the college green, and we were counting on the school to supply a lot of warm bodies.

Steve's team had been there for a week and had done all the things you need to do to build a crowd: distribute flyers, hang posters, make phone calls. They were working on getting the local schools dismissed so kids could come to the rally, and they'd invited three local marching bands to play. Beaubaire had about two hundred eager and energetic students from the college helping us out.

We estimated we could attract between ten and fifteen thousand people if everything went right. Hillary's biggest crowd so far had been twelve thousand at a Kentucky rally put on by another advance team, and Steve dearly wanted to beat that number. The logistics of putting on a rally that size are a major headache. You have to worry about things like street closings, remote parking areas, shuttle bus service, emergency medical services, outdoor toilets, and hundreds of other details. You also need sophisticated sound and lighting. For this event we had ten sound towers spaced throughout the site. They were on delays, meaning that the sound hit each speaker at a slightly different time and created a much more natural effect by reducing echoes. Our press riser alone was about the size of an aircraft carrier.

Steve asked me to run the daily countdown meetings, at which every detail is checked and double-checked. At the first meeting I noticed this huge guy, about six feet seven and dressed in really funky clothes, who looked more like a lost hippie than an advance man.

"What's your role here?" I asked.

"I'm the fetcher," he answered, very serious.

"Fetcher?"

"Yeah, man, fetcher. You know, like when someone wants something from Parkersburg, I go fetch it."

Sharon was working her media magic, and we were getting a lot of play. By the time she was finished every man, woman, and child in Athens knew about the rally.

Since Beaubaire was college age himself, we sent him to infiltrate the opposition and see what it was planning. David had an innocent face, but he was from Chicago, and a Windy City wise guy lurked behind his cherubic appearance. By the day before the rally he'd so ingratiated himself with the folks at Republican headquarters that they gave him their signs to deliver to the protesters. Our event was going to be very clean.

On game day Steve went to Parkersburg to pick up Hillary at the airport. The crowd built nicely, and by the time I got word her motorcade was approaching, we had upward of eighteen thousand people on hand, and folks were still streaming in. We had set things up so Hillary would arrive at the back entrance of the student union, a long, low-slung building. We planned to walk her through the building and out the front, right into the rally. That way we wouldn't have any problem with people at the arrival point, and we had a safe retreat route at our backs. Because we were out in the sticks, our cell phones were all but useless, and we hadn't communicated with the motorcade. Hillary had no way of knowing just how big the crowd was.

I stood by the door as the motorcade pulled up to the back of the building. Steve hopped out of the lead car and rolled his eyes at me, his message unmistakable: Hillary is in a *baaaad* mood. The Secret Service opened the door to her limousine, she stepped out, and I immediately saw the tension and exhaustion etched on her face. She and her staff followed me into the building, and we began the long walk through the halls that would take us to the rally. Everyone was walking on eggshells. Hillary had been working like a demon, sometimes campaigning in five states in one day, and she was at the end of her rope. The last thing she had needed was an hour drive from some dinky airport to take her to a small-town rally. When Kelly Craighead, her trip director, offered her a ribbon to wear in support of some cause or other, she snapped that she didn't want to wear any ribbon. Then she indicated that she thought the rally was going to be a disaster.

"I can't believe you dragged me all the way out here to speak to a bunch of college kids who probably don't even vote. This isn't exactly the best use of my time," she grumbled.

We've got a serious problem on our hands, I thought. We've got twenty thousand screaming kids out there, and she's about to go out and scold them. As we walked the long hallway, my mind raced for something, anything I could do to improve the situation, and then suddenly I decided on a bold course of action. I stopped the procession and looked Hillary squarely in the eyes. "Hillary. Relax. You're with us now. We've taken care of everything. Nothing bad is going to happen."

She looked right back at me. There was a terrible moment when I wasn't sure how she was going to react. Then she let go. The tension drained out of her body, and she visibly deflated. She went from tigress to rag doll right in front of my eyes. I felt bad for her, knew she was on an emotional roller coaster that wasn't going to slow down until after the election.

She switched gears and even managed a small smile as we reached the lobby that led out to the rally. She closed her eyes for a second, and I was afraid she might pass out. I could hear the muffled cheers from the pumped-up crowd. I realized that I now had just as big a problem as I'd had three minutes ago, but this time it was the mirror opposite. If I let her walk through the door and onto the stage in this condition, she was likely to fall asleep on her way to the podium.

Again I stopped her and stared into her eyes. Only this time I also grabbed her shoulders and shook her violently. "Let's go, girl! There are twenty thousand people out there who came to see you! Are you ready?" I began hitting her shoulders like football players do before a game and bouncing her around pretty good. "Let's see some life here!! You going to let those people down? Or are you going to give them what they came for?"

Her Secret Service detail looked on in amazement, their expressions suggesting they were within an inch of wrestling me to the ground and slapping on handcuffs. That probably would have been a mistake right then, since I was in no mood to go gently.

It took a few blows, but Hillary finally responded, and I saw the spark come back into her eyes. The sun was coming out from behind the clouds. She threw her shoulders back and stood up straight, and her face just kept getting brighter and more alert.

"Okay, let's go," she said, and burst through the door and onto the stage. The next thing I heard was Hillary shouting, "Hello, Ohio!" The crowd responded with an earthshaking cheer.

And then things grew quiet, as they always do when Hillary speaks. No matter how big, rowdy, and restless her audience is, it seems to transform from thousands of individuals into one entity, leaning forward, listening. I've seen her do it many times, and it never fails to amaze me.

By the time she finished and came back into the building she was walking about a foot off the ground. The crowd was by far the largest she'd ever had, and she was feeding off its energy. "Pat, I want you and this whole team down in Little Rock for election night," she said. Then she went right to the nearest phone and called headquarters to have the necessary travel orders issued. This was a major reward because we'd been told earlier that each of us was going to be dispatched to some city to help get out the vote. We all wanted to do whatever we could to help assure victory, but by this stage we were pretty well fried. Sending us to some unfamiliar city to help with a field program that had been in the works for months didn't make a whole lot of sense.

She made one other call, to her husband, and we overheard her from the hallway where we were lurking. "Nah-nah-nah-*nah*, I had a bigger crowd than you! Twenty thousand people! Right here in the middle of Ohio!"

Sharon had corralled the police official working on crowd control and gotten him to agree on her estimate of twenty thousand. She then took him over to the press riser and had him give the number to the media. The old reality rule was in effect: It doesn't matter how many people were actually there; the record shows twenty thousand.

Hillary and everyone else were in buoyant spirits as we drove back to the airport. We were about a mile away when the Secret Service got a re-port that Spearmint's plane was about to land and that there was a crowd of supporters at the airport to greet her. "Spearmint" was the Secret Service code name for Marilyn Quayle, wife of the vice president. Since Parkersburg is a very small airport, we were bound to run into her welcoming committee. It was not a pleasant thought.

As we pulled onto the tarmac, I spotted my tall hippie friend Fetcher, whom I'd instructed to guard the airport, thinking he couldn't possibly get himself in trouble out there. He was standing with a big crowd of people waving Clinton-Gore signs. A closer look revealed that only the front row was holding our signs and cheering. The rest of them were holding Bush-Quayle signs and jeering. But from a distance it looked as if old Fetch had organized an airport rally. I ordered the motorcade not to slow down. When we reached the plane, Hillary got out of her limousine, waved at the crowd, and then started toward them. Steve and I both stepped in front of her.

"Hillary, you're running late," I said.

"Very late. You've got that big event in Detroit to worry about," Steve added.

Hillary looked from the two of us over to the crowd. I'm not sure if she saw through our little ploy or not, but she smiled, thanked us again, and got on her plane.

Our stock was rising within the Clinton camp. And I'd never been happier. This campaign was one tight ship: organized, disciplined, entirely professional. You had rules to follow and were held strictly accountable for performance, but you were treated with respect and dignity. Unlike virtually every campaign I'd ever worked on, the Clinton people simply didn't allow infighting. We had a clear enemy, and it was the other side. If you wanted to fight, fight with the opposition. Inside the organization we worked together and stood by one another. If you didn't play by those rules, you went home. The last thing I wanted to do was go home.

So I was very happy when Little Rock called the next day to inform Steve, Jack, and me that we would be needed to do stops on the final swing of the campaign, a frantic forty-eight-hour dash from one end of the country to the other. Headquarters had decided to have Hillary join her husband for this around-the-clock barnstorming tour, and we would be handling her end of three of the stops. Because the itinerary wasn't set yet, we were asked to go to Columbus, Ohio, and await further instructions.

I had requested the last stop on the tour so I could have the satisfaction of seeing the campaign through to the end and flying back to Little Rock with the Clintons. The final blowout was a rally in an airport hangar at Stapleton Airport in Denver at five o'clock in the morning on election day.

My role in the event was fairly limited since Governor Clinton's team was putting everything together. I had to review its setup, be prepared to brief Hillary on her role, and assist her and her staff with anything they might need.

The rally was timed so the morning news shows on the East Coast would have live pictures of Clinton wrapping up his campaign. It was held in a vast hangar with a United Airlines jet as a backdrop. Clinton's lead advance person had found a local band that consisted of nothing but drummers, each playing a different kind of drum. They weren't bad at all, but there was something a bit surreal about ushering a large crowd of people through the snow and into a drafty hangar at three o'clock in the morning accompanied by nothing but drums.

The atmosphere in the hangar was charged with anticipation. Many people had obviously stayed up all night and were giddy with a mixture of exhaustion and elation. Everyone sensed we were going to win this, and the crowd knew it was a part of history, the last campaign stop of the man who was about to become president-elect.

By the time they reached Denver, both Clintons were exhausted but relieved it was over. Governor Clinton had lost his voice. He gave it a brave attempt but couldn't manage much more than a hoarse whisper. Hillary was doing the speaking.

This was the first time I had seen them together, and only the third or fourth time I had met Bill Clinton. The other occasions had been political events in Massachusetts and at the Democratic Convention. I had a hard time focusing on anything except the notion that this man was very likely going to be the next president of the United States.

As they were shaking hands along the rope line, Governor Clinton turned to me and croaked: "Pat, my throat's killing me. Would you get me a diet Coke?"

I just stared at him slack jawed.

"What's the matter?" he asked.

"I can't believe you know who I am," I stammered.

"Of course I know who you are. You work for my wife, don't you? How about that diet Coke?"

I had become someone recognized on sight by the next president of the United States. Incredible.

Hillary meanwhile was using up her last drops of energy shaking hands with the crowd. She was physically beat, with the glazed look people get when they've been pushed to the max and then beyond. As she walked to the door of the hangar to get on the plane for Little Rock, I put my arm around her.

"Good luck, Hillary. Next time I see you you'll be the First Lady. It's been a great campaign."

She brightened. "It has, hasn't it? But I'm still *very* glad it's over."

My friends from the campaign were already in Little Rock when I arrived on the press charter, the first of the three planes in Governor Clinton's traveling entourage to touch down. Steve Graham, Jack Murray, Sharon Kennedy, and Paula Thomasson, exhausted from the rigors of the campaign but bucked up with giddy anticipation of the first Democratic presidential victory in a dozen years, were waiting on the tarmac. Also milling about in the cool morning air were a couple of hundred bedraggled campaign staffers from the warrens of the Little Rock headquarters, looking as if they were seeing daylight for the first time in months, and battle-hardened road warriors from the advance ranks. An electric tension ran through the crowd as a public-address announcer reported that the plane carrying "the next president of the United States" was on final approach. The tight security did nothing to dampen the festive, carnival air. This day had been a long time coming; we had earned our exhilaration.

I was standing next to fellow advance person Julie Hopper and a young girl with curly red hair as we scanned the sky for a glimpse of the approaching jet. A small twin-engine plane ducked in below the cloud cover and lined up its approach.

"Here comes Chelsea on her charter," I announced to laughter all around.

The kid with Julie said, "Oh, that's *my* plane, is it?"

I turned, startled.

"Chelsea?" I managed to say.

"That's me," the gangly twelve-year-old answered.

"I'm Patrick Halley. I work for your mom."

"You must be tired," she said with a smile.

"But it's a good tired."

"There it is!" Chelsea said excitedly, pointing up to the sky.

The Clinton campaign plane taxied to a stop and disgorged its weary but triumphant passengers. Chelsea rushed forward to join her parents, the nearly mute Bill Clinton and Hillary, the woman who had come to mean so much to us over the course of the campaign.

Now all we could do was wait. Little Rock was a town possessed. All downtown had been cordoned off for a celebration, and there was a massive media presence. Block after block was jammed with television satellite trucks, and portable power generators hummed as technicians added to the miles of thick black cable already cluttering the ground.

We finally got to meet the people from the Clinton campaign headquarters who until then had been only voices over the telephone. The headquarters was located in the old *Little Rock Gazette* building. Steve and I were standing in a parking lot across the street, waiting in line to get housing vouchers, when a short, rotund woman in her forties approached. "I recognize those Boston accents!" she squealed. "Steve Graham and Pat Halley! I'm Isabelle. Say something more so I can figure out which of you is which."

I stuck out my hand. "I'm Pat, so you can figure out who this big guy is. Nice to finally meet you."

She grabbed my hand and then wrapped me up in a hug. "You guys saved my job! Things were getting rough for a while there, and you came in and smoothed out Hillary's events. I don't know how to thank you."

Inside headquarters we found the corner designated "Hillaryland" and met Patti Solis, the scheduler, an attractive young Mexican American with shoulder-length black hair; Lucy Naphin and Sara Grote, the hardworking scheduling desk coordinators; and Hillary's chief of staff, Maggie Williams.

We all had a hell of a laugh for ourselves when Maggie, an African

American, first clapped eyes on Steve. She took a long look at him and exclaimed: "Steve Graham! You're a white guy! I'll be damned!"

Steve looked at her, puzzled.

"I've been sending you to do all our black events. You put on half a dozen rallies in black communities. I thought you were a brother!"

He laughed and said: "That explains a lot. I just thought you knew I was addicted to good barbecue."

We went to a place named Yo Mamma's for lunch and sat in cinderblock splendor, eating cheeseburgers and drinking Budweiser from long-necked bottles. Bliss. The place was full of prominent people from the campaign, and we joined James Carville, George Stephanopoulos, Paul Begala, and others who were nervously pushing food around their plates as the wait dragged on.

By midafternoon, exit polls were confirming that Bill Clinton was going to be the next leader of the free world. The Boston Boys stood outside the War Room at the fringes of Hillaryland and compared notes on how the election was faring in various states. The three o'clock exit polls had us solidly ahead in Illinois and Arkansas, winning a large number of states by decent margins, and leading in Ohio, Pennsylvania, and Georgia, all key states targeted by the campaign. Tied in Florida at 41 percent each and holding President Bush to a 39 percent draw in his home state of Texas, we were closing in on the holy grail of American politics.

The campaign had rented every hotel room for miles around to accommodate the hundreds of staffers pouring into Little Rock. Advance teams were assigned to the Markham Inn, a threadbare motel on the outskirts of town. We immediately overwhelmed the place like a horde of invading Mongols. Those of us on the payroll were bunked two to a room, but so many volunteers had made it to Little Rock that most rooms had six or more occupants. The telephone system was swamped with calls from across the country, and the inn's limited supply of spare beds and linen was quickly exhausted.

Having four hundred tightly wound advance people, all with type A personalities in full adrenaline-pump mode, descend upon your establishment is a hotelier's worst nightmare. The poor folks at the Markham basically gave up and sat back, hoping we wouldn't do too much damage. Within an hour someone from our ranks ordered several dozen folding cots from a rental center, someone else called the linen supplier and had a truckload of clean sheets and towels delivered, while a third was manning the hotel switchboard. These were the kind of emergency measures we were used to taking on the road. Never complain, take action. The owners took all this in relatively good humor, but I'm sure they locked their daughters in a safe place.

By nightfall the Little Rock sky was glowing with the surreal ambience of television lights, the crowds were thickening, and the partying was intensifying. Downtown was flooded with people watching the network election coverage, cheering each new development.

By the time President Bush called to concede, the downtown area was so packed with people you practically couldn't move. President-elect Clinton was going to address the crowd from the steps of the old statehouse, about twenty-five yards from the Excelsior Hotel, where we were attending a party thrown by our New Orleans friend Kathy Vick. We had tickets to admit us to the lawn of the statehouse, and I stepped out a side door of the hotel and tried to make my way. I'm very experienced at moving through crowds and know all the little secrets about how to maneuver through tight spaces, but this was different. After what seemed like a half hour of almost fruitless effort I found myself about halfway there, standing near the fence that protected the press riser.

Suddenly I spotted Fetcher, my six-foot-seven-inch hippie friend from Athens, standing near me in the crowd. I enlisted him in a plan to get us both to a place where we could see Clinton's speech. Using his superior size and a lot of apologies, he was able to move us to the edge of the press area by telling people I was a United States senator. I spotted a TV crew that had been with me on the press charter that morning and waved. They waved back, and I shouted that I would be there in a minute to do my "interview." The security staff then gingerly lifted me and Fetcher over the fence and helped us up onto the platform. We had the best view in the house when the Clintons took the stage.

I remember thinking, as the President-elect spoke, with Hillary and Chelsea at his side, that the Clinton family was entering another realm of existence. Ironically, now that they were about to become the most powerful and famous family in the world, they looked more vulnerable to me than they ever had before. I'd read enough history and political biographies to know that no family escapes from the White House unscathed. Ideals, dreams, careers, and friendships perish. The Clintons were claiming their prize, one they'd worked for many years to win. And while I rejoiced at their victory, part of me was sad because I knew what a human toll the presidency would take on these very decent people.

4

NUNSENSE

February–April 1993

THE DAYS AFTER A CAMPAIGN ENDS ARE DIFFICULT FOR A POLITICAL junkie. Cold turkey is tough. Your body goes into a kind of shock, as if you've been running as fast as you can and *suddenly you stop*! Life loses its immediacy and vibrancy. Gone is the sense that at any second something momentous—either in your favor or against it—could happen. Your band of comrades, with whom you've formed bonds tempered under fire, dissolves and drifts apart. After you recover from the exhaustion and re-connect with your friends and family, life can begin to seem pretty boring. Make that *very* boring. You're not shaping history anymore; you're taking out the trash. Maybe the most depressing realization is that for the fore-seeable future you're going to be drinking your coffee from the same cup every morning.

Of course, after a winning campaign the withdrawal is cushioned by the afterglow of victory. We spent the days immediately after Clinton's election in Little Rock celebrating at a host of parties. These ranged from small dinners with folks we'd worked closely with to rowdy bashes with hundreds of people. At one, a small dinner party at Paula Thomasson's cousin Patsy's house, Hillary's trip director, Kelly Craighead, was com-plaining that a young man she'd met on the campaign trail, a handsome medical student from New York, was unable to afford a plane ticket to join the fun. Kelly was a tall California blonde, a former gymnast with dazzling blue eyes and a smile that could make you forget a New England winter. She was in her early twenties, sharp, and intelligent and had a presence that belied her youth and beauty. When things started to get out of hand in any aspect of Hillary's travel, as they inevitably did, Kelly reacted like a marine boot camp sergeant and straightened out the problems right away, with Hillary's well-being always foremost in her mind. Steve and I took pity on Kelly's plight and began a collection to fly the young lad down to Arkansas. People donated cheerfully, with some wag dubbing our noble efforts the Kelly Fun Fund.

The parties culminated with a blowout hosted by the President-elect and Hillary at a mammoth dance hall outside Little Rock. It was the type of joint where good ol' boys in beat-up cowboy hats drink beer directly from the pitcher while college kids who wouldn't know a cow from a zebra try, often with hilarious results, to ride a mechanical bull. A real clash of cultures, exactly the kind of place Bill Clinton enjoyed.

Hillaryland gathered in a back room, and Hillary joined us. It had only been a couple of days since the campaign had ended and the election had been won, but already she was a new woman. The bags under her eyes were noticeably smaller, and the tenseness and rigidity that had marked her posture in the final days of the battle were gone. She still looked as if she would appreciate a weeklong sleep, but her spirits were buoyed. It had been a long road for this independent, fiercely bright girl from the suburbs of Chicago, but she and her husband had snatched the White House from a Republican party that thought it had a permanent lock on the place. The confidence that comes with victory was evident in the tilt of her head, the set of her mouth, the assurance of her gaze. She worked her way through the crowd and then climbed onto a makeshift stage. The room quieted.

"Wow. First, I just want to thank you all from the bottom of my heart. Without your efforts, your commitment, your long, *long* hours we couldn't have done it. This victory belongs to all of us. Bill and I want to thank each and every one of you.

"And what a long strange trip it's been. I remember those freezing mornings in New Hampshire when Todd would pick me up at the hotel at five A.M. for a two-hour drive to some tiny town. It was my job to read the map, and when we'd stop at the gas station, I'd go buy the coffee while

Todd pumped the gas. Thank goodness I was relieved of my map-reading duties when we could finally afford a campaign plane.

"Then we started to pick up steam, and you all showed up in my life and began turning everything I did into a major *event*. The press started following me, and the crowds got big, and we did the best we could to look professional, but sometimes it was still a wing and a prayer. I may have been the one praying, but you folks supplied the wing. And you carried me, and I am *so very grateful*.

"One of the best things that happened was the addition of the Boston Boys to the campaign. You guys made a tremendous difference with your skill and ingenuity. And I understand you haven't stopped."

She looked directly at Steve and me.

"And now I hear we have you to thank for a certain fund to help out Kelly. I just want you to know we all appreciate your efforts."

"Especially me," Kelly piped in.

When the parties ended, I went home. For the moment I was a spectator, watching with hope and fascination as our young and vital new president took over. The beginning of any new administration is an exciting time. The press and public generally greet the fresh faces with a mixture of curiosity and patriotic support; partisan divisions are replaced with a shared sense of responsibility to our nation as a whole. This is the honeymoon, when even the hard-liners from the other party are willing to give the incoming team the benefit of the doubt.

In a harbinger of things to come, Clinton's honeymoon was anything but harmonious. He brought the rollicking, adrenaline-driven, who-the-hell-needs-sleep pace of the campaign to the West Wing of the White House, where it promptly collided with two centuries' worth of culture. Franklin Roosevelt reportedly said a president should be elected with one set of people and govern with another, and I'm not at all sure he had it wrong. On the campaign trail it's very clear: us versus the enemy. Win or lose. Right now. But governing is a gray world. The senator beating your brains in on the education bill today may be your biggest supporter on the tax bill next week—if you don't screw up and personalize the first battle. Democracy moves slowly, and that's not necessarily bad. It took the Clinton administration awhile to learn these important lessons.

Within days of taking office President Clinton appointed Hillary to head his task force on health care reform and issued an executive order banning discrimination against gays in the military. It would be a great understatement to say that neither move met with broad public support. The honeymoon was over before it began.

At the same time, the disturbing right-wing phenomenon of Hillary hating gathered steam. While her supporters saw her as a logical step forward, a first lady who was more than just a figurehead, who took an active, public role in promoting her own and her husband's ideals and agenda, they were drowned out by the venomous cacophony from Republican operatives and their allies in the media. To them, Hillary Clinton represented a threatening encroachment of women into the heretofore male-dominated bastions of power. She wasn't elected, they screamed. What right did she have to take an office in the West Wing and assume leadership of a significant area of government policy? Send her back to the East Wing with a bag of flour and some chocolate chips.

Just as the cookie remark had galvanized support for Hillary among working women and the many men who supported the full participation of women in every aspect of American society, so too had it become a rallying cry for those who wanted to inflict political damage on Hillary by painting her as overly ambitious, a woman who would deny Americans the cozy comforts of a traditional first lady. Their answer was that she *should* have stayed home and baked cookies.

Of course Hillary wasn't the first political figure to be held up to scorn and ridicule. It's an American tradition to demonize our opponents. For years the Republicans have depicted Ted Kennedy as the embodiment of evil, responsible for the deterioration of American values, poster boy for a counterculture cabal that would squander our hard-earned money on layabout welfare recipients (often GOP code words for minorities). Later the Democrats used the same methods on Newt Gingrich: He became synonymous with intolerance, the dismantling of environmental laws, and the arrogance of white males.

However, the intensity and personal tone of the hatred directed at Hillary Clinton were profoundly disturbing. Snide remarks about her looks, her emotional stability, and her sexuality were commonplace on talk radio and even from Republican officials. I remember a news report that showed a Republican official in a midwestern state introducing Elizabeth Dole to an audience of the faithful; he cracked a joke about Hillary's having to fly in the hold with the other dogs. To her credit, Liddy Dole's smile looked pained. Ambition is celebrated in men; in Hillary it was denigrated as ruthless.

Conservative magazines such as the *National Review* and the *American Spectator* delighted in tearing down the First Lady, writing pieces that used shoddy investigative methods to reach spurious conclusions. Rupert Murdoch unleashed his media empire on Hillary. Every allegation was fact; every rumor, truth. Books were written with the sole purpose of attacking Hillary Clinton. This was a vendetta, with no pretense of impartiality, let alone fairness. A particularly ugly side of the American psyche was exposed, and Hillary's gender had a great deal to do with it. Hillary was going where no woman had ever gone before. She was also paying a price for her courage.

Hillary, while somewhat bewildered by their intensity at first, was undeterred by her attackers. If they thought they could turn her into a victim, they didn't know whom they were dealing with. She kept her focus clear, and health care was an issue she cared about passionately. As the first lady of Arkansas she had traveled throughout the state and had seen firsthand what can happen to a family when it doesn't have health insurance. She believed it was a disgrace that the United States was the only developed nation without universal health care. Also, health care ranked high in the polls of issues Americans cared about.

Of course I had my own interests to look out for, and I was thrilled that Hillary was taking the lead in health care reform. It meant she would be traveling far more than previous first ladies, and for that she'd need advance people. I was bored with my desk job in the attorney general's office five minutes after I returned to it.

Isabelle Tapia had been appointed director of presidential scheduling and advance, and she was responsible for all assignments. Because President Clinton had ordered a 25 percent cut in executive branch personnel, there would be only four full-time advance positions, all dedicated to the President. The First Lady would have to rely entirely on volunteer help. Steve and I made it clear we would be more than willing.

Isabelle made it clear that the opportunity to advance for the First Lady (for no pay, of course) would be given only to the favored few. Would I make the cut? Every time the phone rang I jumped.

It didn't take long, thirteen days to be exact, before the call came. The

First Lady was going to Philadelphia in early February to promote her health care initiative, and Isabelle assigned the trip to Steve, Paula Thomasson, and me. Our briefing was no more sophisticated than the skimpy directions we had received on the campaign trail: Go to Philadelphia and do "a health care stop in a white community." With our trademark Boston bravado, Steve and I acted as if the gig would be a piece of cake, but we each sensed the other was nervous about our first foray into official White House advance. We were glad Paula would be along because she'd known Hillary a lot longer than we had and could help us figure out what would work for Hillary, First Lady, as opposed to Hillary, candidate's wife.

The three of us arrived in Philadelphia in the early afternoon, checked into our hotel, gathered in Steve's suite, called the White House to get more details—and couldn't find anyone willing to talk to us. They all were tied up in meetings, even though Hillary's trip was only two days away. We sat there, somewhat stunned at how little guidance we were getting, and tried to figure out what to do.

I suppose we shouldn't have been surprised at the lack of organization at the White House. We were reading the same news reports as everyone else, of late-night bull sessions in the Oval Office, where the opinion of some lowly staffer was given as much weight as Secretary of State Warren Christopher's. There was no doubt this administration hadn't found its sea legs.

"Look for local help" was an advance mantra. These were the folks who knew the lay of the land. The one and only contact our handlers at the White House had given us was a low-ranking aide in Senator Harris Wofford's office. I gave him a call.

"Can you give us a hand?" I asked. "We're looking for a location for a health care event for the First Lady, something in a white neighborhood."

"How about bringing her out to a doctor's waiting room in one of the Main Line suburbs? She can talk to patients," the aide suggested.

"That sounds about as visually interesting as watching paint dry. Do you know of any possibilities in downtown Philadelphia?"

"Sorry, I'm from Pittsburgh. I really don't know the first thing about Philly."

I thanked him and hung up.

"We've got a problem. They want a white event. Central Philly is pretty black," Paula said.

"And trying to find a white health care facility in a black city is like trying to find the best steakhouse in Chinatown," I cracked.

"Rocky!" Steve exclaimed.

"Rocky?" Paula said.

"Yeah, Rocky. He lived in Philly, in an Italian-American neighborhood."

I dialed the hotel's concierge. "Do you by any chance know how we can get to Rocky's neighborhood?"

"Certainly, sir. Just drive south on Broadway."

Clearly, it wasn't the first time he'd gotten that question.

We piled into our rental car, a white Caddie with red leather interior—Steve liked to travel in style—and took off down Broadway. It was a mild, overcast winter day. The blues clubs and rib joints gave way to Italian bakeries and delicatessens. In both neighborhoods the kids hanging out on the street corners wore the same uniform of baggy pants and backward baseball caps. For some reason I found this sartorial integration a hopeful sign. Paula was sitting in the back seat with the Philadelphia yellow pages open to "Hospitals." We called out the name of each street we passed, and she frantically tried to find a hospital or clinic with that address. The whole operation was very high-tech.

"Can you believe we actually represent the White House right now?" Steve said in amazement.

"No," I answered truthfully. None of it felt real. We'd spent a lot of our adult lives trying to win the Big One, and now that we had we weren't entirely sure how to handle ourselves. We all wanted very badly for Hillary to succeed. This was one of her first health care trips, and it had to be good. Just had to be.

"Hey, there's a great-looking hospital! Pull over!" Paula cried.

Steve complied. Sure enough, there was a tall white hospital on our right. Our hopes soared. Then we read the name: St. Agnes.

"You're nuts, Paula," I said.

"No way a Catholic hospital is going to let us bring in Hillary Clinton," Steve added.

Abortion had been a hot-button issue throughout the campaign, particularly in Pennsylvania; we'd been warned that on at least one occasion protesters had tried to hand a fetus to Hillary. It was one of the raw nerves of American politics, and we had no desire to have it overshadow Hillary's message.

"I can just see the whole thing turning into a gigantic antiabortion rally. Wouldn't that be a picnic?" Steve said, lighting a cigarette.

"It's one thing to do events in Catholic neighborhoods. But to go right into a hospital run by the church and hope they won't notice? I don't think so," I said.

"Y'all are prejudging. The people who run these hospitals aren't the loonies we see standing outside our events with pictures of dead babies. We gotta at least check it out."

Steve and I exchanged a look that said: At this point in the game, we don't have much choice.

"All right, we'll check it out. But this has to be covert," Steve said.

"Damn right," I said. "Last thing we want is a headline in the paper saying a local hospital rejected a visit from the First Lady and gave us the bum's rush."

"All right," Paula said. "I'll be Natasha, you two can fight it out for who's Rocky and who's Bullwinkle."

A plaque outside the building informed us that St. Agnes Medical Center was run by the Franciscans. We tried to look nonchalant as we walked into the lobby and scoped the place out. It was sparkling clean, but there were nuns everywhere.

"All these nuns make me very nervous," I whispered.

"Pat, grow up," Paula said.

"That's the problem, Paula. I grew up in a Catholic school. See these knuckles? Notice the scar tissue? Nuns did that."

"Pat, these are *good* nuns," Steve assured me, smiling broadly at a sister as she glided by. At school the nuns had stomped; here they glided. I guess that was a good sign.

"Okay, okay, let's go," I said.

We strolled casually over to the front desk, about to make our first contact on behalf of the White House, yet we didn't have a scrap of official identification. The only means we had of proving who we were was the rental contract for Steve's Cadillac—in the name of the executive office of the president of the United States.

"Good afternoon, Sister," Paula said to the nun behind the desk, flashing her warmest smile. "Could you tell us where the public affairs office is?"

The director of public affairs was a serious middle-aged nun in a light blue habit. Steve put on his best official face and, after introducing us, said, "We're here representing a high-level government official who's interested in visiting St. Agnes."

I held my breath, waiting for her to ask the identity of this mysterious official, but Steve has a lot of authority, not to mention a certain rough-hewn charm, and the director swallowed his story. She even puffed up a little, flattered and impressed.

I busied myself scanning the brochures on the information rack. The hospital had some promising programs, including a managed care unit for union members and an advanced physical therapy program for people injured on the job. I handed several of the brochures to Paula.

"Could we possibly take a look at these programs?" she asked the director.

"Why, certainly," the nun answered. As she led the way, Steve, Paula, and I exchanged conspiratorial glances.

The programs proved exemplary, and we were soon convinced that St. Agnes would be a great place for the First Lady to visit. Now came the hard part: facing the higher-ups.

We walked into the president's office and were greeted by his secretary, a trim young woman who sported a tailored business suit and a no-nonsense manner. She was pleasant enough but had that Philly attitude that screams: Don't feed me any bullshit. I had a feeling our luck was about to run out.

"Hello," Steve said with a big smile, cranking up the charm. "We've been looking around the hospital on behalf of a high-level government official who is considering making a visit. We're very impressed by what we've seen. We'd like to discuss the possible visit with the president of the hospital."

"And exactly which 'high-level government official' might that be?" the secretary asked, impervious to the charm offensive.

"We'd rather not say at this point," he answered.

"Look, I've got a lot of work to do. I don't have time for nonsense. Can you find your own way out?"

"We represent the First Lady," I blurted out.

The secretary laughed in our faces. "Sure you do. Let's see some identification."

"Actually we don't have any identification on us right at the moment," Steve said.

She picked up her phone. "Security, could you please send up a guard to escort three people out of my office."

"Look," I said quickly, "here's what I want you to do. Call the White House; here's the number. Ask to speak to the Scheduling and Advance Office; ask if they sent us."

There was a long pause while she considered my entreaty, during which security arrived. Security looked like Rocky's older brother, the one with the serious muscles. "Why don't you follow this gentleman out to the lobby while I think about this?"

The lobby was painted cheery pastel colors. They did nothing for our mood. The clock was ticking, and if St. Agnes wouldn't have us, then what? The thought was too anxiety-provoking to contemplate. After a very long ten minutes the secretary appeared.

"You really are from the White House!" she said. "I didn't know whether to have you arrested or brought upstairs to our psych unit. President Wilson will be happy to see you."

One down, one to go.

Jim Wilson was thin, energetic, blond, in his late thirties. He wore a blue oxford shirt with his tie loosened. He greeted us warmly, and we explained our mission. He listened carefully and then, without hesitation, said, "St. Agnes would be honored to have the First Lady visit."

I knew it was time to bite the bullet. If there was going to be trouble, I didn't want anyone blindsided by it. "What about abortion? We know it's something the church feels deeply about, and we wouldn't want it to interfere with the First Lady's message on health care reform," I said.

Wilson grew silent, his face thoughtful. After a long moment he said, "The Franciscans' concern is for the care of the whole person. And we know health care needs systemic reform. Those things far outweigh disagreements on any one issue."

I was really beginning to like this guy.

We called the White House with the news and to ask for help pulling all the details of the visit together, but they still seemed preoccupied. Once again we had to fall back on our own wits. We borrowed motorcade vehicles from a Chevrolet dealer and used local contacts to scare up drivers and other volunteers. Interest in Hillary's visit was intense, and we found ourselves dealing with more than fifty media outlets and hundreds of people who wanted to meet her. It was all so seat-of-the-pants. Was this how advance had been done under the Reagan and Bush administrations? I doubted it.

But we pulled it off. Hillary was greeted warmly by the nuns and toured St. Agnes's managed care program; the press made some great pictures. Hillary then did something uniquely her: She spent an hour in a closed-door session with a cross section of the hospital's staff. During the eight years I worked with her, Hillary frequently asked us to arrange this kind of off-the-record meeting. She lived for the free-form exchange of ideas, for serious discussion without distraction. Hillary concluded her visits by taking questions from the media. This combined photo op, closed discussion, press-questioning format worked well because it gave the media what they wanted, and it provided Hillary with the opportunity for some intellectual sustenance.

The format came about through discussions among Steve, Paula, and me about what made sense for Hillary the person as opposed to Hillary the icon. We knew we couldn't ignore the icon, by we also felt we had to nurture the person. Throughout the campaign, and particularly now as First Lady, Hillary was expected to stand before the cameras and make a statement. That gets old real fast. You can't possibly have an honest exchange of ideas with a bank of television cameras trained on you. We knew Hillary was a policy wonk at heart and would relish the chance to dive into a no-holds-barred discussion with people on the front line of health care delivery. Afterward Hillary commented on how much she enjoyed the format.

This was the first time we'd seen Hillary since she became First Lady, and we were dying to chat with her, but the omnipresent television cameras made that impossible—until she broke for the closed-door discussion.

"Well, this looks just like one of my campaign stops. I'm glad to see you guys haven't lost your touch," she said to Steve and me as we huddled outside the conference room.

"Thanks. We have to stay sharp. We'll be running for reelection before you know it," I said.

"My guess is that getting this health care package passed is going to be tougher than the campaign," Steve said. "The Republicans and the insurance companies are going to try to kick our brains in."

"I'm glad to see you two will be around to help. I really appreciate it."

"Don't mention it Hill—your first ladyship—damn! I don't even know what to call you now," I stammered.

"*Hillary* will do just fine," she said with a laugh.

———

By early March 1993 it was clear that Steve had been right. Hillary's health care reform initiative was locked in a public relations war. The Republicans and the insurance companies had started a massive campaign to paint universal health care as a loss of choice, even faintly socialistic. You wouldn't be able to see your own doctor anymore. The feds would dictate everything from Advil to X-rays. Of course they were also making the battle personal. That no-good, domineering, aggressive, unladylike Hillary was behind the whole thing.

The White House was fighting back. It was making the battle personal too. That is, about real people who were being at best ignored, at worst abused, by a health care system more interested in healthy profits than healthy people. Steve and I were dispatched to New Orleans for our second advance trip for the First Lady. As soldiers in the health care war we were on a mission to find the human faces, the stories that would drive home Hillary's message of reform. That's where Glazer Steel came in.

Glazer Steel and Aluminum was the kind of manufacturing company you don't see much anymore. Family-owned, it was housed in an old warehouse in a gritty New Orleans district that looked like something straight out of *On the Waterfront*. The second I set eyes on it, I knew it was perfect. A quick tour of the plant confirmed my opinion: The work force was hardworking and diverse—and had no health insurance. The Glazer family had recently been forced to cancel it when the costs threatened to turn the company into a nonprofit operation. The final straw had come when one employee's cancer treatments had triggered a sudden jump in the premium.

In Philadelphia we had felt as if we were floating in space, free agents for an administration that couldn't believe it had taken power and paid scant attention to the nitty-gritty of governing. Now those days were over. The White House bureaucracy had kicked into gear, and it was scary. Not only did it want us to spend hours on the telephone justifying every decision we made in the Big Easy, but it also buried us in paperwork and expected us to reciprocate by sending it reams of memorandums.

There's a fundamental lesson that people who cut their teeth in Boston politics learn at an early age: Don't put it down on paper. In the immortal words of the dearly departed ward boss Martin Lomasney, "Never write what you can say, and never say what you can convey with a wink or a nod." It cuts down on things that can be used as evidence later on.

The White House bureaucrats obviously weren't from Boston. A staffer in the Public Liaison Office faxed me the guest list for one of Hillary's receptions. Beside each name he had written a comment, some of which were less, a lot less, than flattering. The memorandum was on White House stationery, and to make matters worse, it was sent directly to the hotel fax. I had no way of knowing who had seen it before it got to me. I was horrified by this bush-league blunder and decided to put the fear of God into the perpetrator.

I got him on the phone. "Listen, pal, sending down that fax was a real Mickey Mouse move. Anybody at this hotel could have read it, it was on White House stationery, and worst of all, my name was on it."

I could practically hear the guy puffing himself up with umbrage. "I was doing my job. That memo contains information that you need to do *your* job." He obviously considered *my* job a lot less important than his.

"Well, buddy, *your* job definition may have just expanded to include damage control. The memo was picked up off the fax by a PR person here at the hotel who happens to be the sister of the town's leading political reporter. She made a copy and gave it to her brother. Look for your indiscreet comments to be page one news in tomorrow's *Times-Picayune*."

"But—but—that's unethical. That memo was marked 'confidential.'"

"Welcome to the real world, Johnny Appleseed. I'd advise you to begin planning what you're going to say when the *Times-Picayune* calls you for a comment. Oh, yeah, I'd also suggest you figure out how the hell you're going to explain this mess to your supervisors. Assuming you still have any."

I let the poor lad suffer a sleepless night before I called him back and told him I'd managed to squelch the story. He was most grateful and promised never to be so stupid again. Sometimes tough love and a tall story can work wonders.

There was strong media interest in the Glazer Steel event, and we built a large press riser inside the plant. We'd gone to a lot of trouble putting together a good visual and didn't want the press crawling all over the place and messing it up. The morning of Hillary's visit things were going well until a hyper young producer from CBS arrived. He was wearing an expensive suit accessorized with sneakers and a baseball cap. His long, stringy hair made him look seedy despite the costly threads. With a cameraman in tow, he began to roam the floor of the plant as if he owned the joint. I approached him. "What are you doing?" I asked politely.

"I'm not going to limit my people to the press area," he informed me dismissively.

I'd had experience with network producers before. They were used to being the big kids on the block, and sometimes they acted like real bullies, looking for ways to expand their control.

"If you want to cover the event, you'll have to do it from the press area. Otherwise I'd appreciate it if you'd leave," I said.

I could almost see his blood pressure rise. "What's your name?" he barked.

"Patrick Halley."

"Film this," he ordered his cameraman. "Now, Mr. Halley, I want you to repeat what you told me, this time on camera."

I looked right at the camera, hoping my tie was in place, and said, "My name is Patrick Halley. That's H-A-L-L-E-Y. The CBS camera crew can cover this event from the same place as everyone else. Otherwise you can leave. I might add that if you don't get back into the press pen right now, I'm going to revoke your credentials and have the police escort you from the building. Trespassing is illegal, you know." I closed with what I hoped was a telegenic smile.

The producer sputtered and fumed all the way back to the press area. The rest of the media folks took due note of my approach and behaved themselves very nicely.

Hillary's discussion with the steelworkers made great pictures. She huddled on the factory floor surrounded by a dozen workers in hard hats and work shirts; other employees sat on nearby girders and heavy machinery and listened. The soaring old warehouse and the heavy cranes used to move the steel beams framed the shot. These were the pictures we were always trying to get: Hillary surrounded by real people, not local politicians trying to get their mugs on the evening news.

The stories the steelworkers told were every bit as compelling as the setting. One woman explained that she'd found a lump in her breast, but because she didn't have insurance, she and her doctor were waiting to see what happened before they committed to a biopsy. A middle-aged man said he might have to quit his job after twenty years so his family could go on public assistance; it was the only way his daughter, who had a chronic illness, could get the medical attention she needed.

I was very moved by what I heard, moved and angered. This was the real deal: hardworking, taxpaying citizens of the richest country in history who were hung out to dry because politicians lacked the courage to enact universal health care. Hillary put on a spellbinding performance as she drew out their accounts and consoled them on the difficulties they faced. She never forgot their testimony and often referred to it in speeches around the country.

Even after such an important event, it was hard to remain in a reflective mood for long in New Orleans, particularly when the natives were bent on showing you a good time. Mayor Barthelemy hauled us all off to Mulate's Cajun restaurant on the waterfront, where the delectable andouille sausage and blackened catfish were accompanied by lively zydeco music. This was a far cry from your typical buttoned-down affair at a private dining room. To a Protestant girl from the Midwest and two Catholic boys from Boston, there was something vaguely sinful about dancing during a weekday lunch, but the mayor wouldn't be denied, and soon the lot of us were out there shaking our stuff. Once again Hillary proved that she knows how to have a good time.

Hillary was due to fly back to Washington after lunch, and her motorcade was waiting outside the restaurant, along with enough police cars to invade a small country. In addition, the streets had been closed along her route. She looked at me with dismay. "Oh, Pat, I hate to travel like this," she said.

"Well, you are the First Lady," I said.

"Yes, but I'm not the queen. I hate the idea of people being tied up in traffic just for my convenience."

I approached the police captain in charge, a stocky middle-aged gent who appeared to take his job very seriously. "Do we really need this large an escort?" I asked.

"Son, this is N'aww-lins," he said, as if that explained everything.

I believe in picking my battles, and this was one I was willing to concede. So we were whisked to Lakefront Airport on the shore of Lake Pontchartrain with lights ablaze and sirens blaring. From then on, every time a local police department got carried away and gave us more of a presence than we wanted, we referred to it as the "full New Orleans."

We got Hillary, her staff, a local congressman hitching a ride, and five gallons of gumbo earmarked for the President on board her military jet. As we crossed the tarmac, a car pulled up next to the plane, and a man got out and sprinted toward the terminal building. Two air force guards walked briskly over to us.

"Do you know who that man is?" one asked.

"We have no idea," Steve answered.

It dawned on us all simultaneously: a car bomb. Steve and I ran for cover as air force personnel raced to secure the plane's hatch, and it began to taxi away from the car. Just then the man emerged from the building and ran back to the car, where he was immediately set upon by Secret Service agents. The stunned fellow quickly explained that he was the congressman's aide and had been delivering his luggage for the trip to Washington. His sprint to the terminal had been motivated by nothing more than an urgent bladder. We all got a laugh out of that, but it had a hollow ring. The ugly rants and threats of the Hillary haters echoed in our ears. This incident, while harmless, was a real reminder that the end result of that level of incendiary rhetoric is often violence. I believe there are far fewer than six degrees of separation from the extreme right-wing diatribes against the Clintons to the actions of Timothy McVeigh.

There was quite a bit of downtime after the New Orleans trip, which allowed me to catch up on my work at Attorney General Scott Harshbarger's office. The time I was spending on the road was starting to take a toll. My immediate staff was disoriented by my comings and goings, and the senior management of the office was disrupted by the constant need to brief me on developments I missed. Probably the only reason I wasn't shown the door was that Harshbarger was considering a run for governor in 1994 and he wanted to use my political talents. But I did feel guilt about collecting a paycheck for a job I wasn't performing particularly well.

My problems paled beside Hillary's. The insurance industry had begun running its infamous Harry and Louise commercials. They showed a married couple sitting up in bed late at night, discussing how afraid they were of health care reform. It was a scare tactic, and it worked. Although the ads were shown only in the Washington, D.C., area, they generated enormous press and were a real setback for Hillary's efforts. On a personal level, her father was gravely ill. She had always been particularly close to Hugh Rodham, and she rushed to Little Rock to be by his side as he convalesced at a hospital.

Hillary had a long-standing commitment to speak at the University of Texas in Austin in early April, but her schedule had been suspended because of her father's illness. The Advance Office had assigned the trip to Jack Murray and me but told us there was a good chance it would be canceled. We were scheduled to leave Boston on a Thursday, then got a call Wednesday telling us Hillary would remain in Little Rock through the weekend. Our trip was off.

That Saturday night I was enjoying a pint of Guinness and some Irish folk music at my favorite pub when Lockers, the bartender, told me I had a telephone call. "Some guy says he's with the fookin' White House," Lockers said.

It was the assistant director of the Advance Office, who had managed to track me down. He told me Hillary's Austin trip was back on, and he needed Jack Murray and me to get down there as soon as humanly possible, since she was scheduled to speak on Tuesday. Sharon Kennedy was already on her way down to do the press. Hillary's family had been urging her to take a break from her vigil, and she had finally relented.

I rushed home, threw a few things in an overnight bag, and headed out to Logan airport. I made it down to Austin by Sunday morning. The planning for a visit by the First Lady usually takes three or four on-site days; we had a day and a half. We had a lot of work to do, but fortunately the big pieces—site and audience—were already in place.

If we were going to get the job done, we were going to have to find some way to keep the White House bureaucrats off our backs. A bit of divine intervention came about when I was contacted by the lord mayor of Adelaide, Australia, who was going to be in Austin and wanted to meet Hillary and present her with a gift. I called Sara Grote, my scheduling desk, and suggested she check with the State Department and the National Security Council on how to proceed. She called back a few minutes later and said it would be all right to arrange the meeting, but we needed to "ascertain what the gift would be." I called the mayor's people, who told me he was planning to present her with a crystal kangaroo. Hmm . . . I thought I smelled an opportunity. I called Sara at the White House.

"He's going to give her a kangaroo," I said.

"A *what*?"

"A kangaroo. You know, the funny-looking things with the pouch."

"Oh, my goodness!"

"I'll ask the air force about getting it back to D.C., but you'd better check on how we'll take care of it once it gets there."

That sent the bureaucracy into a full-blown tizzy and kept them out of my hair for the rest of the day. The next morning I got a call from a very concerned Sara, who'd spent the last twenty-four hours learning about the care and feeding of kangaroos.

"We've made arrangements to give the kangaroo to the National Zoo," she said. "You should arrange for the air force to ship it there directly."

"National Zoo?" I said. "It's a crystal kangaroo. Why the hell would you give it to the National Zoo?"

"You bastard, a *crystal* kangaroo? You told me we were getting a live kangaroo."

"I never said the damn thing was alive. I just said it was a kangaroo. It doesn't weigh more than a pound or two. I'm sure you'll have no problem caring for it."

We'd accomplished our goal. The bureaucracy had been too busy dealing with the kangaroo scare to micromanage our efforts in Austin, and we were able to get our work done.

Hillary's event was a forum in the Liz Carpenter lecture series. Liz had served in various capacities in the Johnson administration and was still very close to Lady Bird Johnson. She was most gracious and had the advance staff out to her house, which perched on a hill overlooking the city, for dinner the night we arrived in town. Liz was a firecracker of a lady in her mid-sixties. Pure Democrat through and through, she took great pleasure in skewering what she called tinhorn Republicans. She regaled us with tales from her days in Washington and lamented how infrequently the Democrats had controlled the White House since the days of Kennedy and Johnson.

The forum was going to take place in the Erwin Center, a campus sports complex that seats about fourteen thousand people. Tickets were going fast, and Liz assured me we'd have a full house. She also helped us line up the University of Texas marching band to entertain during breaks in the program.

One of my concerns was Hillary's state of mind. I called Patti Solis, her scheduler and confidante, and tried to get a reading on how she was faring.

"What have you heard from Little Rock? How's her father doing? Just as important, how's Hillary holding up?"

"She's spending all her time at the hospital, and she's not talking to anyone here. She hasn't even called in a few days. We're all giving her as much space as we can."

Hillary was coming to Austin directly from the hospital where her father was a patient. His condition hadn't changed in the past two weeks, and she had finally decided to resume a limited schedule, since no one knew how much longer he might live.

She flew to Austin on a small air force jet, and I hoped the clear, warm weather would lift her spirits some. When the plane landed, I boarded and found Hillary, worn but game, seated in the main cabin's big leather captain's chair. The worry of the past two weeks was evident in her eyes, but she was obviously summoning up her stamina.

"How are you holding up?" I asked. "I know how tough these things can be. Are you sure you're up for what we've got to do today?"

"I guess I'm okay. It's been a rough week, but there's not much more I can do. You've just been through this yourself, Pat. All you can do is tell them you love them and pray."

Hillary had been very kind to me when both my parents had fallen ill at the same time, and I wanted to do anything I could to support her in these difficult times. "Anything you need, Hillary, I'm here," I said.

She laid a hand on mine. "Thank you, Pat," she said simply. We were silent for a moment, and then she said, "Well, I guess what I need right now is a briefing on this event."

"Okay, as you come in, the University of Texas marching band will be on your left, and they'll be playing 'The Eyes of Texas Are upon You.' The press will be straight ahead on a riser. You should acknowledge the band before you take your seat."

"The University of Texas marching band! Don't you think that's a little much for this event?"

"Well, we've got about fourteen thousand people. We have to do something to keep them entertained."

"Fourteen thousand! I thought I was speaking to Liz Carpenter's class of about one hundred and forty kids!"

"Nope. Fourteen thousand people. I've seen them with my own eyes."

"Well, I'll have to read my briefing book a little closer from now on. Let's go."

We drove to the Erwin Center for Hillary's meeting with Lady Bird Johnson. Hillary was determined to meet all the former first ladies to get their takes on the position. This was the first of several such meetings, and it was a lot more cordial than those with her Republican predecessors. Lady Bird looked a little frail, but she still had a clear head and a big heart. She gave Hillary an enthusiastic Texas welcome, and they retreated to a room we had set aside for a few moments of private chat. The press was howling for a photo of the two first ladies, and Sharon had picked a spot with the American Flag, the Texas flag, and a University of Texas banner in the background. I'd arranged for a golf cart to take Mrs. Johnson to the photo op, and when she came out of the room with Hillary, I approached her. "Mrs. Johnson, I have a golf cart here to take you to the photo shoot."

"Son, I'm perfectly capable of getting there on my own two feet, thank you," she answered, and all but sprinted the full distance across the arena.

There was a brief luncheon for the panelists, who included Bill Moyers and Governor Ann Richards. Governor Richards was famous for her wit and her lambasting of "George Herbert Walker Bush, who was born on third base and thought he'd hit a triple," at the Democratic Convention in 1988. She had silver hair, wore bright red lipstick, and was accompanied by two of the largest Texas Rangers I'd ever seen.

After lunch Hillary took me aside. "Pat, I need some index cards," she said.

I had come prepared and handed her a small stack.

"Thank you. Now I want fifteen minutes alone in the holding room."

I stood outside to make sure she wasn't disturbed. Exactly fifteen minutes later she emerged. "I'm ready," she said.

We could hear the huge crowd rumbling and the marching band belting out a tune as we approached the stage. If Hillary had any apprehension about what she was about to face, it wasn't evident. I felt as if I were leading a prizefighter into a ring. She walked with a spring in her step and gathered her focus until she was so becalmed it seemed as if she were in a trance.

Hillary is a powerful, accomplished speaker. Her performance that day in front of a large audience while she was burdened with the emotional stress of her father's failing health was extraordinary. She talked for nearly forty minutes, only occasionally glancing down at the index cards. She spoke eloquently of the need for modern society to come to grips with its crisis of meaning. Many people had a sense that their lives were about day-to-day survival and working hard to keep up, but they lacked any grander, common purpose. It would take a collective effort to lead us out of what she termed a spiritual vacuum, and we couldn't simply depend upon the government or a market economy "which knows the price of everything, but the value of nothing.

"We need a new politics of meaning. We need a new ethos of individual responsibility and caring. We need a new definition of civil society which answers the unanswerable questions posed by both the market forces and the governmental ones as to how we can have a society that fills us up again and makes us feel that we are part of something bigger than ourselves."

The audience listened with rapt attention. I had a great vantage point, standing just to the left of the stage, facing the audience and watching Hillary in profile. I could see and feel the connection she was making with this vast crowd, as if she were sitting across a kitchen table speaking to each of them individually.

Months later I got the White House to provide me with a verbatim transcript of the speech. Verbatim transcripts contain every sound the person makes, every "uh," "um," and "er." In her forty-minute speech Hillary spoke in complete sentences and made hardly any extraneous verbal utterances. Her message was so powerful that the *New York Times* used it as the basis for its cover story in its Sunday magazine on the concept of communitarianism. It was a remarkable performance, and it was 100 percent Hillary Rodham Clinton. No speechwriters, policy wonks, or political pundits had helped.

What the people in Austin saw that day was a direct example of why Hillary is regarded as such an intellectual powerhouse. But unlike so many brilliant people who are all head and no heart, Hillary has a humanity and an empathy that are unforced, as natural as breathing. That day confirmed my belief that she was someone worth working for, even if it called for some personal sacrifice. My commitment to her was growing into something even I didn't understand. I'd been in politics a long time and understood that loyalty is the glue that holds it all together, but Hillary was getting under my skin in a way that no one else I'd ever worked for had. I wanted to protect her from harm, and with every ounce of my Irish heart I wanted nothing but the best for her.

You can't shake every hand in a crowd that big, but Hillary stood at the bottom of the stage and greeted hundreds and hundreds of people. The students poured forward, wanting to get close. You could see the inspiration on their faces. It reminded me very much of a minister standing at the church door after a service, bidding farewell to the congregants. Perhaps because of what she was going through with her father, Hillary had a special grace that day, and I believe it touched all of us.

Hugh Rodham died later that evening.

5

THE NAKED TRUTH

June–July 1993

STEVE AND I GOT OFF THE PLANE AT WASHINGTON'S DULLES AIR-
port and began our search for the White House driver who was to take us
to Andrews Air Force Base. There were no likely suspects in the terminal,
so we walked outside and saw two government vehicles with military
drivers standing by. One was a White House limousine, its driver standing
ramrod straight in full dress uniform; clearly some high-ranking government official was expected. The other was a beat-up van whose driver was
leaning against the side holding a clipboard. Bingo. We walked over to
the van.

"Do you have Halley and Graham on your list?" I asked its driver.

He glanced at the clipboard. "No."

Just then the soldier from the limo approached and saluted. "Pardon
me, sir, did you say Mr. Graham and Mr. Halley?"

"Uh, yes, I did."

"Sir, I'm here to pick you up and take you to Andrews. Do you have any
bags?"

I turned to Steve and said, "I don't think we're in Peoria anymore."

As we were quickly discovering, overseas travel is one of the great perks
of doing advance. Hillary was making her first trip out of the country as
First Lady, accompanying the President to Tokyo for a G-7 Conference, so
called because it's a meeting of the leaders of the seven largest industrial

nations. Like all things governmental, the formal name of the association, the Group of Seven, had been reduced to an acronym. We had done eight trips for Hillary in the United States, but this was a whole new magnitude of advance. Instead of a lonely band of three or four advance staffers living off the land, we'd be one small cog in the traveling White House, part of a massive operation supported by hundreds of people.

When we got to Andrews, we were directed to one of the old Boeing 707s that had served as Air Force One before the 747s came into service. It was maintained and piloted by Fox Airlift Command, the air force wing that services the White House. In a money-saving move, we were hitching a ride to the conference with the deputy secretary of the treasury. We walked on board and were greeted by what looked like acres of open space, couches, worktables, a galley, a video library, and a bar.

"I could get used to this real fast," Steve said.

Unfortunately this was a working flight, and I quickly settled down and reviewed the details of Hillary's schedule. Foreign travel brought our normal concerns to an entirely new level. It wasn't just about presenting a favorable image of the First Lady to enhance her stature and increase our chances for reelection; suddenly it was about how the rest of the world saw America. In addition to the folks in our scheduling operation, those vigilant guardians of Hillary's image, we now had to pass every event and every guest by the National Security Council. The NSC staff carefully considered every angle and detail, including reviewing the texts of speeches and vetting the guest lists of our events.

This trip was as important politically as it was diplomatically. Clinton's first months in office had been rocky, at best. The latest controversy had been over the firing of the staff at the White House Travel Office, the folks who make arrangements for White House staff and the traveling press. The people in that operation had been around for a long time and were set in doing business their own way—the Republican way. Instructions to be more flexible to accommodate the needs of busy staffers were met with an attitude that screamed, "We really run this place; you're only here temporarily." They'd do things like require you to stay over on Saturday night after completing a business trip so they could get a lower airfare. You missed a day with your family, and they looked good on their balance sheets. It was a bad culture, and it set a tone for all the other professional elements that supported the administration. For once the President authorized immediate and direct action: termination of the entire staff. This move was so out of character for a guy who'd spent his first few months trying to please everyone that some folks were convinced Hillary was behind it.

With the Clinton haters and media jackals trying to fan the ember of Travelgate into a firestorm, the President needed a boost domestically. One of his great strengths was his ability to be statesmanlike on the world stage, to communicate his gravity, intelligence, and purpose. Clinton needed this trip to establish his authority, not only with world leaders but with the American people and his political opponents. Nothing plays better at home than a president shining abroad.

We stopped to refuel in Alaska, and by the time we landed in Tokyo we were exhausted. There's a thirteen-hour time difference, and our body clocks were all out of whack. We had to fight the urge to crawl right into bed and get some sleep because that would only prolong the jet lag. It was the first time any of us had been in Tokyo, a big, bright, noisy city, crammed with people and full of energy. It's also amazingly clean. After checking into the elegant Hotel Okura, one of the world's most expensive, Steve and I decided the best course of action was to stay up as long as we could to get ourselves in sync with local time. Why not explore a bit? And since we were staying up anyway, why not grab a few drinks? After all, they'd probably help us sleep through the night once we finally knocked off.

Drinks in Tokyo, like everything else, were incredibly expensive. The first few places we hit charged about ten bucks for a beer. No way. I was on a per diem, and whatever I didn't spend I took home with me. We finally found a neighborhood joint, off the beaten path under a highway overpass, called the Blind Pig. It was a *suntory* bar, Japanese slang for "no frills." It was a bit seedy, but the beer was a mere five bucks a pop. After several rounds we met some Japanese kids who had gone to college in Boston, and somehow or other we lured them into a friendly arm-wrestling contest. Losers bought the next round.

Steve is built like a linebacker. While the Japanese aren't known for their size, they're a very determined lot and were eager to see if they could take him. None met with any success, but they were having a great time trying. Steve wrestled one after another while I combed the place for new victims. By the time Steve's arm gave out we each had ten beers lined up at the bar. We finally headed back to our hotel at about four in the morning, knee-walking drunk.

Back at the hotel, Steve bade me good night, and we went off to our separate rooms. I sleep in the nude, and as I took off my clothes, I did my usual check to make sure my wallet, flashlight, and room key were handy. No room key. Anywhere. Shit. No doubt I left it in the door when I came in. So I stepped out into the hall wearing nothing but my birthday suit, and the door slammed shut behind me. I *hadn't* left the key in the door. Now I was naked and drunk in the eighth-floor hallway of one of the most expensive hotels in the world. No problem. After all, there was a maid stationed on each floor ready to answer a guest's every need.

Unfortunately the maid took one look at me and ran away screaming as if her hair were on fire. Hmm. Now I really was in a bind. I didn't know the room number of anyone else from our team, and knocking on random doors might lead to a misunderstanding. So I got on the elevator and headed down to the lobby. When the front desk staffers saw me approaching, they turned en masse and scampered into a back room. I was beginning to think the Japanese were very uncomfortable about nudity.

I was left standing at the desk ringing the bell and hollering for assistance. After a considerable wait a clerk ventured out, shading his eyes with his hand. "May I help you, sir?" he muttered.

"Yes. I've locked myself out of my room and need a new key," I explained calmly.

"Do you have any identification?"

"I have a mole on my ass. Would you like to see it?"

"I am sorry, sir, according to hotel policy, that is not an acceptable form of identification."

"Listen, my friend, I need a new key, and I need it *right now!*"

Just then two members of my team, David Neslin and Paula Thomasson, got off the elevators, on their way to check out the city's fish market for a possible presidential visit. They saw me. "Shock" is too mild a word to describe the expressions on their faces.

"Pat, you're naked," Paula said.

"Yes, Paula, I'm aware of that fact."

She promptly took off her baseball cap and handed it to me. I promptly put it on my head.

"*Damn it, I want a new key!*" I bellowed at the clerk, who at this point looked as if he were about to burst into tears.

Paula snatched the cap off my head and directed it to where it would provide a bit more strategic cover. She then asked the clerk to issue me a new key, and for some strange reason she had more luck than I did. I was finally able to get some much-needed sleep.

I can't claim that I woke up with a clear head, but I quickly dived into the tasks at hand. Unlike domestic trips for Hillary, where I was often the guy calling the shots, here I was pretty far down the food chain. Security, communications, and policy staff totaled 750 people. There were folks from the State Department, the Secret Service, the National Security Council, and a couple of three-letter federal agencies that like to stay in the shadows. We took over the whole hotel, which is massive.

The White House Communications Agency required an entire floor. The first thing it does on every trip is set up its satellite uplink dish so you get a White House dial tone on all the telephones in the work areas. You can reach anyone by dialing his or her five-digit extension, and you can dial directly anywhere in the world. The whole system runs through military communications satellites, and the sound is clear as a bell.

The State Department handles foreign travel for the White House. It pays all the costs and issues the travel orders. The American embassy in every foreign nation provides a control officer for every principal. That person is supposed to assist us in dealing with local politics and customs and make sure we don't do anything to create an international incident. Hillary's control officer for this trip was Robin Berrington, the embassy's cultural attaché, a slight, quick-witted gentleman of about sixty. Robin and his embassy colleague Charles Walsh, whose job was to help us with the media, worked hard to help us understand the ways of our Japanese hosts and vice versa.

The Japanese Foreign Ministry had put together a spouses' program. It included seven events over two days, the most interesting of which was a visit to the Imperial Palace and the most unusual of which was a tour of the Meguro trash incineration plant. Lawry Payne insisted on negotiating each detail with our hosts, who had everything timed to precision, as in:

"The First Lady's motorcade will leave the hotel at ten thirty-two *and thirty seconds.*" Getting them to make even the slightest change was next to impossible. I quickly learned a new Japanese term, "maybe no," which translated to "no way on God's green earth." We heard it a lot.

We'd been briefed on the special importance the Japanese placed on the royal family, which went back over a thousand years, and I assumed the palace would be ancient, filled with cavernous halls, carved wood-work, and secret passageways. I was wrong. It was a modern two-story building of glass and concrete. If the building wasn't ancient, the attitude of the palace household certainly was. We were led on the walk-through by its "Grand Master of Ceremonies," Mr. Samir, and its press liaison, Mr. Nonoyama. Both spoke English with clipped British accents.

These guys gave new meaning to the word "inflexible." They were the keepers of ancient and sacred traditions, and we were clearly lesser beings. They led us to a nondescript spot in the palace, an entry hall outside the main ballroom.

"This is where the official photo will be taken," Mr. Samir informed us.

It was a horrible setup, a narrow passageway clogged by a big display case with a glass wall behind it.

"I'm not sure this is the best possible spot," I said. "The light will reflect off the glass and ruin the picture."

"This is where the official photo will be taken because it is where the crown prince had an official photo taken at a banquet," Samir replied pointedly.

"Could we see a copy of the crown prince's photo?" I asked.

"No. The reflection from the glass ruined it."

They then insisted we take the first ladies on a tour of the palace's "lower garden."

"May we see the lower garden?" I asked.

"No, you are not of sufficient social standing to walk on the ground there."

After some intense negotiations, Samir relented and bestowed the priv-ilege on us. The path down was steep and slippery, and the whole area was little more than a mosquito-infested swamp with a few lily pads floating in it. After more tense negotiation the garden was struck from the itinerary.

It was a hectic week, but by the day of the Clintons' arrival we'd negotiated, with the help of Robin and Charles, all the fine details and had actually won a few battles.

I stood in front of the hotel to greet the First Lady. She was riding in the President's limo, and as usual her luggage was in a van a couple of vehicles behind. The Clintons entered the hotel, and I waited while the van was unloaded. I was flabbergasted by the amount of luggage Hillary had brought. She was a tidy traveler on domestic trips, but this time it looked as if she had packed every stitch of clothing she owned. Her bags just kept appearing out of the back of the van. For an experienced and organized traveler, she had certainly packed heavy.

I had learned by then that Hillary is obsessed with her luggage, her one real insecurity. I always found this fascinating but was never able to come up with a plausible explanation. It couldn't be security because the bags were sniffed by bomb-detecting dogs at every turn. Hillary always insisted her luggage travel in the motorcade with her, and if she was going to an event before checking into her hotel, the bags came along. When she arrived at a hotel, it was like a fire drill in reverse as all trusted hands were commandeered to grab a bag and make a beeline for her suite. She then took an immediate inventory. The bags could never be left with hotel staff. I knew that an advance person had won her trust when she allowed him or her to supervise the movement of her luggage.

Luggage wasn't the only excess baggage we were dealing with. As was typical when we visited a foreign country, the Japanese security forces insisted on having a detail work with the Secret Service to protect the President and the First Lady. Since this was her first trip overseas as First Lady, Hillary wasn't prepared when the number of bodyguards around her suddenly doubled. In some countries these agents were unobtrusive; in Japan maybe no. Her customary detail of four agents became two rings of four, with the Secret Service closest to her and the Japanese agents forming an outer perimeter. It looked as if she were moving in the middle of a rugby scrum.

As she entered the Hotel Okura lobby, Hillary spotted a friend from her college days. Her face broke into a huge smile, and she headed toward her. Her Japanese bodyguard, Mrs. Fukahara, immediately grabbed Hillary by the arm and spun her around. With lightning speed Tom McGeorge, her Secret Service agent, grabbed Mrs. Fukahara and pinned her to the wall as the rest of Mrs. Clinton's Secret Service detail closed ranks and kept the Japanese security people at bay. Hillary was wide-eyed with shock and amazement but quickly grasped the situation and told her friend she'd give her a call. She then walked calmly to the elevator, her composed manner helping defuse the situation. There were immediate high-level talks between the Secret Service and the Japanese security forces, and the rules for protection, chief among them that you *never* touch the principal, were explained in detail.

Hillary had an unusually small advance team, just two people, to handle her schedule. This was because State Department expectations were based on what previous first ladies had done while overseas. They soon realized that Hillary Rodham Clinton was never content just to attend the spousal program; every overseas trip was an opportunity to highlight the role of women and children in that country's society. So we always put together a discussion with the country's prominent women, women notable in their own right, not simply the wives of prominent men. Hillary was interested in having open, unhindered exchanges, so these events were closed to the press, except for a photo op at the beginning. These meetings were similar to the private discussions held at each health care event back home. They allowed Hillary to get intellectual sustenance without having to guard every word, and they resulted in a dynamic network of contacts around the world.

Our first event in Japan was the women's discussion at the ambassador's residence. With the embassy's help we pulled together about twenty women from business, government, academia, and the media. Melanne Verveer, Hillary's policy maven, sat in, and I observed from the corner of the room. Hillary began with a brief explanation of how happy she was to be in Japan and a quick overview of some of what was going on in American politics and culture. She then went around the room and asked each woman what she thought were the most pressing issues facing Japan. This was followed by an open discussion, which flowed pretty well considering that some of it required translation. After an hour or so of this structured back-and-forth, the women mingled and chatted in smaller groups. Hillary seemed inspired by the exchange of ideas, and any lingering jet lag was whisked away by the intellectual stimulation.

The next day saw one of the more bizarre events I ever did with the

First Lady. For some unknown reason, the Japanese were immensely proud of the trash incineration plant in the Meguro neighborhood and insisted the spouses pay a visit. The drive was long, and the day was warm, and when we arrived, we were greeted by the overwhelming stench of burning garbage—oh, yes, and scores of adorable schoolchildren bearing flowers and singing. As incineration plants went, it was a nice one, but well, it was a *trash* plant.

Our hosts wanted to take a photograph in the control room, where the plant operators, wearing white jackets and hard hats, sat at a computer console and monitored the flow of trash from one end of the plant to the other on a huge electronic map. Their original plan called for the ladies to look up at the screen and follow the trash. That would have given us a compelling shot of seven backs. We'd convinced them to turn it around so the ladies stood behind the console and faced the cameras with the map behind them.

As the women lined up for the picture, I noticed a gap between Mrs. Clinton and Mrs. Helmut Kohl, the German chancellor's wife, where Mrs. Kiichi Miazowa, the wife of the Japanese prime minister, was supposed to be. As I frantically scouted for the missing spouse, I suddenly caught a glimpse of dark hair bouncing up from behind the console. It was the top of the tiny Mrs. Miazowa's head. I'd inadvertently turned the G-7 spouses into the G-6 spouses. As the photographers snapped away, the first lady of Japan was jumping up and down, trying, vainly, to be seen.

Hillary had a free day at the end of the conference and decided she wanted to visit the seaside town of Kamakura, about an hour's train ride from Tokyo, with her mother, who had joined the First Family in Tokyo. Hillary treasured time away from the press, when she could sightsee and absorb foreign culture undisturbed and at her own pace.

The day went smoothly, too smoothly. I should have known my luck would never hold. When we returned to the train station for the trip back to the city, all hell broke loose.

The Kamakura train station is in the town square, surrounded by a shopping district. When we advanced the site with our Japanese counterparts, I told them we'd better have some rope ready to restrain any spontaneous crowds in case the First Lady decided she wanted to do some souvenir shopping before she got on the train. Their response was that she couldn't go shopping; she had to get right on the train. I explained that if the First Lady wanted to go shopping, we were going shopping.

When we turned into the square of what until then had been a peaceful little village, there was a crowd of about five thousand people lining the streets. Hillary was very popular in Japan, and word had gotten out that she was in town. She couldn't have reached the shops in a tank.

I was riding in the vehicle in front of Hillary and immediately passed word through the Secret Service to all the drivers in our motorcade: "Go directly to the train station."

The crowd followed, and not at a walk. We stepped out of the cars at the station to see five thousand people charging toward us, yelling, "Hee-ra-ree! Hee-ra-ree!"

The First Lady turned to me. "What do we do, Pat?"

"Run, Hillary!"

We bolted into the train station and took refuge in the stationmaster's office. Within minutes the crowd had completely overrun the station and flooded the platforms. The police moved in and linked arms to hold them back. Word arrived that our train was pulling in. We left the safety of the stationmaster's office and wormed our way through the tiny path the police were struggling to keep clear, all to deafening screams of "Hill-a-wee! Hill-a-wee!" The mass of humanity seemed to ebb and flow with each breath, and we were in real danger of being trampled. I finally managed to shoehorn the First Lady, her mother, and the rest of our party into the car and then hopped aboard myself, my suit torn and my shirttail hanging out. Hillary and her mother sat there dazed and breathless.

"Well, that was something, wasn't it?" Hillary said as I made my way down the aisle.

"Sure was," I said. "Can I build a crowd or what?"

6

SEEING RED

July 1993–January 1994

JUST NINE DAYS AFTER I RETURNED FROM TOKYO, ON JULY 20, 1993, ONE
of the saddest and ugliest episodes of the Clinton years began. The shaky
start and frenetic, almost manic, pace set by a president bent on making
significant changes in American policy proved too much for Vince Foster,
assistant White House legal counsel and trusted confidant and friend to
both Clintons.

Foster had been a senior partner and mentor to Hillary at the Rose Law
Firm in Little Rock and followed the Clintons to Washington, where he
became their go-to guy in the legal office. He had been intimately involved with some of the more volatile decisions of the young administration, including the ongoing debacle of selecting an attorney general. Zoe
Baird and Kimba Wood had been nominated and then had their names
withdrawn, Baird because she had failed to pay Social Security taxes on
her child's nanny, Wood because of a somewhat too colorful past that included a stint as a Playboy bunny. President Clinton was finally able to get
Janet Reno, the crime-fighting district attorney of Dade County, Florida,
confirmed as the nation's top law enforcement officer.

It was widely speculated that Hillary was the one insisting the new attorney general be a female and Vince Foster was seen as her agent in the
selection process. Vince had never been exposed to the level of infighting,
intrigue, and scathing press criticism he faced in Washington, and it took
a terrible toll on him.

Shortly after lunch on that steamy Washington Tuesday, Foster told his secretary he was leaving for a meeting, got in his car, and drove away from the White House for the last time. His lifeless body was discovered by a tourist not long afterward in a public park on the Potomac, a single bullet hole in his temple, an antique handgun once owned by his father at his side.

Hillary and the President were devastated. It was six months to the day since President Clinton had taken the oath of office.

Far from observing a period of mourning and respect, the Clinton haters leaped on Foster's suicide like vultures on carrion. As the Clintons did what little they could to console his widow and assist in the funeral preparations, rumors and innuendo began echoing through the streets of the capital and soon found their way into print. Vince Foster was murdered to cover up what he knew about the Whitewater land deal. Hillary and Vince Foster were secret lovers. Vince Foster was a closeted homosexual and was about to be exposed. The right wing fanned these baseless lies through their network of hate-radio hosts and other media allies and outlets. Once again these people proved they had no shame.

About ten days after Foster's death the President called a meeting of his staff to discuss the lessons of the tragedy. Although I wasn't present, I was told that he talked about the importance of retaining a sense of perspective. Don't put in so many hours that you lose contact with your family and friends. Don't take matters personally, and please understand these are policy battles, not matters of life and death. Work hard, be successful, but don't sacrifice your life for it.

I saw Hillary about a week later when I advanced a trip she took to Orlando, Florida. She was subdued but otherwise in good spirits, pleasant and focused. I avoided any mention of the tragedy in Washington.

I asked to do the trip because my father and mother lived about an hour away, and it would give me a chance to visit them and for them to meet Hillary. After Hillary's event, there was a small reception for local Democrats at the airport before her return flight. Unfortunately my father's failing health kept him homebound, but my mother was waiting when Hillary arrived. I brought her over to the First Lady. "Hillary, I'd like you to meet my mother, Ferne Halley. Mom, you know who this is."

"Well, hello, Mrs. Halley, it's so nice to meet you. Your Patrick has been taking such great care of me, and all over the world! You must be very proud of him."

"We certainly are. And we're proud of you too. You're doing such a great job as First Lady. My husband John's a dyed-in-the-wool Democrat, and he's sorry he can't be here today, but he asked me to give you his best."

"How is he feeling?" Hillary asked. Mom shrugged. "I'm so sorry he isn't well. You'll tell him how much the President and I appreciate everything Patrick's doing for us, I hope."

In all the time I worked for Hillary, both she and the President always took a genuine interest in meeting staff members' families. You never felt it was an imposition. On the contrary, they seemed to delight in expressing their appreciation for work well done. I can't tell you how much that means to people who put in a lot of hours, sometimes for very little pay.

Everything I knew about the Clintons suggested that their eagerness to share a few moments with the relatives of staff members was just part of their nature, but I also think that Vince Foster's suicide underscored the importance they placed on reaching out to their staff and making sure everyone kept the pomp and circumstance of the White House in proper perspective.

That perspective was to prove invaluable to Hillary and her staff in the escalating war over reforming the nation's health care system. In late September the Universal Health Care Initiative was formally launched in a ceremony in Washington. The President made a speech in the East Room of the White House and shared the dais with his wife. Hillary brought all her passion and energy to the enterprise, but there was already a vague sense that maybe she had bitten off more than she could chew. The insurance companies and their allies in Congress had succeeded in painting the program as government intrusion. Hillary traveled around the country during the rest of the year, pushing the initiative, but it was all uphill, and I think the trip she and the President took to Moscow in January of 1994 was a welcome respite.

I'm afraid I'd been spoiled by the trip to Japan, with its balmy weather and luxury hotels, not to mention the courtesy and efficiency. The preadvance team had warned us conditions in Russia were somewhat spartan, and I found out pretty damn fast that they weren't kidding. In January the country is also basically one big open-air freezer. I'd prepared by packing boots, gloves, long johns, a down vest, a ski parka, and as much bottled water and food as I could cram into my luggage.

I flew commercial, alone, and landed at night. I looked for an embassy driver holding a placard with my name printed on it. I searched high and low without success and was about to give up when two very scruffy-looking Russians appeared; one held a beat-up piece of cardboard covered with nearly illegible scrawls. After studying the letters for a minute, I thought I made out "Halley."

"Are you fellows the drivers from the embassy?"

"No speak English," one said as the other nodded.

Then they grabbed my bags, and I figured I'd better follow. Out in the parking lot they opened the back of a rust-pocked green van and tossed my luggage in. With some trepidation I climbed into the vehicle. The interior was filthy, and the side windows were covered with curtains hanging off frayed elastic rope. My two greeters jumped into the front seat and, after several attempts, got the engine started. It was snowing, and the van slipped and slid on its bald tires as we crept toward Moscow. The gentlemen in the front seat passed a vodka bottle back and forth, and every so often one of them used a greasy rag to wipe the frost off the inside of the windshield. I began to wonder if I'd been kidnapped by Russian mobsters and had visions of being held in a basement somewhere while tense negotiations took place.

By the time we reached the city limits, I was thinking seriously of bolting from the van the first time it stopped at a traffic light. When I spotted my hotel, I cried out like a shipwrecked sailor spotting land after a month in a life raft. My charming hosts toasted our successful arrival by polishing off the bottle of vodka and giving me broad, tooth-challenged grins.

I was staying at the Radisson Slavjanskaya Hotel, across the street from Moscow's main train station. The hotel had begun as a joint Russian-American venture, but the American partner was later murdered and his Russian partners were considered by some to be suspects. The lobby was nice, and the desk clerk spoke English and informed me I had a suite. As I rode up in the elevator, I began to think the place might be decent after all. Then I opened the door to my "suite" and found a small, stark room with two twins beds, towels so thin I could see through them, and a refrigerator that made so much noise I unplugged it. When I turned on the water in the bathtub, it came out the color of bourbon. I figured they just hadn't rented the room in a while, and I'd let the tap flow to get the rust out. After filling three tubs, I gave up and took a shower. The rust collected on the soap so quickly that by the end of the shower I felt as if I were scrubbing myself with a Brillo pad. Hey, exfoliation is supposed to be good for the circulation.

As was the case on most foreign trips we made with the President, our rooms were in a secure area near his staff's temporary offices and were protected by marine security guards, who demanded to see the identification badge of anyone who approached. There also was a large orange sign in each of our rooms that read THIS ROOM NOT SECURE FOR VERBAL COMMUNICATION—translation: "You're being bugged." The marine guards accompanied the hotel housekeepers when they cleaned our rooms and conducted regular searches to make sure we hadn't left any official documents lying around. We held all our countdown meetings at the embassy, and even that wasn't regarded as totally safe. For sensitive discussions, we were encouraged to use the embassy's "conversation tank," a room that had soundproof walls and debuggers.

When the National Security Council staff arrived at the hotel, the paranoia level ratcheted up a notch. Video cameras were set up in the hallways that led to the council's temporary offices, and the rooms themselves were stripped down to the studs and wrapped in thick insulation. In the end, the place looked more like a series of padded cells in a mental hospital than the top secret nerve center of American foreign policy. I can think of a few recent administrations for which that analogy is pretty apt.

The embassy control officer for the First Lady's visit was Nancy Sambaiew, the consul general and our third-ranking diplomat in Russia. Nancy's husband, Vladimir, an American of Russian decent, also worked for the State Department. He was responsible for figuring out how to transport the nuclear weapons we were buying from Ukraine and other former Soviet republics to the United States. I guess Federal Express had passed on the job. We were very fortunate to have Nancy, not only because she was kind and worked hard but also because her position gave her stature and credibility with the Russians.

The dynamics of this trip were very different from those in Japan. This was a bilateral summit meeting, not a gathering of world leaders. In Japan we just had to fine-tune the spousal program to fit Hillary's needs. Here we'd have to establish and negotiate her whole itinerary with the Russians.

With Nancy's help, I began discussions with Kirill Koupliakov, from President Boris Yeltsin's office, and Olga Malanovsky, a senior diplomat with the Ministry of Foreign Affairs. Our first meeting was held in Olga's office, and I was accompanied by three members of my staff. I couldn't help admiring the enormous portrait of Lenin on the wall and the hammer and sickle emblems on the three single-line telephones on her desk. The Communists had been out of power for only twelve months, and I guess the interior decorators were running behind schedule. Olga and Kirill were friendly and cooperative, and everything was going fine until Aleksey Kabakov, the representative from the Russian Federal Security Service (formally the KGB), showed up and bullied his way into the conversation. He was belligerent and stern to the point of parody, frowning, shaking his head, and raising objections to nearly everything we suggested. I'd been warned that the Russian security forces liked to throw their weight around and that I should meet fire with fire. No problem. The first time he raised his voice I let him have it.

"Who the hell do you think you are, telling the representatives of the First Lady of the United States what we can and can't do? In America we don't let our security people dictate our schedule, and it's not going to happen here either! You have a problem with that, let me know right now. Otherwise keep a lid on it."

The room was quiet. The members of my team sat there cringing. Olga and Kirill were deadpan. Kabakov narrowed his eyes, deepened his frown, and then, after an excruciatingly long pause, nodded and said, "Yeah-yeah, okay-okay." From that moment on he was a big pussycat, helpful and almost charming.

Unfortunately I can't say the same for the wife of the American ambassador. Our first event was to be a coffee with Naina Yeltsin at Spaso House, the ambassador's residence. I arranged a meeting with our hostess and her household staff to review the details. Spaso House is an ornate mansion donated to the American government by the Russians. In a city where most structures were decrepit and dirty, this well-maintained stately palazzo was a welcome exception. We cleared security at the outer gate; a servant met us at the door and escorted us into a parlor to meet our waiting host.

The ambassador's wife was a middle-aged woman with a lot of nervous energy and a pinched face. She was wearing a designer dress and looked as if she'd been pacing back and forth. Her deep-set, darting eyes were the first tipoff to her very odd personality. She seemed somehow offended that I wanted to have any input on the event. I explained to her as politely as I knew how that "Just leave everything to me" didn't cut it. I asked for a walk-through of the house so my team could draw the necessary site diagrams, and her irritation grew. When I told her we wanted to open the front door and have the two first ladies pose for a picture on the porch, she went ballistic.

"I don't think that's a good idea *at all*," she said. "The front doors have been sealed shut for the winter. Opening them would be very disruptive. There's a great deal of snow out there. Besides, I don't care for that view of the house. It's unattractive. There must be a better place for your picture."

"The preadvance team felt strongly that it would make a good picture. They even took some trial shots to find the best angles. They'd be very unhappy to hear that all their efforts were for nothing because the doors couldn't be opened. I'll pay for the plastic to have them resealed. You have my assurance that we'll leave everything just as we found it."

Her face tightened, and she glared at me. "This is my home, and I run it as I see fit."

"Well, my concern here is finding the best picture for the First Lady. That happens to be on the front porch. By the way, we're going to build a large press riser on the lawn. It's the only way we can be sure of getting the picture we want."

I smiled, as if to say, "It won't be all that bad," but I guess she didn't see it that way. She was rattled and all but threw me out of the house.

There was a countdown meeting at the embassy that evening, and when it was over, a young embassy staffer who was responsible for the residence approached me. "I have a direct message from the ambassador's wife," she said somewhat apologetically.

"Shoot," I answered, steeling myself.

"She thinks you're rude and resents you invading her house and turning it upside down. There will be no photo on the front porch, and that is final."

I paused a moment to give my blood pressure a chance to subside, then said: "Would you be so kind as to give her a direct message from me? Tell her it isn't *her* house, it belongs to the United States government, and we'll use any damn porch we please."

About midnight I had a telephone call in my room from Brady Williamson, the President's lead advance man for the trip. "Pat, I got a call from the ambassador. It was no fun. He spent a half hour telling me how upset his wife is."

"Brady, the woman is impossible."

"But she's married to the ambassador."

Protecting Hillary's interests was my job, and letting this affair escalate wasn't going to help me do it. "Listen, why don't I meet with the ambassador's wife first thing in the morning? I'll be on my best behavior and get everything straightened out."

I reported to Spaso House the next morning and was escorted into another parlor. A minute later the ambassador himself burst into the room, and I figured my goose was cooked. But to my great relief, the ambassador, a member of our career diplomatic corps, gave me a warm, calm smile. "It's a pleasure to meet you. Tell me what you need," he said.

Since he didn't mention his wife's behavior, I wasn't going to bring it up. I had a feeling it wasn't the first time she'd put him in this spot. I outlined my requests, and he took careful notes and even helped pace off the area on the front lawn where I wanted to put the press riser. His wife's name was never uttered, but he assured me there would be no further problems.

We worked long hours but still managed to scrape together a little recreational time. Moscow was a city of sharp contrasts, the beauty of the architecture offset by the abject poverty of so many of the people. As we drove around, I saw what I at first thought were long breadlines. They turned out to be impromptu beggars' markets, with people selling whatever they could: a single can of peas, one shoe, a broken hair dryer. These fledgling capitalists spread dirty towels on the smog-darkened snow and offered fish or discolored pieces of meat for sale. No packaging and definitely no USDA stamp of approval. The formal marketplaces weren't much better or much cleaner. At one of the large open-air markets on the city's outskirts, we saw people peddling everything from military night-vision goggles and army rifles to packages of marshmallow chicks stamp-dated the previous Easter. One man was dragging a bearskin around on his back, shouting out a price. The traders all wanted American cash, but we'd been warned that was illegal and instead carried wads of Russian rubles. The bearskin was tempting, but I decided to pass.

We managed to find a pizzeria and an Irish pub, both within three blocks of the Kremlin. I got a kick out of sitting in Rosie O'Grady's Saloon overlooking the onion domes of Moscow, drinking Guinness with Irish bartenders. There were casinos all over town, but they were run by mobsters, and even if you could avoid the crossfire from one of the frequent gun battles, the gambling tables weren't straight.

A few nights before the Clintons arrived I hosted a dinner for my Russian counterparts at a very nice restaurant they chose. There were five of them and five of us, and Russian tradition dictated that the senior male from each side had to propose one toast for each person on his team. The others could just take a small sip, but as lead I had to gulp down the whole shot, five for our people and five for Kirill's people. My first toast went something like: "To two great nations and two great peoples. May we co-exist in peace and friendship for centuries to come." My tenth toast was along the lines of: "Here's to the Boston Red Sox. You've got your Reds, and we've got ours." It was a great bonding experience, and since we were drinking good vodka, the hangover was manageable.

At the last minute President Clinton decided to make a brief stop in Kiev on his way to Moscow. That meant the First Lady would be arriving from Washington separately.

One of Hillary's idiosyncrasies is that she hates arrival ceremonies. She went to great lengths to avoid them, even flying into countries in the middle of the night. She liked to get off her plane, get in the limousine, and head to her first event. Her arrival in Moscow was at about four o'clock in the morning, so I managed to scale the airport greeting party down to just Olga Malanovsky and my old friend the ambassador's wife.

I boarded Hillary's plane amid the usual scurrying about by staff and air force stewards and found Hillary and Chelsea in their private cabin. "Better bundle up, girls. It's colder than Jesse Helms's heart out there, and we've arranged a fresh blanket of snow for your arrival."

"Pat! What brings you out so early in the morning?" Hillary asked with a laugh.

"Well, I was going to let you take a cab, but I figured you might have trouble finding one in this snowstorm."

It had been a year and a half since I first met Hillary, and we'd been through a lot together. Goodness knows we'd seen a lot of territory, from the sunshine of Florida to this frozen Russian morning. But it wasn't just the miles that I marveled at; it was the change in Hillary herself. She'd begun to grow into the role of First Lady and seemed able to differentiate the criticism she was getting for her health care initiative and her other political beliefs from attacks on her as a person. It couldn't have been easy to take that sort of abuse and even raw hatred, but she appeared to have developed an ability to compartmentalize it. To the outside world she presented a dignified and guarded profile. Behind the scenes, like those few moments on her plane, she was the same old fun and feisty Hillary.

The ambassador's wife insisted that she ride in the First Lady's limousine. When we arrived at Spaso House, Melanne Verveer, the First Lady's deputy chief of staff, jumped out of the limo and pulled me aside. "Pat, you certainly didn't make a friend of the ambassador's wife. She spent almost the entire ride complaining about you."

"How did Hillary respond?" I asked, pretty sure what the answer would be.

"She told her in no uncertain terms that she stood by her staff one thousand percent."

That's why we love Hillary so much.

For some reason, the ambassador's wife didn't speak to me for the remainder of the visit.

Just for the record, the photo op of Hillary and Mrs. Yeltsin on the front porch of Spaso House made the evening news on every network and ran as a two-page spread in both *Time* and *Newsweek.*

We'd scheduled a photo op for Hillary in Red Square that same day after a luncheon in the Kremlin's ornate Tzarina's Room. Immediately after that, she was going to join the President at the Ostankino television studio, where he was scheduled to address the Russian people. Hillary was supposed to exit the Kremlin in her motorcade and get out in front of St. Basil's Cathedral, the beautiful onion-domed masterpiece that's the signature of the square, and be photographed with a touring American hockey team. We'd set up barricades to hold back the press corps, which numbered about a hundred. There were a few spectators milling around, but everyone was behaving himself, and no one had strayed into the secure area.

The event started quietly enough, and we quickly got the photograph we were looking for. Then Hillary spotted a mother holding her baby, and her maternal instincts took over. She went over and admired the infant, whose parents immediately handed her the toddler.

In a split second all hell broke loose. The press corps swarmed out from behind the barricade to get the picture of Hillary cradling the baby. We tried to hold back the hordes, and the whole thing quickly degenerated into a massive pushing contest. Within moments we were surrounded, and there was no clear path back to the motorcade. The Secret Service sensed it was losing control of the situation.

"Clear!" went the shouted order. This was the Secret Service equivalent of code blue: Get the First Lady back to her car by *whatever* means necessary.

Instantly we were in the middle of an all-out brawl—with bodies flying and blood flowing—as the American agents surrounded Hillary and shielded her from harm while they pushed through the crowd to get back to the car. Russian security agents, recognizable by their expensive fur hats and flashing blackjacks, appeared out of the crowd and began to clobber people. The American agents were playing defense, and the Russians were playing offense, opening up people's heads with their clubs. There was total panic as the now out-of-control press went *mano a mano* with all the different agents. A few Russian civilians joined in just for the fun of it.

We managed to get Hillary back to the motorcade. Once I saw she was safe, I rushed to get into the lead car so we could take off. A photographer blocked my way and, trying to get a picture of Hillary in her limo, pushed me. I hit him square in the face so hard I thought I'd broken my hand. His nose exploded in an eruption of blood, and I was able to shove him out of the way and jump into the lead car. Doug Burke, the lead Secret Service agent, had worse luck. He'd been poked in the eye and was holding a handkerchief over what was soon a serious shiner.

When we got to the television studio, I found some ice, and Doug and I sat in the holding room, taking care of our wounds. When the show was over, we were supposed to fold into the President's motorcade for a joint movement back to the Radisson. But the President, characteristically, decided to hang around and tape some interviews for the networks back home. The First Lady, anxious to get ready for the state dinner, didn't want to wait and asked us to take her back to the hotel. When we told the Russians we were going to separate Hillary's motorcade from the President's, they said we couldn't because they didn't have the manpower to do a separate movement. We explained that that was unacceptable and told them we were going to leave immediately, with or without them. They reluctantly agreed to accompany us.

The Russians had a unique way of clearing traffic. They'd send out a couple of police cruisers with their sirens screaming and lights flashing. A police officer would hang out the window and wave cars off to the side with a long black and white baton, which with great understatement is called a *pazhaluysta* stick, being Russian for "please." If a car failed to pull over fast enough, the officer would whack its side with the baton. If the driver still didn't respond, he'd lean out a little farther and smack the front windshield where it meets the roof, spiderwebbing the glass. This *never* failed to get the motorist's attention and clear the street.

The first part of our trip back to the hotel was uneventful because the Russians had already started to close the streets for the President's motorcade. But when we got a little over halfway, we hit traffic, and out came the *pazhaluysta* sticks. The officers later claimed they set a record for the number of popped windshields.

That night there was a state dinner, followed by entertainment in St. George's Hall. When the evening's program was over, President and Mrs. Yeltsin invited the Clinton family to join them on a private tour of the Terem Palace, the sanctum sanctorum of the Kremlin, rarely seen by outsiders. There were eleven of us on the tour, and five were named Clinton or Yeltsin. We spent almost two hours exploring the ornate rooms that had served as the seat of the Russian Empire.

I was fascinated by the interaction between President Clinton and President Yeltsin, who spoke through an interpreter. Their body language communicated a certain discomfort, but at the same time it was obvious that each man was trying to reach out. They later developed a real rapport, and this was clearly an early bonding experience. As we walked through the historic rooms and I watched the two world leaders and their wives, I found myself quite moved. This was some gig I had.

The Clintons stayed overnight in the Kremlin, in a suite of rooms on the third floor. The following morning we were scheduled to do two formal departure ceremonies, one at the Kremlin and the other at the airport. The Russian security forces had issued me an identification pin that gave me free run of the Kremlin. I wandered around a little bit to see if anyone challenged me, and no one did. I couldn't help thinking back to all the times I'd crawled under my desk as a schoolkid, practicing for a Russian attack. Now here I was strolling around the capital of the Evil Empire as if I owned the place. Amazing.

When I reached the guest wing where the Clintons were staying, I ran into Capricia Marshall, the First Lady's personal assistant, who told me Hillary had asked to see me. After passing the final security checkpoint, I started down the private corridor toward their suite. On one side there were high windows overlooking a courtyard, and on the other was a series of doors that opened into parlors, anterooms, and dressing rooms. Suddenly one of the doors opened, and the President walked out wearing a baseball cap, briefs—and nothing else. I was shocked and embarrassed but had nowhere to turn. He and I got along, but I wouldn't say our friendship had reached that josh-around-in-your-underwear phase. I mean the guy was *the President.*

"Morning, Pat," he said with his trademark smile, as if this whole underwear thing were no big deal.

"Good morning, Mr. President. I'm, uh, sorry to disturb you it's just that, well, the First Lady, ah, asked to see me."

"Oh, yeah. She's in the bedroom."

"Is she . . . uh?"

"Yeah, she's dressed. Go on in. I've gotta go put some clothes on," he said, telling me something I already knew.

I found Hillary and Chelsea packing up the last of their things. Chelsea had bought a fur hat, and Hillary was trying it on. "Mom, you're not going to wear my new hat, are you?" Chelsea protested.

"Chelsea, how often do you borrow my things?"

"True. I *guess* it's all right if you wear my hat."

Hillary perched the hat on her head, and the three of us went out into the hall to meet the President, by now, to my relief, attired in a blue business suit.

"How do like my hat?" she asked.

"I like it a lot," he replied, "but the first ceremony's inside, so you won't want to wear it just yet."

With that Hillary took off the hat and handed it to me. We walked out of the guest wing and were joined by the usual entourage of aides and bodyguards for the walk to St. George's Hall for the departure ceremony.

These ceremonies tend to be formal and dull, and I could see the President and First Lady slipping into their official personas, serious and erect. I was holding the hat in my hands as if it were a cat. I realized this looked ridiculous and decided to have a little fun. I put the hat on my head, where I'm sure it looked even more ridiculous. The Russian agents were the first to notice and laughed quietly. That got the American agents' attention and they broke up too. The President glanced back to see what was so funny and grinned broadly. Then Hillary turned around, her eyes grew wide, and she said, "Lose the hat, Pat!" At this point everyone was laughing, and the good mood carried us right through the ceremony.

7

NO MORE YEARS

March–April 1994

I WAS ENJOYING LUNCH AND A GLASS OF AN OUTSTANDING MERLOT AT A small restaurant in the Napa Valley when the call came that former President Richard M. Nixon had died. Hillary was doing a series of events in Northern California, and his death meant a quick shuffling of her schedule. I headed down to Southern California to advance the funeral.

Advance for a funeral is, to say the least, a bit unusual. This particular funeral would involve four past presidents and dignitaries from around the world, and since the Republican old guard was running it, the atmosphere was a bit strained.

Our first meeting was at the Nixon Library in Yorba Linda, a small town in Orange County, about forty miles southeast of Los Angeles. The county is quite affluent and, until the recent of influx of Hispanic and Asian immigrants, was a Republican stronghold for years. One of the routes into Yorba Linda is a privately developed and operated toll road for those who don't mind paying a little extra to scream along in their luxury SUVs and avoid the rush-hour traffic. The Nixon Library is run-of-the-mill as presidential libraries go, its highlight being the president's boyhood home, which stands on a small plot behind the main building.

By the time I arrived for the countdown meeting the line of mourners extended out the front door and snaked down the walkway. I walked quietly through the large air-conditioned room where the body was laid out in a flag-draped casket. I was disappointed that it wasn't an open casket; Steve Graham has asked me to make sure the rascal was really dead.

I soon learned that all the arrangements were being handled by President Nixon's daughters, Tricia and Julie, whom the old guard referred to as the girls. Any mention we made of them as "the Nixon daughters," "the family," or "Mrs. Eisenhower and Mrs. Cox" was quickly and emphatically corrected to "the girls."

President Nixon was going to be accorded full military honors. As with presidential inaugurals, the armed forces play a major role in planning and executing presidential funerals. The military prides itself on being the keeper of the American image and is expert at pomp and circumstance. Sadly, since the military has to bury its war dead, it's also had a great deal of experience with solemn and dignified funerals.

After the countdown meeting I went to the nearby El Toro Marine Air Base to greet Hillary, who was arriving via motorcade from Los Angeles; the President was arriving separately from Washington. I can't say she seemed particularly saddened by Nixon's passing, but I couldn't help wondering if she was checking it all out and imagining what it would be like when President Clinton (or she herself) passed into that gentle night.

After the President's arrival our motorcade set out for Yorba Linda. The caravan stretched far into the bright California afternoon. As we made our way along the highway, the crowds began to form, at first just on the overpasses and then, as we got closer to Yorba Linda, along the roadside. By the time we reached the outskirts of town people were standing five and ten deep. Some waved American flags, some sported Nixon signs, some Clinton signs, and some cheered. Most simply stood in respectful silence.

We were greeted at the library by Governor and Mrs. Pete Wilson and the Reverend Billy Graham, who escorted the Clintons to their seats in the front section. The service was to take place in a courtyard behind the library. There was an electric buzz in the crowd, an excitement you could feel, natural when a large group of powerful and famous people are gathered together, especially in close proximity to the full national press.

Most of the Democrats I'd seen up close before, but this was the first time I'd laid eyes on Gerald and Betty Ford, George and Barbara Bush, Henry Kissinger, and Ronald and Nancy Reagan. The crowd was almost exclusively white and older, and it had that country club look of folks who had never punched a time clock. The women looked like department store mannequins—old department store mannequins.

Reverend Graham presided, and his measured, pious tone and stirring voice quickly quieted the assemblage and brought the proper level of dignity to the proceeding. It was easy to see why he was considered America's pastor. The service progressed with a mixture of music, religion, and political speechmaking. The speeches were punctuated with hymns by the Army Chorus and somber musical interludes by the Marine Corps Band. The former President, who once tried to dress the White House guards in uniforms that looked like something from the court of King Louis XIV, would have been pleased. Governor Wilson, who had started his career in politics as an advance man for Nixon, spoke with passion about Nixon's career and went so far as to imply he had actually won the 1960 election but had decided not to contest the outcome "for the good of the country." Noticeably omitted was any mention of Nixon's legacy of criminal activities and conspiracy.

As the speeches came to a conclusion, I moved to the burial plot with the rest of the Clinton advance team so we would be in position to escort the Clintons back to the library after the interment.

Nixon was going to be buried beside his childhood home, next to his wife, Pat. The earth had been dug up, and its rich black texture stood in sharp contrast with the red carpet ringing the grave. Only the immediate family and the former presidents were present for the actual interment. It was more than a little eerie to watch the Nixon girls, their husbands, Reverend Graham, and the five living presidents—Ford, Carter, Reagan, Bush, and Clinton—and their wives bow their heads as Graham intoned a final prayer asking the Almighty for forgiveness and salvation. The Nixon girls dabbed at their tears with white handkerchiefs.

While a soldier in full dress uniform began to fill the grave, a sailor played taps, and the military issued a twenty-one–cannon salute. The cannon fire was so loud and percussive that it set off car alarms, and the silence between rounds was pierced by their wailing.

We moved forward and escorted the Clintons along the walkway and back to the library. As we did so, a man approached the President and attempted to engage him in conversation. About fifty, he was sweating profusely in a light-colored suit. He was clearly out of place, and I wondered how he had crashed the scene since the area was tightly secured. The President nodded respectfully and kept walking. As we reached the entrance to the library, the man tried to follow President Clinton inside. My colleague Wendy Smith and I, thinking that this might turn ugly, body blocked him and made sure the door was closed and locked with our new friend on the outside. In a situation like this, there's a fine legal line that the Secret Service is wary of crossing. If a person doesn't appear to be an immediate threat to the President or First Lady's safety, it's up to the staff to intervene. Since this fellow was doing nothing but trying to talk to the President, his actions were deemed more of a nuisance than a threat.

There were three gatherings after the service: one exclusive to the presidents and their families, another for the diplomatic corps, and a third for the remaining dignitaries. Our first stop was the small gathering downstairs, to which only the Nixon girls and the former presidents and their wives had been invited. Betty Ford and Barbara Bush quickly engaged in deep conversation with Nancy Reagan; Rosalyn Carter and Hillary chatted with the presidents and each other. Nancy Reagan didn't look anywhere near as mean as I had imagined, and surprisingly it was Mrs. Carter who was giving off negative vibes. She seemed to be very uncomfortable, wearing a pained expression and looking distracted. The Nixon girls were quite composed and circulated among their guests, thanking them for coming.

It was fascinating to see all of the living presidents and first ladies in one place and witness their interaction. It was, on balance, very cordial. I suppose that's natural for such accomplished political figures, but I couldn't help recalling that Presidents Ford, Carter, and Bush had each been denied a second term in bitter, bare-knuckle campaigns. Yet they and their wives mingled with one another like suburban couples getting together for a barbecue.

I was surprised at how much President Carter had aged and how good President Bush looked, clearly rested and refreshed. At one point Presidents Clinton, Bush, and Ford came together, and I sidled over, eager to hear their exchange.

"I envy you, having all the time in the world to play golf," Clinton said to Bush.

"There's no doubt about it, golf is a lot better for your health than governing," Bush bantered.

"That's true, unless you happen to be a spectator when I'm playing," President Ford cracked.

Standing nearby was Ronald Reagan, a mythic figure, a giant in American politics and history, a man whose iconic visage—and hair—were burned into every American's consciousness. Now I was staring at him in the flesh, not five feet away.

He must have noticed me staring because he approached at an amiable shuffle and stuck out his hand. "Hello, I'm Ronald Reagan. What's your name?" he asked with a big smile.

"Patrick Halley, Mr. President. It's an honor to meet you."

"Halley, huh? Good to see they've still got an Irishman or two kicking around the White House. My folks were from Ireland, you know."

"Yes, sir, and I remember you calling into the South Boston St. Patrick's Day breakfast when you were president. It was the best reception a Republican ever got in that part of town."

"Well, I did my best. Nice to meet you."

Ronald Reagan was a larger-than-life character, and I was amazed that in person he seemed so small. He was at least four inches shorter than President Clinton and an inch or two shorter than President Bush. His famous hair, caricatured in countless cartoons, was a brownish red, not the jet black I'd always imagined. There was a lot of whispering in political circles and in the press that he was already showing signs of Alzheimer's disease—many even claimed the symptoms first appeared during his second term as president—but the old Gipper certainly seemed all there to me, right down to the famous twinkle in his eye and his movie star presence. I had absolutely no use for the man's politics, but I'd be less than honest if I didn't admit a certain thrill at meeting him.

A little later I saw President Carter talking to a member of the library staff, obviously making some sort of request. I overhead the man answer, "I can't help you with that. You'll have to find it on your own." Beyond being shocked at the man's rudeness and lack of grace, I felt bad for President Carter. I approached him. "Excuse me, President Carter, are you looking for a men's room?" I asked as respectfully as possible.

Carter looked a little taken aback, no doubt still reacting to his previous encounter, and then explained, "No, I'm not looking for the men's room. I want to leave."

I looked around and didn't see any aides or Secret Service agents attending him or Mrs. Carter. Strange. "May I arrange a ride for you?" I asked.

"No, I don't want a ride. I just want to leave."

This was quickly going from bad to worse. "How did you get here?" I asked.

"I have a motorcade, Secret Service agents, and everything!" the somewhat exasperated former president said, no doubt thinking they just didn't make presidential aides like they used to.

I got on my radio and was able to track down the Carters' Secret Service detail. A short while later they were on their way.

We moved upstairs to a larger reception for former Nixon aides and members of the diplomatic community. There were a couple of hundred people milling about and schmoozing as they would at a cocktail party. It was a sort of Irish wake for a WASP president, one that was quickly starting to feel like an out-of-body experience. All the political figures I had read about as a young man were suddenly rubbing elbows with me. It was as if a history book—open to the rogues' gallery—had come to life. John Dean and John Ehrlichman floated by, as did Dan Quayle. Chuck Colson, Henry Kissinger, and a raft of other famous Nixon aides hovered about.

Suddenly Capricia Marshall grabbed my arm and yanked me close. "Oh, my God, it's him!" she whispered. I turned to look, and she hissed, "Don't look now!"

Just at that second, G. Gordon Liddy slid by like a shark in an aquarium. Liddy was the Nixon aide who had been the White House go-between with the Watergate burglars; he was a certified whack job. He had once held his hand over a burning candle at a cocktail party to prove how tough he was; the other attendees, sickened by the smell of his burning flesh, asked him to stop. At the height of the Watergate investigation he had offered to take the fall for Nixon. He had said he would stand on a Washington street corner and allow them to shoot him dead; they just had to tell him where and when to appear. He had served time in prison for his Watergate involvement and now hosted a radio talk show on which he had referred to government agents as jackbooted thugs; he had even instructed his listeners on how to avoid the agents' body armor when shooting at them. Liddy was a scary-looking fellow with a permanent scowl and a mad look in his eye, and he wasn't talking to anyone. He'd walk up really close, look at you dead-eyed, and then just drift away. You felt as if he were still working for Nixon, casing out the enemy, hatching sinister plots deep into the night. After he passed by, Capricia relaxed her grip on my arm. A cold drop of sweat made its way slowly down my spine.

Eventually we moved into the main hall of the library for the final reception with all the invited guests. We had requested some sort of rope and stanchion receiving line, but the Nixon girls had said no, so the room was basically a free-for-all. By this time Hillary had had enough of the Republican crowd and was anxious to get going; we worked our way quickly across the room, shaking hands and avoiding any lengthy conversations.

"I think we've paid our respects. Let's let these people go on with their reception," she said as we stood near the door.

The President was following behind, but as usual was stopping to talk with anyone who showed any interest. At the rate he was going we would have been there for hours.

Hillary sat down on a bench near the door. "Pat, please tell the President it's time to go," she instructed me.

"Hillary, he has three of his own people there to keep him moving."

"They're obviously not capable of doing it. You know how he is. I want *you* to go get the President."

I made my way back through the crowd, slid past his aides, and got close enough to make eye contact. He got the message and began to follow me toward the door. Everything was going great until we ran into Chuck Colson. Colson had been known as Nixon's hatchet man, the guy behind a lot of the dirty deeds, and he had pleaded guilty to obstruction of justice in 1974 for helping plot the Watergate cover-up. While serving a lengthy jail term, he had become a born-again Christian. He stuck his hand out, said hello to the President, and that was it. Clinton seemed fascinated with what Colson had to say, a soliloquy on ethics, prison reform, and religion, and settled in for a discussion. He wouldn't budge. For the next fifteen minutes I tried everything short of tugging on his sleeve, but no dice. Finally, in desperation, I started clearing a path between the President and the door, figuring that he might get the hint.

Pete Dowling, a Secret Service supervisor, grabbed me by the arm. "Get lost, Pat," he said forcefully.

I glared back at him and said, "As soon as you let go of me, I'll think about moving."

Dowling released my arm, and I retreated to where the First Lady was waiting. "Why isn't the President with you?" she demanded.

"I did my best, but you can't win them all. It's going to be a few more minutes."

Her silence spoke volumes. Fortunately for me, the President finally shook off Colson, and we were able to leave.

Pete Dowling's actions had puzzled me. I'd always worked closely with the Secret Service agents and been told I was one of their favorite staff people. I'd never so much as had cross words with one of them before, much less a physical confrontation. I later learned that the Secret Service was very much on edge that day because of our sweaty friend in the light-colored suit who had accosted the President in the courtyard. It seems that he'd been under watch for threatening presidents in the past and had somehow slipped through security. As if that weren't bad enough, this fellow had told reporters that the Secret Service wasn't doing its job. Pete later apologized, and we resumed our friendship.

The sun was setting and the sky was a deep red as we drove back to the air base. It had been a weird day, sort of like going back home to visit your parents after all the kids have grown up and moved out. Everyone looks familiar, but somehow there's an emptiness. The Nixon crowd, the folks who had run the country in my youth, were all over the hill, and now we controlled the White House. We got to fly on the big plane. And I was able to report to Steve Graham: Yes, the rascal really *was* dead.

8

CODE BLUE

May–October 1994

JUNE BROUGHT THE FIFTIETH ANNIVERSARY OF D-DAY, THE NORMANDY invasion that marked the beginning of the liberation of Europe and the turning point of World War II. President Reagan had used the fortieth anniversary ten years earlier to deliver a stirring speech on the windswept sands of Normandy in which he saluted "the boys of Pointe de Hoc" for their valiant contribution to the longest day. The speech had bolstered Reagan's already formidable lead in his race for reelection. President Clinton hoped to use the occasion to catch lightning in a jar for the second time.

The midterm elections, the first chance that voters would have to register their feelings about the Clinton administration, were only five months off. The entire House of Representatives and a third of the Senate seats would be contested. Representative Newt Gingrich, a nettlesome backbencher from a suburban Atlanta district, was leading the charge for a Republican takeover of the House. Gingrich was almost as fascinating, and repellent, a figure as Richard Nixon. Portly, with pinched features, and a thick mop of gray hair, he possessed manic energy, read history voraciously, purported to love animals, had risen from a modest background, and was one of the most partisan, angry, and destructive individuals in American political history. He almost single-handedly changed the tone in Washington from one of civility and honest disagreement to one of personal destruction. Gingrich's politics were extremely conservative, and he dragged the entire Republican party over to the far right.

For more than ten years Gingrich had methodically recruited and cultivated a host of young disciples, almost a cult, to whom he regularly mailed inspirational tapes. He was grooming this cadre of humorless young men (there were few, if any, women) to run for Congress in their home districts across the nation, and scores of them ended up on the ballot. Gingrich was calling for nothing less than a second American Revolution and in language that was incendiary. At one point he sent his followers a list of words with which to label their opponents and their platforms; these included "grotesque," "bizarre," and "despicable." By June, Gingrich was getting the first whiffs of impending victory, and he was doing everything he could to derail Clinton's agenda and frame the debate coming into the fall. Because he had avoided the draft during the Vietnam War, the President was vulnerable on military issues, and his trip to Normandy was an opportunity for him to shore up this weakness and to demonstrate his stature on the world stage and his extraordinary abilities as an empathetic orator.

David Gergen, a Republican who had served as director of communications in Reagan's White House, had signed on as a senior adviser to President Clinton and was playing a major role in the planning for the trip. Gergen came aboard at a time when it was widely believed that the White House needed some "grown-ups" to bolster Clinton's young and inexperienced staff. He was an old Washington hand, having served in the Nixon and Ford administrations before leaving Reagan to become editor of *U.S. News & World Report.* He was tall and stocky, with thinning blond hair and a booming bass voice. While his politics weren't exactly my cup of tea, I have to admit that he brought a welcomed sense of strength and order to what had been until then a chaotic atmosphere.

Gergen called a large meeting in Washington for everyone working on the trip. Those of us who couldn't make it in person participated by speakerphone. He painstakingly laid out the rationale for the trip and told us what he hoped the President could accomplish: "President Reagan used this same trip in 1984 to rally America's spirit around the brave deeds of our soldiers. He made Americans remember the sacrifice and courage that made us one of the most powerful nations in history. The veterans who will be reuniting on Normandy Beach changed the course of history, and they deserve our utmost respect and honor. President Clinton's trip has to be tasteful, respectful, and, above all, understated. No advance gimmicks here. Remember the veterans. It's their day."

Most of us attending the meeting were born well after the Second World War, and he took a good deal of time sensitizing us to the remarkable achievement of the Army Rangers at Pointe du Hoc. In reverential tones he recounted how they had scaled a steep cliff to take out a German machine-gun nest that was raining death on the American soldiers disembarking on the beach below. Half the unit had died in the effort. "Imagine the courage it took to jump onto that rope and start climbing when the guy right ahead of you, your buddy, has just been shot and killed. These guys operated on sheer courage, and their guts and determination saved hundreds of American lives." He wanted to be absolutely certain everyone on the White House staff treated the returning veterans, all in their seventies now, with the utmost respect.

Gergen's meeting was an interesting exercise for a second reason as well: It was the first and only time the senior staff at the White House shared its goals for a trip with the advance staff. It gave us all a common point of reference and, I think, contributed greatly to the success of the trip.

President Clinton, as President Reagan had done ten years before him, delivered a powerful, moving tribute to the heroes of Normandy Beach. Despite his sometimes frosty relationship with the military, the veterans welcomed his sincere expression of gratitude on behalf of the nation. For many of these veterans it would be the last time they'd see this hallowed ground on which, half a century earlier, they'd risked their lives to save democracy.

I was assigned the Paris leg of the trip, which came after Normandy. Lawry Payne was Hillary's lead, and my assignment was primarily to explore some fun things the Clintons could do if they found any spare time. Every job has its challenges, but few are more daunting than tooling around Paris with a car, a driver, an unlimited expense account, and the help of the embassy staff, trying to find amusing ways to while away a few hours. I was close to trading in my scally cap for a beret.

The most memorable part of our advance planning for the trip was a visit to the American Cultural Center, a new Frank Gehry–designed building about fifteen miles outside Paris, which Hillary had been asked to dedicate. Connoisseurs of architecture may have appreciated the design, but to me it looked hopelessly confused and half finished, as if five contractors had worked on the construction simultaneously using five different blueprints. It was a jumble of odd shapes and assorted materials.

The edifice may have been eccentric, but it couldn't hold a candle to the art inside. The ground-floor galleries were nearly empty. The director, a middle-aged woman dressed from head to toe in black, including thick black oval glasses, explained they were still moving in and that there would be more to see by the time the First Lady arrived. The main gallery upstairs was filled with upside-down packing crates. Brown paper bags containing workers' half-eaten lunches rested on top. There was also a twenty-seven-foot-long green kitchen cabinet and a stepladder with a paint can on it. Despite the building's ugly exterior, this was an attractive space.

"When are you going to install the exhibits?" I asked the director.

She shot me an icy look. "These *are* the exhibits," she huffed.

Oh, boy. Just then Armando Servin, the lead Secret Service agent for the trip, came over and tugged on my sleeve. He'd been looking at a mobile hanging from the ceiling. Its panels were made up of photographs. "Pat, you've got to look at this. I think we have a problem."

I walked over to the mobile and couldn't believe what I saw. The photos in this particular "work of art" were of a man masturbating. The conclusion was explosively graphic. It reconfirmed my notion that the people who call this stuff art should be spanked and sent to bed without their dinners.

As we jumped into our van and beat a hasty retreat back to downtown Paris, I told Lawry we had to cancel the First Lady's visit to the center. He was reluctant to offend the folks who ran it, so he used his cell phone to call Patti Solis for her opinion. He talked with her for about ten minutes, outlining this and that problem with the site, but beating around the bush, if you'll excuse the expression.

Finally I became exasperated and grabbed the phone. "Patty, one of their major works of art is pictures of a guy whacking off. I mean real vivid pictures," I said.

"Oh, my God!" Patti yelled. "We can't take Hillary there!"

My point exactly. Case closed.

The Clintons were staying at the ambassador's residence, which was a few doors away from the Élysée Palace, the home of the president of France. The ambassador, Pamela Harriman, had done a little redecorating, and the mansion was extraordinary.

As was Pamela Harriman. Considered one of the twentieth century's great beauties, with elegant features and porcelain skin, she was in her early seventies, a widow who'd been married three times. Her first husband, whom she married when she was nineteen, had been Randolph Churchill, Winston Churchill's son; her second, the legendary show business agent Leland Hayward; and her third, Averell Harriman, former governor of New York State and heir to a great railroad fortune. Pamela Harriman was an ardent Democrat and longtime Clinton supporter and fund-raiser. The ambassadorship had been her reward. I was prepared to encounter an overbearing socialite and instead found a charming and gracious woman who was clearly comfortable in her own skin.

When I went to her residence to check out the suite the President and First Lady would be using, I was surprised to find Ambassador Harriman there to greet me personally. She had on a very pricey suit, wore her hair swept up and back, and still projected an air of poise and beauty.

"Welcome to the *little place* they give the ambassador to live," she said, tongue firmly in cheek, sweeping her arm to indicate the opulent parlors and a manicured garden visible through tall windows. "I really hope you'll make yourself at home, and if there's anything at all I, or the household staff, can do, please let me know."

I was smitten. "This is an extraordinary house, but the art doesn't strike me as typical State Department issue. Did you add to the collection?"

"Yes, I brought a few things from my place in New York. I hope you enjoy them," she said casually.

"Listen, I've got nothing against Degas or Monet. And isn't that an early Picasso?" I said, proud to show off a little of my newly minted knowledge of French art.

She tilted her head and gave me a sly little smile. "Why, yes. I see the White House sent the right man to Paris."

Hey, it's not every day you get to flirt with a legendary beauty, one who is an ambassador to boot.

The Clintons arrived late on the evening of June 6, after a long and emotional day at Pointe du Hoc. After being greeted by Ambassador Harriman, Hillary headed off to the bedroom suite. President Clinton lingered for a moment, discussing his plans for the next day with Mort Engelberg, the lead of his advance team. Mort was very close to the President, enjoying the same type of relationship with him as I did with the First Lady. When the President realized there was some free time in his schedule, he said, "I want to go to the Cathedral of Notre Dame."

Mort looked a little disgusted and said, "We looked at that, but it's too touristy. I think we should walk through the Île de la Cité and visit a café."

"Mort, I'm going to the Cathedral of Notre Dame."

"Yeah, yeah," Mort muttered as President Clinton turned and walked away.

The President got about halfway down the hall, turned around, and walked back to where Mort and I were standing. "Damn it, Mort, I'm going to the Cathedral of Notre Dame. Is that clear? I won't get on that plane until I've been to the cathedral." He stalked away again.

"Yeah, yeah," Mort said again, winking at me.

That stopped the President in his tracks. He spun around and bore down on me. "Pat," he said.

"Let me guess, Mr. President," I said. "You're going to the Cathedral of Notre Dame and you won't get on your plane until you do."

"Right!" the President said as he clapped me on the back. "Damn! I'm glad someone around here listens."

Mort made kissing lips at me: you suckup. The three of us burst out laughing, and the President disappeared down the hall.

Hillary had an ambitious schedule that included a visit to the Paris Opéra House to watch a ballet performance, lunch at the Matignon Palace with the French prime minister, and a tour of the Rodin Museum.

Lunch with the prime minister should have been a piece of gâteau. It wasn't. Lawry had gotten it into his head that he didn't want the First Lady to leave by the palace's front door with the President because the two of them heading in separate directions would make an awkward photo. He badgered his counterparts to let Hillary leave by the back door. This offended their French sense of protocol, and they refused to consider it. The more Lawry pestered them, the more intractable they became. The fight went on for several days and was never settled. So, on the day of the event Lawry, Hillary's staff, and her motorcade all were waiting at the front door for her to emerge from the luncheon. They waited and waited and waited. President Clinton emerged and departed. No Hillary. The guests started departing. Still no Hillary. Finally Lawry asked where the First Lady was. He was told she had left sometime before, *by the back door.*

I was at the Rodin Museum listening to all this on the walkie-talkie and couldn't believe what I was hearing. It sounded as if Hillary were lost on the streets of Paris.

The back door of the Matignon Palace opens onto a small street two blocks from the front gate. Hillary had been let out amid profuse apologies for the modesty of her exit and told her rude and high-handed staff had insisted. She emerged to find an empty street and started walking around the block in search of her motorcade, which by that time was going around the block in the other direction. To say she was angry doesn't begin to describe her mood.

She was still steaming when she got to the Rodin Museum.

"Hello, Hillary," I said cheerfully. "Come right this way, and I'll introduce you to the director of the museum."

Nothing. Unless you want to count a glacial stare. She followed me silently, and I could tell she would have rather been getting a root canal than traipsing through the Rodin Museum with one more member of her bungling staff. The visit was perfunctory and ended with Hillary's posing for a photo with a group of schoolchildren in front of *The Thinker.* Even the adorable kids in their cute little uniforms didn't improve her mood.

"That was a nice picture," I said hopefully as I led her back to the motorcade.

"It was contrived," she shot back. "I don't happen to travel with twenty kids in school uniforms, so anyone will know it was a setup. Why did you put me in such an awkward setting? You could have found a better picture, or you could have skipped the whole thing."

It was turning into a long afternoon. Back at the ambassador's residence she gave Lawry an earful.

The following morning the Clintons slept late, and everyone was waiting in the motorcade when they came down. Lawry, who normally would have been waiting dutifully outside the bedroom suite when they emerged, was still recovering from the blistering Hillary had given him and was sitting with me in the support van. We saw President Clinton get in one side of the limousine and a blond woman get in the other, and off we went. One of the embassy people in the van said it was about a half hour ride to the airport. I told him we weren't going to the airport; we were going to the Cathedral of Notre Dame. He insisted I was wrong and was amazed at my prescience when the motorcade veered off the road and came to a stop outside the cathedral.

Lawry and I approached the limousine on the left side, Hillary's side. The doors were opened, and to our surprise Ambassador Harriman got out. Where was Hillary? I peered inside the limo. She's got to be in there somewhere, I thought. No dice. The blond woman we had seen getting into the car was Pamela Harriman. Hillary was still back at the residence! Lawry had managed to lose her for the second time in two days.

By the time we got back to the residence Lawry was sweating bullets and asked me to go in and get Hillary. I did as requested and found her in the second-floor bedroom suite. She had remained behind to finish packing and dressing, but was now more than ready to leave. I could see that she was in a less than perfect mood, and I tried to cheer her up. "Did you see the nice photograph in the *International Herald Tribune* of you and the schoolchildren at the Rodin Museum?"

"I did."

"See, the event wasn't that bad. We got a great picture from it."

"There's no accounting for taste," she growled.

"My, we've got our claws out today, don't we?" I replied.

That did it. She broke out laughing and apologized for snapping at me. This time the motorcade really did go to the airport.

––––––––

The summer of 1994 was a long one for Hillary. Opposition to the Clinton administration's universal health care plan grew, and in late August it was pronounced dead by congressional leaders. The legislation Hillary had worked so hard to promote for the previous year and a half, and along with it her dream of providing quality affordable health care to *all* Americans, expired silently and ignominiously.

Newt Gingrich leaped on the failure as one more indication of the Clintons' ineptitude and allegiance to big government. It was close to Labor Day, the traditional kickoff of the election season; Gingrich and his fellow Republicans sensed blood in the water. Virtually every speech they delivered, every press release they produced, singled out Hillary for vilification. There could be no doubt: They wanted voters to walk into that booth with her failed health care plan uppermost in their minds.

In the face of all this criticism her spirits were clearly flagging. I was worried about her and knew that with the election looming life was going to get worse before it got better.

Hillary's birthday is October 26, and Steve Graham and I were slated to do a trip to Chicago with her for that day. Chicago is one city I was always delighted to be sent to, for three reasons: It's Hillary's hometown, the people are incredible, and in my epicurean opinion it has the best cheeseburgers and pizza on the planet.

I was packing when Steve phoned me. "Pat, I just got a strange call from the White House. All they said was that we should unpack our Chicago bags and pack for the Middle East."

"That's it? Didn't you pump for more?"

"Believe me, I tried. But they were very abrupt and told me the line wasn't secure."

A last-minute overseas trip is highly unusual for the president of the United States. Moreover, this one was to the Middle East, the world's tinderbox. As I repacked, my curiosity and excitement grew. The politician in me knew that we were just weeks from the midterm elections, and no doubt the White House was trying to create favorable coverage for the President and steal headlines from the hard-charging Newt Gingrich and his minions. But the eager traveler in me was thrilled at the thought of visiting such a fascinating part of the world.

At one in the morning Steve called back. "We're going to Israel for the signing of a peace treaty between Israel and Jordan," he told me. Prolonged diplomatic negotiations between the two countries had finally borne fruit, and they were scheduled to sign a peace accord within the week.

"Why all the secrecy?"

"Israel is considered a dangerous assignment at the moment."

The week before, a terrorist bomb had destroyed two city buses and killed a number of people in downtown Tel Aviv. In addition, three people had been killed in a shoot-out a couple of blocks from the King David Hotel, where we would be staying. The militants who didn't agree with the peace accord figured the best way to derail it was through violence.

When our plane landed at Ben Gurion Airport in Tel Aviv, we were spirited into an armored car for the ride to Jerusalem; we could barely see through the bulletproof glass. It was late at night and we were jet-lagged by the time we got to the hotel, but we all were called to an immediate security briefing by the embassy's residential security officer (RSO). I've heard RSO briefings all over the world, and they all boil down to the same recommendation: If you stay in your room, under the bed, with the door double-locked, and don't answer the phone, you *might* survive your stay in the country. It's the same message in Ottawa as in Beirut. The reason is simple: The RSO doesn't want the headache of springing you from the local slammer, and there's a hell of a lot of paperwork involved if you get injured in his jurisdiction.

This briefing was a little different for two reasons. First of all, the RSO told us to try to blend in with the population. Don't wear clothing that will give you away as an American. Speak Hebrew if you know how. There were about fifteen advance people, and Steve and I were the only two who weren't Jewish. Both of us are Irish Catholic, and we look it. Scottish we might pass for. Israeli? Forget about it.

The other unusual thing was that we were given a specific list of places that were off-limits. We couldn't visit the Old City, particularly the Arab section. The West Bank was not to be entered, neither were the Dead Sea and Bethlehem. Don't even think of going anywhere near the Jordanian border.

When the briefing was over, I looked at Steve. "Did you get that list of things for us to see tomorrow?" I asked.

"Got it," he replied.

The next day was Saturday, the Sabbath, and everything in Israel was closed, so we had the day off. Steve and I knew there was no way we'd be able to blend in, so we put on American flag T-shirts and headed straight for the Arab section of the Old City, where we bought straw cowboy hats.

Our outfits earned us some puzzled looks, but everyone left us alone. We figured that if we couldn't be inconspicuous, the next best thing was to be totally obvious. People would think we were either crazy or heavily armed, maybe both. We went to the Wailing Wall, the Dome of the Rock, and the Al-Aqsa Mosque. We drank coffee and haggled with merchants over the price of souvenirs. After lunch we went back to the King David and found our driver.

The State Department always supplies cars and drivers for White House advance teams. State long ago figured out that it was a lot cheaper to pay someone to haul us around than to settle all the damage claims that would result if we drove ourselves. Drivers on foreign trips come in two distinct varieties: drunks and spies (or some combination of the two). They don't all work for the host country's intelligence services, but you can be sure they report, and in many cases record, every word you say in the car.

Our driver in Israel went by the name Ghazy. He didn't look like your typical livery service driver: He was trim and fit, and he wore nice clothes and an expensive wristwatch.

"Ghazy," I said, "we've got a busy afternoon ahead of us. We want to go swimming in the Dead Sea and check out the West Bank, particularly the areas near the Jordanian border."

Without missing a beat, Ghazy answered, "No problem."

Ghazy drove a black Mercedes and was greeted at the checkpoints like a long-lost brother. The people in the cars in front of us had to open their trunks and present papers. Not Ghazy. We were waved through with a friendly smile. When I bent over to pick up something off the floor, I noticed an Uzi machine gun under his seat. Nice touch.

We went all the way across the West Bank to the shores of the Dead Sea. It's so salty that you can't sink. You just lie back and enjoy floating; you're your own raft. After a nice swim and a cold shower to wash off the salt, we headed back through Jerusalem and onward to Bethlehem. Despite the air-conditioned comfort of our Mercedes, it was possible to imagine what life had been like here in the desert for the past two thousand years. The land was barren except for the occasional scrub brush, and we saw local boys leading a camel toward town. Bethlehem was a jumble of narrow, winding streets lined with sandstone houses with uneven roofs. Take away the electrical wires and occasional television antenna, and it probably still looked something like what Joseph and Mary saw as they searched for a place to spend the night. We visited the Christ child's birthplace and even posed for pictures with some of the security forces. All in all, we had a grand time for ourselves without a spot of trouble.

The next morning we had a meeting with our Israeli counterparts in the ballroom of the hotel. The executive secretary of the National Security Council presided. The Americans were impeccable in suits and ties; most of the Israelis were wearing blue jeans. After mutual introductions, one of the Israelis said something innocuous about the arrival ceremony, and the children of God went beserk and began screaming at one another and throwing things. Within moments the ballroom looked like a scene from a Marx Brothers movie. We sat there in shock and watched the donny-brook. I knew the Israelis were a volatile and emotional people, but this was wild. After a few minutes of pure pandemonium, the senior Israeli stood up, took off his shoe, and banged it on the table like a gavel, yelling for everyone to shut up. His colleagues slowly took their seats and quieted down. There was stunned silence from our side as we tried to make sense of what we had just witnessed. Then one of our folks asked a question, one of the Israelis replied, and the whole mess started all over again. It was going to be a long week.

With such short notice all the attention had been focused on the President, with little thought given to the First Lady's schedule. Steve and I contacted Eitan Haber, Prime Minister Yitzak Rabin's chief of staff, for help. He invited us to come right over for a meeting. His office was in a small, heavily fortified building where the prime minister and cabinet members had offices. When we arrived, Haber's secretary informed us he was stuck in an unscheduled meeting. We sat in his outer office, and a few minutes later the door opened and Prime Minister Rabin emerged in shirtsleeves and open collar, smoking a cigarette. He was a slight man in his sixties, whose craggy face and wise, penetrating eyes gave him a grand-fatherly appearance.

"Hello, Mr. Halley, Mr. Graham, I'm Prime Minister Rabin."

"A pleasure to meet you, sir," I managed to get out.

"Could you possibly spare me a few minutes?" he asked.

"I think that could be arranged," Steve said.

He led us into his office and offered us seats. As world leaders' offices go, it was a modest affair. The windows were thick bulletproof glass, and papers were strewn all over his desk and on a table behind it. You definitely got the sense the place was for work, not ceremony. The prime minister showed us to seats at a coffee table and called out to an aide, holding out his index and middle fingers, first together and then spread slightly apart. I was at a loss to figure out what that meant until a moment later when the aide returned with three glasses of scotch and a small bowl of cigarettes.

"I am so happy that the First Lady is going to accompany the President. I am a great admirer of her work and want to do everything I can to make sure she enjoys her stay in Israel," he said. He was warm and charming, a regular guy, completely unaffected by the weight of his office.

After a few minutes of friendly conversation the encounter was over. "I'll let you get to your meeting with Eitan," he said, leading us to the door. "By the way, those suits are nice, but you boys don't have to dress up in this heat. Enjoy your time with us, and let me know if there's anything we can do for your First Lady."

We thanked the prime minister and walked across the hall to where his chief of staff was waiting for us. Haber was an intense fellow in his fifties, who talked in machine-gun-like bursts and somehow managed always to be doing more than one thing at a time. Like the prime minister, he was working in shirtsleeves, which were rolled up to expose thick arms extending from a barrel chest. As he spoke to us, he also yelled at his secretary, talked on the phone, and signed the multitude of papers his aides kept putting in front of him.

Steve is a history buff, and he engaged Haber in an animated discussion about Israeli warfare. When Steve gets into a subject I'm unfamiliar with, I'm never sure if he's on the level or tapping into the Irish gift for embellishment, and I was concerned that he might be stretching his credibility with some of his assertions. At one point he mentioned a specific battle in which he thought the tank maneuvers were brilliant. I was sure he was making it up. Haber excused himself and left the room. A minute later he returned with the general who had led the battle Steve had been rhapsodizing about. I was impressed.

In Israel the prime minister is the head of government and the president is the head of state. The prime minister is the guy with all the power, but the president is involved with anything having to do with pomp and circumstance. The president of Israel at the time was Ezer Weizman, a retired air force general with a stiff, formal manner. Weizman didn't get along with Rabin. We were told by Rabin's people that we would have to get information about the role Mrs. Weizman would play in the visit directly from his office. We contacted his chief of staff, who invited us for breakfast the next morning at the president's house, where the staff had its offices.

Our driver delivered us to the gate of the two-story mansion, and we were checked in by heavily armed soldiers. It was a modern structure with a large, well-landscaped courtyard in front and imposing carved wood doors leading to the main entrance. We had no sooner begun our meeting than President Weizman walked in. He was tall and trim, in his mid-sixties, dressed in a blue suit with a starched white shirt and a necktie. No open shirts for this ex-general. Apparently he had heard that the prime minister had given us an audience and he wasn't about to be outdone.

He joined us for what turned out to be a working breakfast. The talk was mostly one-sided as he told us what his wife's role would be in the visit. Even his casual speech dripped with the air of authority. In fact, he didn't so much speak as give orders.

When we were done, he escorted us out. As we emerged from the mansion's front gate, we ran into President Clinton's advance team, cooling their heels, waiting to get in; it was to be the site of one of President Clinton's meetings. They were having a hard time getting access and were shocked to see Steve and me being led out by the president himself, who clapped each of us on the back and wished us farewell. We'd been in Israel for less than forty-eight hours, and already we'd visited every site on the off-limits list and met with the Israeli prime minister and president.

Our daily meetings with our Israeli counterparts to coordinate details for the trip were moved from the King David Hotel to the Israeli Situation Room, a bunker located on the government campus that had thick bombproof doors and all the latest high-tech gizmos: electronic maps, video screens, and sophisticated communications gear. No wonder these people were so good at winning wars. A major point of contention in our ongoing negotiations was whether or not President Clinton would visit the Wailing Wall, since doing so might be construed by some in the media as American recognition of Israeli claims on disputed territory.

There was still no resolution to this last issue when the Clintons arrived. The President's people finally nixed a stop at the wall, fearing it could incite violence. Hillary, though, wanted to visit and asked the national security staff and the Secret Service if it could be done safely. There was a big meeting in Hillary's suite to discuss the matter. I walked in at the tail end, and everyone was laughing, Hillary loudest of all.

"What's so funny?" I asked.

My question ignited renewed gales of merriment, in which I detected a somewhat conspiratorial tone—to wit, *I* was the butt of the joke. I gave Hillary the hairy eyeball, but she acted all innocent. We got back to business, it was determined that Hillary could indeed visit the wall, and the meeting broke up.

"What was that about?" I pressed Steve.

He started to laugh again, but I shot him a look that wiped the grin off his face. I wanted to get to the bottom of this.

"Well, Pat, Hillary asked the head of her Secret Service detail if he could assure her safety, and he said he could. He explained that he would just have you put on your best game day face and then send you to the wall first. He said you're so damn scary-looking when you're in the zone that all the troublemakers would take one look at you and run for their lives."

Ha-ha-ha.

It wasn't long before I got a chance to use that fearsome game day face for real, at Hillary's birthday party, which turned out to be a disaster. It was hosted by Mrs. Rabin and Mrs. Weizman, who got along even worse than their husbands, so the guests, almost all women, were basically split into two camps. We insisted that Hillary's table be roped off. She *hates* being disturbed when she's eating, and it happens all the time. People come up, put their arms around her, and have their pictures taken. On some level, people really do think they own celebrities.

Unfortunately the situation at this luncheon was the worst I'd ever seen. People were crawling over the ropes and asking for her autograph or snapping her picture. As soon as we would chase someone away, she'd be replaced by two others coming from the other direction. It was like trying to bail out a sinking rowboat with a child's pail. The two hosts didn't help matters; they were continually trying to one-up each other by diving into the crowd and returning with more "admirers" to impose on Hillary. No amount of pleading for help from the Rabin and Weizman staffs did any good. We were outnumbered and outmaneuvered. In the middle of it all, in direct contradiction of our carefully negotiated plans, one of the Israeli staff people opened the doors, the press poured into the room, and the crowd broke into "Happy Birthday."

The song ended, Hillary quickly thanked her hosts, sat down to eat, and the hordes immediately began to descend again. She looked at me. "Patrick, isn't there anything we can do?" she implored.

"We can leave," I said.

Hillary thought about that for a quick second, placed her napkin over her entrée, and got up. As we were leaving the room, one of Mrs. Rabin's staffers, who had been completely uncooperative from the start, pulled me aside and in a loud and threatening voice demanded, "Where are you going?" Sit back down! You can't leave yet. What will we do with the birthday cake?"

"Stick it up your ass," I said as I escorted the First Lady to safety.

Our modest greeting party at the Wailing Wall consisted of the mayor of Jerusalem and two thousand Israeli troops. It was dusk, and the heat was beginning to moderate. My palms were sweating anyway. The soldiers parted like the Red Sea, and Hillary walked down to the wall, where she said a prayer and, as is the custom, inscribed a brief note that she then stuck in a crack in the wall. The Wailing Wall is strictly segregated by gender, and we managed to observe this protocol by borrowing female agents from the President's Secret Service detail. The photo of her at the wall ran on the front page of the *Washington Post* the next day.

Hillary never told me what the prayer was, but I thought it might have had something to do with bringing peace to this troubled part of the world and perhaps to her own life, which had hit a low point with the health care defeat and faced further uncertainty in the midterm elections.

She was now one of the world's most recognized women; she had become a global icon. To the Clinton haters and people threatened by women's progress, she was a pariah. To progressives and champions of women's and children's rights and human rights, she was a hero and pioneer. In Paris and now in Israel I'd witnessed how the pressures took a toll on her normally cheerful personality. I hoped that she included a prayer for the return of some personal tranquillity.

We returned to the United States a mere ten days before the midterm election, a seminal event in the Clinton presidency.

9

WHIPPED LIKE A RENTED MULE

November–December 1994

STEVE AND I WERE SITTING IN PADDY BURKE'S PUB, OUR FAVORITE watering hole, watching the election returns on television. It was early, but already the Democrats were dropping like flies. First Senator Harris Wofford went down in flames in Pennsylvania; then James Sasser crashed and burned in Tennessee. Steve was making notes on a dog-eared newspaper he'd been carrying around all day, and a few stools away a couple of very shocked staffers from Senator John Kerry's office looked as if someone were measuring them for a casket. It was going to be a long night.

Paddy's occupied a pie-shaped building near Boston's North Station and the Fleet Center, and on any given night you were bound to find cops, criminals, politicians, and professional athletes crowding the joint. We were partial to the second floor, presided over by dry-witted barkeep Jim Loughlin, known as Lockers. The Dublin-born Lockers could give Mr. Dooley a run for his money when it comes to political wit. Steve called for another round of Guinness as the carnage continued.

"I've seen the likes of this Gingrich character before," Lockers said as he pulled a couple of fresh pints. "When it comes to helping people, he's got long pockets and short arms."

On television, a talking head spoke portentously of the end of a generation of Democratic control of Congress.

"Looks like Clinton's a one-termer," Steve said, grabbing our drinks.

"Yeah, and worse than that, we're going to have Newt Gingrich as speaker of the house," I moaned.

On television, another pundit was officially declaring it the year of the "angry white male," referring to the voters who were turning out in record numbers to express their disdain for the first two years of the Clinton administration. It didn't take a brain surgeon to figure out exactly who these guys were angry at: our boss, Hillary Rodham Clinton.

"I feel bad for Hillary," I said. "She's taking the heat for everything from the budget deficit to static cling. The fat white boys made her the demon, and it's working like a charm, particularly in the South."

Newt and his minions had run a national campaign and called it a Contract with America. Those who called it a contract *on* America had it right. They wanted tax cuts for the rich, prayer in schools, mandatory drug sentencing, and a crackdown on immigrants and all those freeloading welfare cheats. Abortion would be illegal, but discrimination against homosexuals would be legal. The agenda was small-minded, fiscally irresponsible, and intolerant. It ignited people's prejudices and was fueled by their fears. All in all, seriously depressing stuff.

The ass whuppin' continued as Democrat after Democrat lost their seats, thirty-seven incumbents by the end of the night. Not a single Republican incumbent was defeated. The mood in Paddy's grew gloomier by the minute. The staff people from Kerry's office were disconsolate, knowing that the senator would have to run again in two short years. I longed for a nice cheery Irish wake.

"They got both chambers, and that means they get to call the shots on legislation and chair all the committees. This is bad. Real bad," Steve said.

"And we can count on Newt's running in '96," I said as I finished the last of my beer. "That ought to be a barrel of laughs."

On television, a parade of gasbags were writing off President Clinton. With Republicans in control of the Congress, any meager chance he had of passing major legislation was gone. It seemed as if the next two years would be the political equivalent of pushing a rope up a hill.

We ordered another round of Guinness to drown our sorrows. The rout continued. Governor Mario Cuomo went down in New York; in Texas it was the feisty Ann Richards, losing to George W. Bush.

"Do you think Canada would take us as political refugees?" I asked, wanting only for this sad night to be over.

The tide we had felt building over the past couple of months turned out to be a real tsunami. By the time it receded, the Republicans had picked up ten governorships, a total of fifty-three seats in the House, and seven seats in the Senate. It was the first time they had controlled both chambers since 1955, a lifetime ago.

The days that followed were cruel ones. We went through the motions of our lives, but we were numb, in shock. Down in Washington the White House descended into a deep funk. The people I chatted with every day on the phone sounded as if they were suffering from posttraumatic stress syndrome. The modus operandi went from hyperactive proactive to bunker mentality. There was a whole lot of soul-searching and finger pointing going on behind the scenes as the President and the staff sorted through the rubble and tried to make sense of the rout. For those of us in advance, the loss soon translated into a burden we'd feel on almost every trip.

Gone were the helpful Democratic governors, senators, and House members from many key states. Instead we'd be dealing with Republicans who would go out of their way, through press statements and other things, to make the Clintons look bad. A lot of once-friendly territory became hostile overnight.

In the weeks that followed, the media went into a hysterical frenzy. You couldn't pick up a newspaper or turn on the television without being assaulted with stories on the demise of the Clinton presidency. The 1996 election was two years distant, but journalists were already crawling all over one another to pen the best Clinton political obituary.

It was a bleak time indeed for the Democrats. A significant portion of the country had just flipped us the bird. But a closer examination of the returns revealed some reason for hope. The voting had been heaviest in precincts that were heavily white and heavily evangelical Christian or Roman Catholic. Blacks, Hispanics, and women simply hadn't been motivated to turn out. Gingrich had fired up his constituency to a remarkable degree. Ours had sat at home. We could never let that happen again.

There were a few bright spots. Senator Chuck Robb held off Ollie ("The Traitor") North in Virginia, and Ted Kennedy beat back Mitt Romney. Also in Massachusetts, my boss, Attorney General Scott Harshbarger, won reelection handily, getting nearly 70 percent of the vote.

He celebrated by firing me. I can't say I was particularly surprised since

I'd been spending the majority of my time working for the First Lady, not tending to business at the attorney general's office. I'd been with Harshbarger for twelve years at that point, and the day-to-day battles with the state's politicians and petty bureaucrats held little interest for me. Alas, I could hardly bear a grudge; Harshbarger had been indulgent of my political wanderlust for a long time.

Suddenly I was unemployed, and it looked as if Hillary would probably join me in that category in two years. I had to make a big decision. Did I keep on working for the White House on the same trip-by-trip basis I had been, with its erratic income, or did I go out and find a good job in Boston? All in all, it wasn't a happy time.

I needed a break, so I flew out to South Dakota to spend Thanksgiving with friends. In addition to sympathetic ears for my plight, I picked up a nasty case of the flu. I returned to Boston and went right to bed with aches, chills, and a burning fever. As I lay suffering, the phone rang. "Pat, it's Isabelle, I *need* you."

"Not in my present condition you don't. I've got a killer flu. I'm half dead."

"Well, you half dead is equal to two people at full steam."

I've always been a sucker for cheap flattery. I sat up. "What's up?"

"Miami. The President and Vice President are hosting the Summit of the Americas, twenty-five Western Hemisphere countries discussing economic and environmental issues. The First Lady is going to have a significant role."

"Isn't it kind of late in the game to be sending down her advance team?"

"Her advance team has been there for almost a week. Things aren't coming together. Hence this phone call," Isabelle said, the anxiety obvious in her voice.

I can never resist a challenge, and I was also eager to see how Hillary was holding up a month after the election debacle.

"How soon do you need me?"

"Two days ago. Pack yourself in ice, and hop on the next plane."

As she had done at previous summits, Hillary was going to promote her belief that a first lady should play an activist role in her country's civil society. In the past this agenda had been met with enthusiastic support by some of the younger first ladies, and a great deal of skepticism by some of the older ones, who basically considered summits wonderful shopping vacations interrupted by a few dull dinners and a couple of photo ops. At this summit Hillary's key event was going to be a discussion on the importance of a free and open press. Since she was the host first lady, it had to run smoothly.

My physical condition had improved dramatically by the time I landed in Miami, and it was a good thing because there was a lot of work to do. In addition to a heavy schedule of spousal obligations with the President, Hillary was going to visit a hospital, tour an elementary school, and host both a formal dinner and the aforementioned working session on the press.

The advance team was staying at the Sheraton Bal Harbour, a beautiful hotel right on the ocean in Miami Beach; both the President and the Vice President would be staying there as well. The summit itself was at the luxurious Biltmore Hotel in Coral Gables, an elegant Spanish-style establishment that first opened in the 1920s. Security at both venues was incredibly tight.

Even though we were in the United States, the trip was being funded by the State Department because of its diplomatic nature, meaning we had an additional layer of security provided by marine security guards. We received an operational security (OPSEC) briefing every day from the Secret Service, reminding us not to leave sensitive documents lying around, to watch what we said in public and on cell phones, and to report anything suspicious right away.

Two days before the summit officially began, the first of the dignitaries arrived. The security people had our hotel locked down tight. I returned from work late that night and noticed a suspicious-looking package near my room, beside a fire door at the end of the hallway. It was about a foot square, wrapped in brown paper and tied with twine. I was immediately wary and tiptoed closer. I saw grease spots, a telltale by-product of certain types of plastic explosives.

I called down to the Secret Service, which evacuated and cordoned off the entire floor and then called in the Miami Fire Department's bomb squad. The squad members arrived in protective suits that made them look like astronauts. After about a half hour of careful poking and prodding, they determined that the package contained . . . leftover Chinese food. With no. 2 you get the bomb squad.

That first twenty-four hours of the summit proved to be among the most difficult I ever had on the job. Hillary arrived, but I was too busy to greet her. On opening day she, the President, the Vice President, and Mrs. Gore were scheduled to do five receptions and a state dinner back to back. That's a lot of standing around having your photograph taken, probably the most boring and physically demanding chore in the political world. The heads of state, all men, were going to have their dinner in one function room at the Biltmore, and the first ladies were going to have an identical dinner in another, the Alhambra Room. As I mentioned, Hillary was the host for the latter.

Unfortunately, the Alhambra Room was also being used for one of the receptions, so we had only two hours to prepare for the formal dinner. We had to dismantle the reception arrangement and then bring in tables and set them with White House linens, candelabra, and china. There were endless details of seating, security, protocol, table settings, microphones, amplifiers, you name it.

As soon as the last guest left the reception, we swung into action, and for the next 120 minutes the ballroom looked like a movie being run in fast motion. Staging flew out of the room, and risers were whisked in. Flowers and hand-lettered place cards magically appeared on white linen tablecloths; the orchestra tuned its instruments. I was running around as busy as a one-armed paperhanger, but I was still feeling the effects of the flu and was sweating profusely. The hotel staff was superb, working in perfect coordination with the folks from the White House, and with about twenty minutes left on the clock I was beginning to think we were actually going to make it.

Then I looked down the long hotel corridor and saw Hillary approaching. It didn't look as if the five receptions had done anything for her mood. Trouble was walking right in my direction.

I rushed over to where the bomb sweep guys were working with the dogs. "Get these dogs out of here pronto," I told the commanding officer.

"You don't have the authority to call off this sweep," he said.

Just then the First Lady walked into the room and approached us. "Nice dogs. Are they staying for dinner?" she asked sarcastically.

I smiled and greeted her. No response.

She sat down at the head table and ordered the food served as soon as possible. The other first ladies would be arriving in fifteen minutes, and Hillary obviously wanted the dinner to start—and *end*—ASAP. Her order created a real problem since we hadn't planned to bring on the appetizers for another forty-five minutes; the kitchen was nowhere near ready. I was racking my already frazzled brain for how to handle the situation when she called me over. "I'm not happy with these seating arrangements," she said.

"Let me go get the lead," I said, thinking—or, more accurately, hoping—that the woman who had been designated as Hillary's lead for the trip, someone who normally worked for the President, would be the best person to handle the First Lady's complaint. I was also starting to think that maybe a well-paying job in Boston might be a very nice thing.

"I want *you* to take care of this. She doesn't work for me; she works for my husband. *You* fix this."

Yikes. The embattled lead had walked up in the course of this little vote of confidence and heard the whole thing. It was a very awkward moment, and in retrospect I wonder if Hillary's mood and manner that evening were a reaction to the results of the midterm elections. There must have been mutual disappointment, and perhaps laying of blame, between her and the President. Was she taking out some of her feelings toward her husband through his advance woman?

Those thoughts came later. At that moment my only concern was to fix things to Hillary's satisfaction, as I did. She thanked me and even managed a small smile, but I could tell that she was walking wounded. In the past three months she had suffered two massive setbacks. I've known enough losing politicians to know that it's impossible not to take defeat personally. First Congress and then the American people had rejected her. Had she overplayed her hand? Been outmaneuvered? I also knew that she was determined to learn from her mistakes and was no doubt replaying events of the last two years over and over in her head, figuring out where she had gone wrong. What could she do better the next time? Would there be a next time?

Hillary wasn't the only one doing some soul-searching. Back in Boston, my own funk continued. My loyalty and commitment to the First Lady hadn't wavered, but I had myself, and my mortgage, to think about. During the last two years my work for the White House had been paid for by the state attorney general's office under the guise of "intergovernmental cooperation." The job at the AG's office had made it all possible, but now, without that paycheck, I was flying without a safety net. There were still no White House advance jobs dedicated to supporting the First Lady, so that wasn't an option. I was torn between wanting to continue traveling with Hillary and the need for secure and steady employment. Somewhat reluctantly, I updated my résumé and made a few exploratory phone calls.

One night I called Steve and asked him to meet me back at Paddy's for a heart-to-heart talk. The place was back to its usual convivial self, and as we sat and enjoyed our Guinnesses, I laid out my dilemma and asked for his advice.

"Look, Pat, you have to weigh things. Clinton is probably going to be a one-term President, right?"

"Looks that way."

"And then we'll both be out on the street with very little dough in our pockets, right?"

"Yeah."

"All right, weigh that against three facts. First, Hillary needs our help digging herself out of this hole. Second, we've had a blast working for her. Third, you'd be bored out of your mind being a desk jockey after running all around the world like it was one big playground." Steve gave me a big smile and raised his glass in the air.

I hesitated for maybe half a nanosecond. "Here's to two years of having fun, raising hell, and making life miserable for Republicans!" I said.

And we toasted that.

10

THE GREAT ESCAPE

March 1995

WHEN YOU'VE BEEN IN POLITICS AS LONG AS I HAVE, YOU BEGIN TO think you've seen everything. Then came Pakistan.

The First Lady was about to embark on a long-planned tour of the Asian subcontinent, and I was asked to be lead in the colonial city of Lahore. This was to be my sixth trip for Hillary since the midterm election, and I'd watched as she'd gradually come to grips with her setbacks. In her public statements she was already beginning to acknowledge that she had made mistakes in the way she'd run her campaign for universal health care. She had asked the American people to embrace wholesale change without adequately explaining what that change would mean. She had developed the legislative shape of her initiative in a series of meetings and forums with interested parties but had excluded the press and the public from these gatherings. She had also allowed an image of herself as autocratic and mirthless to take hold. Three parts of the political strategy to rebuild her image were: admitting her mistakes, allowing the American people to see that she was a well-rounded, fun-loving wife and mother, and bolstering her stature as a representative of the United States abroad. This trip was an important step in that strategy.

Lahore is the capital of Pakistan's Punjab Province and supplied the setting for Rudyard Kipling's *Kim,* the mystical adventures of a young street urchin, Kim O'Hare, the illegitimate son of an Irish soldier in the

British Army and an Indian woman. Kim travels through exotic worlds of holy lamas and colorful thieves before becoming a British intelligence agent. Kipling's story opens with Kim sitting astride a cannon, an apt metaphor for my entire trip.

The situation in Pakistan at the time was very tense. Radical Islamic groups were trying to unseat the government of Prime Minister Benazir Bhutto by inciting street violence, and there was a massive daily death count coming out of Karachi, the country's largest city. Just ten days before I arrived, a van carrying employees of the U.S. consulate in Karachi had been ambushed and two American diplomats had been killed.

The flight to Pakistan was long and grueling. For some reason, the Travel Office booked a route that included stops in New York, Athens, Cyprus, and Kuwait. With layovers, we were to be in transit for more than twenty-four hours. As I was waiting in New York to board the flight to Athens, I spotted Congressman Bill Richardson, a friend and later U.S. ambassador to the United Nations, who had quite a reputation for negotiating the release of hostages. "Bill, we're on our way to Lahore to advance the First Lady's trip. I'm counting on you to come through if we're taken hostage."

Bill laughed and said, "Pat, any terrorist group that takes you hostage will be calling me to get us to take you back."

Cyprus was fun. We spent six hours sitting on the runway in a stifling plane that observed strict Muslim doctrine. In other words, no alcohol. It was March 17. Happy St. Patrick's Day!

TWA had managed to lose my luggage on the New York to Athens leg of the trip. This proved to be a real problem when I switched to Kuwait Air since passengers were expected to identify their luggage personally on the tarmac before it was loaded on the plane. When I told the security people I didn't have any luggage, they regarded me with intense suspicion and weren't going to let me board. I asked them how I could possibly harm the plane with something I didn't have. That got them thinking, and after a long conversation in their native tongue, much arm waving, and a couple of cellular phone calls, they let me board.

We finally arrived in Lahore at four-thirty in the morning. The first thing I noticed as we stepped off the plane was an acrid, smoky smell that reminded me of the dump fires in the small town where I grew up. In a matter of seconds my eyes stung and my throat hurt. I assumed there was a dump near the airport. Nope. That's the way the entire city smelled. All the time.

My deputy for the trip was fellow Bostonian Jack Murray. As I waited with my team for *their* luggage, a man in a military uniform carrying a machine gun approached. "Which of you is Mr. Halley?"

"That's me," I said, hoping Bill Richardson was right.

"Okay. Your bodyguards are standing by."

The Punjab police had thoughtfully provided four guys with machine guns and an open jeep to follow us everywhere we went. The jeep had one of those big fifty-caliber guns mounted on it and looked like something from *The Rat Patrol*. Not only that, but our bodyguards were going to work in shifts and take up positions outside our hotel rooms while we slept.

We were staying at the Avari Hotel, whose motto was "The hotel where everything works." This was true—if you excluded the elevator, the air conditioning, and most of the staff. After a brief nap Jack and I headed out for a look at the city. Our bodyguards hadn't figured out who was who in the large American delegation, so we were able to slip out of the hotel without them. I like to move around a new place as inconspicuously as possible, and I thought the gun-toting soldiers might have drawn a little attention.

Lahore was like no other place I'd ever been. The sheer volume of people, noise, pollution, and constant furious motion soon had me experiencing sensory overload. We saw oxcarts, horses, buses so stuffed with passengers that they were hanging off the roof, little motorscooter putt-putt taxis, minivans crammed with twenty-five people, a car with six children riding in the open trunk, and a family of five on a motorcycle. The hot, sticky air was fouled with fumes from leaded gasoline, and there was a relentless din of honking horns, screeching tires, and music blaring from tinny radios. It seemed the entire city was suddenly swollen with people gone completely mad, rushing about in some cataclysmic spiral that could come to no good end.

———

Hillary wanted to visit a rural village and lead a discussion on women's and children's issues. The preadvance team had found a village it thought would work, and the next morning we set out to see it. I took my team and drove out of the craziness of the city into the craziness of the countryside, followed by our jeepful of bodyguards. The roads were choked with dust, and the level of vehicle and foot traffic "out in the country" was about what you'd see downtown in a medium-size American city.

The trucks in Pakistan are folk art on wheels. Every one we saw, from small pickups to 18-wheelers, was festooned with a unique mishmash of colored lights, ornaments, clocks, neon signs, slogans, and life-size portraits of politicians, sports stars, and religious leaders. We'd be driving through blinding dust, and suddenly one of these phantasmagoric vehicles would appear like a ship coming out of a fogbank.

The village the preadvance team had chosen was off the main road south of Lahore. It consisted of a series of shacks made from straw and clay mixed with cow dung. The cows shared the shacks with the people, coming and going at will. The sewage system was a shallow open trench that drained down to a small stream. The chickens that drank from it scattered as we walked past.

The place was teeming with children, scores of them, and, not the least intimidated by our uniformed guards, they rushed to see what we were all about. The adults were a bit more circumspect, and it took some coaxing to get them to come forward. After touring the "lower village," we were invited to visit the home of the wealthiest man in town. His house had brick walls, three or four small rooms, and no cows inside. It was ridiculously modest by any Western standard, but he was the big dog in his own world. He'd obviously entertained foreigners before–and knew of our phobia about drinking the local water—because he made a big ceremony out of opening the chilled bottles of Pepsi and inserting clean straws.

The only problem with the village was that there was nothing special about it. The school was adequate but unremarkable, and there was no hospital. Crowd control would be a major headache because the village was wide open and people could easily pour in from the countryside.

After thanking our host and giving him some White House pens and a key chain, gifts the State Department provided us with to thrill the locals, we headed back to Lahore. Jack and I met with a Pakistani employee at our consulate, and in a few minutes we had a list of other villages that might work. We sent the rest of our advance staff, trailed by those ever-vigilant bodyguards, on a bogus fact-finding mission and slipped away with just a driver.

The first village on the list was called Burki. It was northwest of Lahore, and we drove through some pretty barren countryside to get to it, at one point passing a garbage dump the size of a small mountain. We were saddened to see children picking through the debris and even more depressed when our driver told us that they lived there.

Burki was similar to the first village, but it had an all girls' school and a small health clinic. It was also a walled village, which was a godsend in terms of security. With the police chief serving as my interpreter, I met the school principal, a couple of prominent residents, and a worker at the clinic. I was sold.

We had been in Lahore for three days now, and I still didn't have my clothes. I'd at least found out they were sitting on a runway in Tehran, Iran. On the way over, I'd removed the White House tags from my carry-on bags in case of trouble on the plane or in the airports, but it hadn't occurred to me to take them off my checked luggage. Silly me. I'm sure those tags attracted a lot of attention in Tehran. In fact, I kept watching local television to see if I could spot an Iranian political leader wearing one of my suits. The clothes I did have with me had about reached their limit, so I went out and bought a shawakameeze, the native dress for men that has balloon pants and a tunic top. The Pakistanis absolutely loved my new look and greeted me with enthusiastic cries of "Sahib! You look so nice today in your shawakameeze!" The Americans thought I had lost my mind. I found the outfit remarkably comfortable, the only drawback being that it had no pockets. So I bought a vest to carry my cell phone, pager, and notebook. Like Kipling's Kim O'Hara, I looked the part of a Lahore native of Irish decent.

It's not uncommon for a host government to practice surveillance, but the level of eavesdropping in Pakistan was phenomenal. My counterpart was Colonel Nasir Abbas, director general for protocol in the Punjab region. Before that he'd been in military intelligence for the Pakistan Army, and he hadn't lost his touch. Every night we Americans would hold a countdown meeting in a "secure" conference room at the hotel and develop a list of things we needed from the Pakistanis. Without fail, Abbas would call me about a half hour after the meeting and answer each request in the order it had been discussed! The surveillance was so obvious we began to use it to our advantage. When the hotel ignored our repeated requests to fix the air conditioning, we complained at a countdown meeting about Pakistani inefficiencies and said we hoped it wasn't indicative of their ability to support the First Lady's visit. Within hours our air conditioning was humming. One afternoon Jack and I slipped away from the hotel without our bodyguards. We were in the middle of the shopping bazaar with thousands of people around us when my cell phone rang. It was Colonel Abbas, who informed me we'd just passed the bookstore that sold American books. We should go back; it was having a sale.

One morning I left my room and walked down the hall to the staff office. When I returned a couple of minutes later, I found my key wouldn't work because the door was locked from the inside. I called the front desk, which sent up an officious manager who insisted that the lock was broken. He went into an elaborate explanation of how they would have to remove the lock and replace the hardware. I went back to the staff office, and less than five minutes later he came and got me. "The lock's fixed. You can return to your room now."

"Do I need a new key?"

"No, the old one will work fine."

Keep in mind this was the Avari Hotel, where it took ten minutes for the front desk to answer to the phone.

Nighttime in Lahore was scary. The terrorist group that had been killing people in Karachi was trying to gain a foothold in Lahore. Each morning's newspapers were filled with stories of explosives and weapons caches seized in the city. Almost every night we'd hear automatic-weapons fire outside our hotel. I'd be lying in bed at two in the morning, the air conditioning not working, a guard snoring outside my door, and suddenly there'd be a raging gun battle just below my window. The street fighting usually died down by about three-thirty, and I'd just be getting to sleep when the Muslim call to prayer would blare from speakers throughout the city. The first couple of times I heard this unfamiliar chant I shot up out of bed with every hair on my body at attention, ready to meet my maker.

The Secret Service in Washington told us it had a pool on whether or not we'd live through each day. Someone would call and find out what site visits each of us had lined up and adjust our personal odds accordingly. One day, as we were leaving the heavily fortified consulate, we were delayed by a gun battle just outside the gates. This one was a bit unusual in that it was taking place in broad daylight. We decided to cool our heels at the consulate for a while.

About our only diversion was the chance to have a couple of beers in the staff office at night. Pakistan is a strict Muslim country, and in order to drink alcohol legally, you have to apply for a one-day license certifying you are a "non-Muslim alcoholic." The big drawback to this, beyond the obvious bureaucratic hassle, is that you have to drink Pakistani beer, which is preserved with formaldehyde and tastes like camel piss. After one near-death experience with the putrid brew, we gave up and requisitioned several cases of St. Louis Holy Water (aka Budweiser beer) from the consulate commissary. My bodyguard took umbrage with my drinking beer without a license and said he was going to arrest me.

"You can't arrest me. You're my bodyguard," I said sternly.

"It's illegal to drink beer without a license," he replied.

"That may be, but it says right in the bodyguards' manual that you can't arrest your protectee. You *did* read the bodyguard manual, didn't you?"

"Of course I did," he said rather sheepishly, and never bothered me about it again.

About a week after we arrived, the colonel took us to the Pakistan-India border, where we were guests of honor for the changing of the guard ceremony. Despite their frosty relations, the two countries open the gate once a day and perform an elaborate military ritual that includes a lowering of flags and much saluting. The guards are the tallest Indians and Pakistanis you'll ever see. The colonel explained that each country sends its tallest soldiers to the border in a game of one-upmanship. I recommend that any NBA scouts vacationing in the area should detour over for a look-see.

For obvious reasons the security for the First Lady's visit was elaborate. The Pakistani government brought in twenty-six thousand soldiers with automatic rifles and posted them every six feet on both sides of every route we took.

Knowing how much she hated long ceremonies, I met with Abbas to review plans for Hillary's arrival. "Do not worry," he assured me. "There will only be a few greeters."

"And just how many are a few?"

"Oh, no more than two hundred. Maybe two-fifty. Small ceremony."

"A few to me means five or less."

He was crestfallen, but after some back-and-forth, mostly forth, I got him down to a little more than a dozen.

The city was sweltering in its usual midday heat and humidity when Hillary's plane touched down. Security at the airport was very tight, with soldiers ringing the landing area. I waited for the red carpet to be rolled out and went aboard the plane. "Welcome to Lahore. I'll be your tour guide today. We have a modest thirty-car motorcade and twenty-six thousand armed soldiers here to greet us," I said.

Hillary and Chelsea were dressed in slacks and sensible shoes for our visit to the rural village and greeted me warmly. "Nice to see you in a suit again, Pat. They told me you'd gone native," Hillary said with a mischievous grin.

"Only until I got my clothes back from Iran. Luckily the CIA finished interrogating my shirts this morning."

"Too bad. I brought my camera to get a picture of you in the Pakistani clothes," Chelsea commented.

For the third year in a row Hillary had timed a trip abroad to coincide with Chelsea's spring break. They cherished the chance to spend time together and explore exotic places. They shared a voracious curiosity and sopped up an area's history and culture and made determined efforts to get past the official façade and connect with real people. Chelsea was maturing quickly. Gone was the gangly twelve-year-old I'd met on the airport tarmac in Little Rock. She was a bright, personable teenager who actually enjoyed sitting in on Hillary's meetings with world leaders and prominent women.

Hillary's visit to Burki village and her address at a Lahore university, in which she applauded the teaching of modern science and stressed the importance of including women in every aspect of Pakistani society, went smoothly. That left one major event, the one I'd been dreading, the state dinner at the Lahore Fort, an imposing red-brick remnant of the Mogul days that has a spectacular hilltop setting. The preparation for this event had included one of the few face-to-face meetings I ever had with undercover CIA operatives. Our intelligence boys didn't want us to do the event. They pointed out it would be after dark at a location clear across the city from the American consulate. The consulate offered the security of a "hard room," a fortified room where protectees could be placed if trouble arose. Pakistan had recently arrested one of the terrorists wanted for the February 23, 1993, World Trade Center bombing and had allowed the United States to extradite him. His comrades seemed bent on revenge and had plenty of guns, ammunition, and bombs in the area. The fact that the first lady of the United States, and possibly the prime minister of Pakistan, would be in attendance made the dinner a very inviting target.

I spent a considerable amount of time on the secure telephone at the consulate discussing the dinner with Patti Solis, Hillary's chief scheduler, and top brass at the Secret Service. The matter went all the way to the director of the Secret Service, who, after several conversations with his counterpart at the CIA, told us to go ahead with the event.

The night itself was beautiful and cloudless with a yellow quarter moon hanging low in the sky. The fort was lit up and looked magnificent as we approached. Hillary and Prime Minister Bhutto were greeted by hundreds of costumed dancers and a large fireworks display. As we walked through the fort's outer reaches, we passed "dancing" camels—the beasts were wearing beaded robes and shuffling and gyrating to flute music—and folk musicians. We entered a dark passageway leading to the heart of the fort, and suddenly the atmosphere changed. We walked down torchlit ancient corridors on beautiful Persian rugs and were serenaded by soothing sitar music. Incense burned on lily pads floating in pools, filling the night air with a sweet aroma. The whole atmosphere was calm and soothing, but I think I would have enjoyed it more if my palms hadn't been sweating and my short hairs standing up. I expected a bomb to go off at any second. It was the only time I ever saw our Secret Service agents working with their automatic weapons out.

The dinner was held in an open-air courtyard, with the special guests seated at a head table under an ornate awning. The First Lady was seated between the governor of Punjab, who was hosting the event, and Prime Minister Bhutto. Hillary and Chelsea looked fetching in their colorful

Pakistani dresses. We'd been very cautious about the food, and our medical people had inspected the kitchen and assured us the sanitary conditions were up to snuff. I'd raised such a fuss about spicy food that the fare they served—chicken with white rice and very little spice—was so bland that even my pedestrian Irish palate didn't object.

About halfway through the dinner, one of the prime minister's aides approached me and said that Benazir would like to accompany the First Lady to the airport. I told him we'd be honored. He offered a ride in the prime minister's limousine, but since it wasn't armored, I said that was out of the question and suggested she ride with Hillary. After a bit of soul-searching he reluctantly agreed.

When the feast ended, the prime minister got in our limousine with Hillary and Chelsea, and we set out for the airport, about a twenty-minute ride. I wish the *Guinness Book of Records* had been there, because I'm sure it was one of the longest motorcades in history. There were thirty-two vehicles in Hillary's entourage, the prime minister had about thirty in hers, and the chief minister of government and the governor of Punjab had about twenty-five each. The total was well over a hundred. I rode in a limousine immediately in front of Hillary's. Directly behind her were two Chevy Suburbans that carried her Secret Service detail and a counterassault team.

As we started out, things seemed to be going well from our vantage point. Then we turned on our radios and heard screaming and sirens from behind us. I radioed to Jack Murray, who was riding a few vehicles back.

"Pat, the whole thing is completely out of control! Everyone is trying to get to the front of the pack so they can be in the picture at the airport. Cars are passing left and right and cutting each other off."

Then I got a report from a staffer in one of the press buses near the back of the motorcade: "It looks like the Gumball Rally! The ambulance has passed us three times, and we've passed it three times!"

We got to a slight hill and looked behind us. It was pure pandemonium with lights flashing, horns blaring, and cars careering every which way. Troops lining the route were scrambling out of the way as vehicles rode up on the sidewalks and shoulders. The Secret Service supervisor riding in the front seat of my car looked as if he'd seen a ghost.

"We're going to get run over when we get to the airport," he croaked.

"There's only one small gate at the airport," I said. "Have the Suburbans block it after we go through. We'll put the First Lady, Chelsea, and the prime minister in the VIP holding lounge and sort this all out."

"Great idea," he said, and radioed instructions to the drivers of the Suburbans.

When we got to the airport, we zipped through the gate and got our principals to the safety of the VIP lounge. I went back outside. The Suburbans were blocking the entrance, and the resulting traffic jam looked like the climactic scene from the *Blues Brothers* movie. There was much screaming, shouting, jumping up and down, and waving of guns as people tried to get through. I wondered: All this Sturm und Drang for the chance to be in a photo op?

I quickly learned that this had nothing to do with a photo op and that I had committed a grave diplomatic error. By having the prime minister ride in our limousine, I'd inadvertently separated her from her aides and bodyguards. I now had their leader in a building without any of her own people nearby. No wonder they were going crazy. They were claiming I had *kidnapped* Bhutto. I heard them shouting my name and using the world "abducted." Hmm. This was not a good situation. I hightailed it onto Hillary's plane and directed the rest of the operation by radio.

When Hillary and Chelsea were safely on board, we opened the gates. The Pakistanis raced across the runway to the steps of the plane and demanded that I get off and explain my actions. I refused and stayed on the plane under the armed protection of the U.S. Air Force until we landed safely in New Delhi. Hillary was a bit surprised to find Jack and me stowed away aboard her aircraft.

"I thought you boys were going to stay in Pakistan for the wheels-up party."

"No way, Boss. I have no desire to experience the hospitality of a Pakistani jail."

She got a laugh out of that and remarked that despite it all, we were still extremely well groomed, our suits pressed, not a hair out of place. "You're still my bandbox boys. Here, let me take your picture."

With that she grabbed my camera and snapped a shot of Jack and me with frozen smiles on our faces. It beat the hell out of having our mug shots taken in Lahore's city jail.

Fortunately the Pakistanis decided to let bygones be bygones, and I never heard any more about my little escapade with their prime minister.

11

YAKETY-YAK

April–September 1995

A MARINE IN DRESS BLUES AND WHITE GLOVES OPENED THE NORTH Portico door to the West Wing of the White House and let me in. That's how staffers know the President is in the Oval Office. When he's gone, so are the marines. The White House, part museum, part stately function hall, part home, is also a workplace, a warren of activity. There's a certain hushed dignity about the place and three distinctly different environments.

Upstairs the family's living quarters are sanctum sanctorum. In this case the boss really does live above the store. Then there are the public spaces people see on the tours: the East Room, Green Room, Map Room, etc. But there's another whole area of the White House where the work actually gets done. That was where I was headed, up a narrow staircase to Hillary's second-floor office next to the White House counsel's suite.

I was on my way to see Pam Cicetti, Hillary's executive assistant. It was April 19, Patriot's Day, which is to Boston what the Kentucky Derby is to Louisville and the Oscars are to Hollywood. The whole town shuts down and parties. The party consists of a twenty-six-plus-mile race, the Boston Marathon, and a lot of middle-aged men putting on tricornered hats and Revolutionary War uniforms to reenact the battles of Lexington and Concord. I've always suspected the real reason for celebration is that we've just made it through another winter and want to bust out of our cocoons and see what we look like without six layers of clothing.

Most years I'd be hard pressed to miss the festivities, but this year I had more important fish to fry or, more accurately, to *catch*. A job. My travels on behalf of Hillary were at different times paid for by five or six different organizations. Sometimes I undertook them as a volunteer, but since being canned from the Massachusetts attorney general's office the previous December, this ad hoc arrangement had really lost its appeal. I needed a regular gig, and Pam Cicetti was helping coordinate my search, which was a bureaucratic nightmare.

Pam's office was right next to Hillary's; the First Lady was upstairs in the residence. It was a little after 10:00 A.M. We had just sat down and were still catching up on the latest scuttlebutt when a uniformed Secret Service officer stepped into the room. "Sorry to bother you, ma'am. There's been a report of trouble at a federal facility, and we're just checking the building. Everything is under control."

With that he turned and left. His words had been vague enough that neither Pam nor I gave them a second thought. After all, the White House campus—the mansion, the Old Executive Office Building, and the buildings across the way on Jackson Place and Seventeenth Street—is the most heavily guarded real estate on the planet. It's not hard to feel secure once you're inside.

Shortly after our meeting broke up, I stopped by the Secret Service office to pick up a new hard pin, the small rectangular pin issued to close aides to the President and First Lady. Distribution of these lapel pins, accepted on sight by agents anywhere in the world, is, as you might imagine, tightly controlled. My white one was expiring, and I needed to sign for a new green pin. I took one step into the office and stopped dead in my tracks.

After a career in law enforcement, I knew how professionals steel themselves and focus in, laser sharp, when there's an emergency. Nothing matters but what they're chasing. These guys, about fifteen of them, were in full crisis mode. They spoke in strained voices, punched furiously at telephone keypads, and pored over papers with lists of names, some circled in bright red.

"What's going on?" I asked George Rogers, the head of Hillary's detail.

"There was an explosion at a federal building in Oklahoma about an hour ago, and a lot of people got killed, including some of ours."

"A lot of people?"

"A lot."

I felt numb for a second, trying to grasp the news. Then a chill raced up my spine. "Was it a bomb?"

"We think so. This place is locked down tight until we get a handle on it. I hope you weren't planning on going anywhere."

I shook my head.

The rest of the morning passed in a suspended state of shock as everyone at the White House gathered around televisions to follow the story. The early focus was on the magnitude of the disaster. More than a hundred people, including small children, were known to be dead, and rescue workers were combing the rubble of what had once been the nine-story Alfred P. Murrah Federal Building for survivors. The gruesome footage from the scene showed bloodstained victims and heroic emergency workers, many of them risking their own safety in the frantic search for survivors.

At lunchtime I found myself sitting in the executive mess with Kelly Craighead, Hillary's trip director. The mess is next to the White House Situation Room, a large, heavily guarded conference room filled with high tech gizmos that allow decision makers to get up-to-the-minute information during a crisis and direct the response. A steady stream of steely-eyed agents from the Secret Service, the FBI, the National Security Council, and the CIA paraded in and out.

"I've never seen anything like this, Pat," Kelly said.

"If it was a terrorist bomb, all bets are off. You never think something like this could happen here. In Oklahoma City no less."

She looked at me. "It's scary, isn't it?"

I nodded.

The lockdown was called off in early afternoon, and I was able to get to National Airport for the shuttle back to Boston. The normally bustling corridors of the terminal were eerily silent as folks gathered around televisions. Parents were clutching their children protectively.

While America was to become all too familiar with massive terrorist attacks in September 2001, at the time an attack of this magnitude was unprecedented. We had been largely immune to bombs and senseless bloodshed on our native soil, and the only parallels in my lifetime for the sense of shock, horror, and loss that swept across the nation were the assassination of President Kennedy thirty years earlier, the far less lethal attack on the World Trade Center in 1993, and perhaps the explosion of the *Challenger* space shuttle in 1986. Suddenly we seemed vulnerable in ways we hadn't before.

While the nation's response was an immediate outpouring of help, support, and love, those first hours also saw something darker. Those same hate-radio hosts who had been so ugly and vociferous in their denunciation of President Clinton and Hillary almost immediately, and without a shred of evidence, began blaming the bombing on "towel-headed terrorists." On station after station across the country, conclusions were leaped to, racist views against Arabs and Muslims were openly expressed, a call for revenge went out. How ironic that the murderer turned out to be a right-wing zealot, one of their own.

Two days later Timothy McVeigh, arrested for a minor traffic violation on the day of the bombing, was identified as the chief suspect, and the nation had to absorb another shock: This dastardly crime had been committed by an American. And not some obvious madman like Theodore Kaczynski, but a blond, blue-eyed, clean-cut army vet in his early twenties, a young man consumed by rage at his own government.

The memorial service for the victims of the blast was held in Oklahoma City on Sunday, April 23. I was in New York City, preparing for Hillary's visit to speak at New York University the following Tuesday, and I watched the ceremony from a temporary staff office at NYU. I was moved by President Clinton's eulogy and agreed with his assessment of the perpetrators as "evil cowards." Hillary was by his side, solemn and obviously deeply touched by the grief of the victims' families. Among the dead was Alan Whicher, a Secret Service agent who had transferred only a couple of months before from the White House. The Clintons had known him well.

The bombing, the revelation that it had been committed by a right-wing American extremist, and President Clinton's pitch-perfect response all combined to set in motion a sea change in American politics. The fast-growing militia movement—groups of citizens arming themselves and undergoing military-style training with the express intent of protecting themselves from their own government—began to look far more dangerous than the government it hated. The rhetoric of the Republican leadership, particularly that of the angry and inflammatory Newt Gingrich, suddenly sounded ominous, expressing beliefs scarily similar to some of McVeigh's. Congresswoman Helen Chenoweth of Idaho had even introduced a so-called militia protection bill. Gingrich's explicit calls for a second American Revolution lost their power overnight. The seemingly unstoppable Republican juggernaut that had swept into power the previous November was, if not stopped in its tracks, certainly stalled.

On the other side of the coin, a president who on the very day before the bombing had felt compelled to declare plaintively at a press conference, "I'm still relevant," found his footing in tragedy. The nation needed a unifier, someone to make sense of what had happened, to speak for all of us and to comfort us. Handsome, dignified, eloquent, empathetic, this brilliant politician rose to the occasion and then some. In the days and weeks after the bombing he connected deeply with the American people. His popularity soared, and it never really faltered—no matter how hard Ken Starr and the Republicans worked to destroy him, no matter how reckless and adolescent his own behavior—during the remaining six years of his presidency.

Hillary's trip to New York was to promote Americorps, the volunteer program that was a centerpiece of the President's domestic policy. I was eager to touch base with the First Lady to tell her how impressed I was with the President's response to the bombing. I managed to grab a couple of minutes alone with her, in a room of a dormitory suite at NYU that we had converted to offices for the downtime between events. She had a large pile of papers spread out on a desk and took off her reading glasses as I entered the room.

"Hillary, I just wanted to tell you that I think the President has done a magnificent job helping the country get through this."

"Thank you, Pat, I'll tell him. These are tough times for all of us."

"And you're okay?"

"It was very emotional in Oklahoma City. Those families have been through an awful lot. But I was moved by their courage. It really puts things in perspective when you see something like that."

Although my employment status was still in limbo, it suddenly didn't seem all that important, while working for Hillary seemed more important than ever. So three days later I took off for Ukraine. No sooner had I landed than I received a call from my mother telling me that my eighty-seven-year-old father was gravely ill. He'd been in declining health for some time and was now hospitalized and not expected to live much longer. I called my desk at the White House and told them. With the help and support of friends like Paula Thomasson and her cousin Patsy Thomasson, who was in charge of the Administrative Office at the White House, I was airborne and heading to my father's bedside within the hour. I managed to make it to Tampa in time to spend a few precious minutes with him before he passed away.

I took a month off after my father's death to spend time with family and friends. Two close Irish friends were married in Tralee that summer, and I spent two glorious weeks in the west of Ireland celebrating their union.

About a week after I returned to the United States, on July 19, to be exact, I received a call from Pam Cicetti telling me that a decision had been made to hire me and that I would be receiving a call shortly from Harold Ickes, the deputy chief of staff at the White House. A month later I *still* hadn't heard from Harold Ickes. But once again I was made an offer I couldn't refuse, a trip to Mongolia. Hillary was the honorary chair of the U.S. delegation to the United Nations Fourth World Conference on Women, in Beijing, and a side trip to Mongolia was on her schedule. Visions of Genghis Khan, the windswept steppes, yurts and yaks danced through my head. Who could resist?

Preparations for the trip were clouded by China's arrest of American human rights activist Harry Wu, a first-generation Chinese immigrant who had infuriated Beijing twice by entering the country using an alias and then shooting documentary footage in forced labor camps. Wu became a very hot topic as the world debated China's human rights policies and the UN's decision to hold a major conference in the world's only remaining Communist powerhouse. Wu's wife wrote to Hillary, asking her not to attend the conference. Public opinion in the States ran against her going, and for a while it looked as if the trip would be canceled. In the eleventh hour the State Department was able to negotiate Wu's release from prison, and our trip was on.

The history I'd read about Mongolia was fascinating. Mongol warlords, Genghis Khan foremost among them, had conquered much of the known world thousands of years ago. The Great Wall of China, history's largest public works project and the only man-made structure visible from outer space, was built to protect the Chinese from these fierce aggressors. Once the two-thousand-mile-long wall was completed, Genghis Khan promptly marched around it and overthrew the Chinese Empire. He then installed the Yuan dynasty, which ruled China for the next century.

Modern-day Mongolia was equally fascinating, albeit far less powerful. It's one of the most sparsely populated countries on earth. In 1992 it had thrown off the yoke of an unelected Communist regime, held an election, and promptly elected a Communist president. More than half of its two and a half million people were nomads who lived in one-room tentlike structures called gers on the Gobi Desert; most of the rest lived in gers in the cities. The capital, Ulaanbaatar, is reputed to be the coldest on earth, with extended periods of 20 degrees below zero temperatures. This freezer effect is more than offset by summer's arid oven, when the temperature can easily top a 110. During our visit the country seemed eager to show off its intense mood swings: It was over 100 the day we arrived and was snowing when we left twelve days later.

Our hotel in Ulaanbataar was a recently renovated structure owned by a Japanese corporation and catering to business travelers. Like everything else in the city, it was spartan in nature. Hot water was available for only about an hour a day, and you never knew which hour. I'd get up early in the morning and run periodic tests as I did my paperwork. Sometimes I'd get my shower at eight o'clock, other times at nine or ten, and then there were the days I went without. The telephone system was barely capable of reaching the front desk, and when I had to return a call from the White House, I was led to the fax machine in the hotel's basement. It was a charming place: dirt floor, single hanging lightbulb, spiders crawling on every surface, including my legs.

The Mongolian visit had been added to the China swing for a number of reasons. First, it was someplace Hillary had always wanted to visit. Second, it afforded us the opportunity, if the China trip was a success, to build on that success with the traveling press corps; if China was less than successful, we'd have a chance to respond to any problems that arose before we were back on the home shores.

It was to be a state visit, with an ambitious agenda that included a meeting with prominent women, lunch with the president and his wife, a visit to a nomadic family to discuss children's issues, a visit to an orphanage, and a major speech on democracy in an academic setting.

So off I set in search of a nice photogenic family of nomads. Our ambassador to Mongolia, Don Johnson, was a tall, thin man with a midwesterner's folksy manner and the political savvy of a beltway insider. He was a career diplomat, not one of our politically appointed ambassadors, but his cooperation was as great as that of any ambassador I ever worked with. He displayed a true affinity for the country and its people. As we careered through the Gobi in our four-wheel-drive motorcade, led by a guide from the embassy, more than one family knew Johnson, and everyone greeted him warmly.

Our search afforded me my first up close look at a ger. It's round, made of dried animal hides stretched over a wooden frame, and held together with thick homemade rope. It has a stove in the middle, with a chimney extending through the roof, and beds that double as seats arranged around the perimeter. Every ger we visited also had meat drying on rope that was stretched across the interior, which naturally drew a squadron of flies. Since we're talking about the desert, water is in short supply, and bathing becomes, at best, an irregular occurrence. In addition, the nomads have a habit of smearing animal fat over their exposed skins to lessen the effects of the wind, sun, and cold. Combine the meat, the flies, the limited bathing, and the animal fat, and the inside of a ger tends to be a rather fragrant place.

Ambassador Johnson explained that the typical family moved its ger about six times a year, with two big moves, north in the summer and south in the winter, and then two more each season to reach fresh grazing land. We needed to find a family willing to delay its trip into the desert's interior for a few days.

Jack Murray, my second-in-command, brought along a Polaroid camera and made instant friends with the kids at each encampment we visited by taking their pictures and then presenting them in an elaborate ceremony. In no time he had gathered enough admirers to be elected governor of the province. Our guide, Bullgar, seemed to know where every family was located and directed the motorcade over hill and dale, around twists and turns, and delivered us to encampment after encampment.

Like most Mongolians, he used only one name. It's a vast country, but every one of its inhabitants seemed to know every other. There are no street addresses per se, even in the city, and just how the mail got delivered remained a mystery to me. There must be amazing mail carriers.

As we made our way across the countryside, I was reminded of the high plains of Montana where they meet the mountains. The land was wide open and pristine, with cool, thin air. At one point we came to what looked like a huge junk pile in the middle of the road, and the ambassador ordered the motorcade to stop and told everyone to get out. The pyramid-shaped pile was made up of rocks, bottles, empty beer cans, sticks, currency, you name it. It was topped by a tattered cloth waving in the breeze.

"This is an ovoo," Ambassador Johnson explained, "a shaman shrine meant to ensure good luck while traveling. We must show respect by walking around it three times counterclockwise and then adding something to the pile."

Our Mongolian guides eyed us carefully to see that we didn't invite bad luck by messing with the spirits, so off we went, twenty or so high-level representatives of the U.S. government, traipsing around the pile in the middle of the Gobi Desert like kids playing ring-around-the-rosy.

After a morning of searching high and low, we located a family that would fit the bill nicely. It had three generations under the same roof, and its encampment was in a spectacular setting on an open plain overlooking a distant mountain range. As was the custom, the family had us in to say hello and made the traditional offering of mare's milk and dried something or other that looked like beef jerky and smelled like cow manure. I became very expert at faking a sip of the mare's milk and palming the something or other. By the end of the day I had a pocketful of the stuff, which I fed to a grateful horse.

I had hoped to see a yak during our travels and told our driver to let me know if we came across any. As we were heading back to the city he suddenly began to shout and point, "Yak, yak, yak!"

Sure enough, there was a small herd of the noble beasts. I asked him to pull over so we could get a good look. They were about the size of buffalo and had big, shaggy coats. There was a large black one just across a narrow ravine, and I decided he would make a nifty photograph. But I needed to get a little closer. I bolted to the ravine, jumped across, and started running in the yak's direction. He took off at a much higher rate of speed than I would have thought possible for an animal of his size. I continued my pursuit, hoping he'd stop and pose. After a minute he did indeed stop, but instead of posing, he turned, snorted, pawed the ground like a bull, and lowered his head in preparation for a charge. At me. This was cause for great concern since the animal weighed about a ton and was a whole lot faster than I was. I took off at a much higher rate of speed than I would have thought possible for a human of my size.

Jack and the other members of the our party, safely on the other side of the ravine, had taken pictures of me chasing the yak and now captured pictures of the yak chasing me. They seemed to find the whole incident amusing. I didn't. In fact, a newspaper headline flashed in front of my eyes: WHITE HOUSE AIDE KILLED BY ANGRY YAK.

Luckily my wits didn't entirely desert me, and I realized that an animal that size couldn't turn quickly on a downward slope. I raced toward the ravine. The yak, no fool, stopped in its tracks, raised its head, and gave me a look that said, "And don't try it again, buddy."

Our choice of academic settings for the First Lady's speech on democracy was similarly limited. We looked at a couple of high schools before settling on the National University of Mongolia. As we were touring the modest campus, our host took us to a lecture hall he thought would be a perfect venue for the speech. The podium stood in front of a gigantic mural of Engels, Marx, and Lenin—hardly the three musketeers of democracy. We finally chose the school's main auditorium, a grand hall with high ceilings and beautiful (nonpolitical) murals framing the stage.

The night before Hillary's arrival, we moved from the hotel to the Mongolian state guesthouse, where she would be staying. The guesthouse is on a sprawling estate east of town that is overrun with deer, moose, and assorted other wildlife. It's an imposing structure that has played host to the Dalai Lama, among other dignitaries. I selected a bedroom on the same floor as the master suite. It was late by the time I retired, and I was exhausted. I collapsed on the bed, which then collapsed on me. I found myself on the floor with the mattress enveloping me like a hot dog roll. I was so tired I didn't bother to get up and spent a surprisingly comfortable night wrapped in a Mongolian mattress.

The next morning I rose early to shower before I went to the airport. I was prepared to find only cold water but was shocked when my faucet did nothing but hiss air at me. There was no water, hot or cold, to be had at the state guesthouse. Hillary would be thrilled. I ended up using bottled water to shave and bathe as best I could.

The scene at the airport was anything but usual. The motorcade vehicles the Mongolians had brought looked like something out of an automotive museum. They were ancient and in obvious disrepair. The press bus was so old it looked as if it could have transported Mark Twain, and the lead police cruiser had bald tires with visible patches on them. Out on the tarmac I got word from our military folks that the First Lady's plane was on final approach, due on the ground any minute, when suddenly about a hundred Mongolian women in army uniforms paraded out onto the runway.

"Who are these people and what the hell are they doing here?" I screamed at my counterpart from the Foreign Ministry.

"They're the Army Woman's Honor Guard. They're here to salute the First Lady."

"Well, you'd better get them off the runway. They could get killed out here."

"Don't worry, they know what they're doing."

They stood in a line right about where the plane would make its turn to get to the motorcade. I knew we had a problem. The big Air Force jet put out such tremendous exhaust, called jet wash, that a carelessly placed minivan had been blown over a few months before. We had been trained in how important it was to stay out of the way of the jet wash, just as one would avoid getting too close to the back end of a horse. The Mongolians knew horses; jets they didn't have a firm grasp on yet.

As Hillary's plane taxied and turned, the straight line of women soldiers in their blue skirts and military caps was sent sprawling. Some hit the deck, others turned and ran, and hats flew down the runway like confetti. Luckily no one was hurt.

I boarded the plane and did my best to prepare Hillary for the spartan conditions. "Mornin', boss. It may look like I did a bad job shaving this morning, but that's because the state guesthouse, where you'll be staying, doesn't have any water. None at all. I hope you took a shower before you left Beijing."

She laughed and examined the stubble on my face. "I'm sure I'll survive. I'm glad you didn't do more damage to yourself shaving without water. I wouldn't want you to bleed to death on my account."

"How was Beijing? I haven't been able to get any news out here."

"I think it went fine. People seemed to react well to my speech, and we didn't run into any major problems. But let's talk about today. Give me the rundown on what we're going to be doing."

I delivered my briefing.

The First Lady's visit began with a motorcade into the desert to visit our nomad family. They proved to be gracious hosts and gave Hillary the mare's milk, which she sipped cautiously and then suggested the assembled press corps should have the pleasure of sampling. Luckily she was spared the something or other. The children also put on a display of horsemanship. These youngsters, ranging in age from five to ten, rode as if they'd been born in the saddle. They had on colorful outfits, green and red silk tunics, and the boys wore the pointed caps unique to Mongolia. Their routine looked like the Blue Angels on horseback as they zoomed at one another, cutting off at the last possible second, and did elaborate turns and formations. The kids put a lot of heart into their performance, and Hillary was enthralled.

The rest of our day went equally well, and Hillary completed her official schedule by giving a well-received speech to a large crowd at the university. It was still early, and we couldn't very well take the First Lady to the hotel's karaoke bar. I'd done some scouting around and discovered that the National Folk Theater was putting on a show that night. And what a show it was! The costumes alone were worth the price of admission. The performers dressed as dragons, lions, and giant snakes seemed to *become* those mythic animals. A pair of contortionists performed feats that would make pretzels green with envy. The highlight was the throat singers, an art unique to Mongolia. By singing *over* a continuous drone created deep in the larynx, the singers actually create two notes at once. It's piercing, eerie, and amazingly melodic. It was a fitting end to a truly exotic adventure.

The following morning I walked Hillary to her plane.

"This was a wonderful trip, Pat, thank you."

"It was my pleasure. And I've enjoyed the opportunity to work for you."

"What do you mean?"

"I've decided to move on. The White House seems to be incapable of providing me with employment. And as exciting as these trips are, I need to make a living. This is my last trip on your behalf."

Hillary looked startled. "You mean nothing's been settled since our discussion back in April?"

I nodded.

"Could you give me twenty-four hours from the time you get home?" she asked.

"Of course."

With the Oklahoma City bombing, the ensuing reversal of the President's political fortunes, my father's death, my roller coaster job situation, and now this extraordinary trip, it had been a jam-packed and very emotional five months. Looming on the near horizon were a presidential trip to my homeland and, just beyond that, the kickoff of the President's 1996 reelection campaign.

But would I be around for the fun?

12

GOING HOME

September–December 1995

HILLARY WAS TRUE TO HER WORD. WITHIN TWENTY-FOUR HOURS OF MY return from Mongolia I got a call from Harold Ickes's office and was told I'd been put on the Democratic National Committee payroll effective September 1. My duties were to work for the First Lady in any capacity she requested.

So, after all that, I was employed again. No office. No desk. No telephone. But a regular paycheck at a very healthy salary. I could stay home in Boston when I wasn't traveling. My check would be deposited in the bank every two weeks like clockwork. Life was good.

Two days later I got a call to head to Scranton, Pennsylvania, for a Rodham family gathering. This was strictly a family trip, with no public events. The Rodhams had a tiny, rarely used cottage on a lake in the Poconos. It was really rustic, no telephone, primitive plumbing, sagging porch. I guess for nostalgic reasons the clan had decided to use it for the celebration of the christening of Hillary's nephew Zachary, her brother Tony's child.

It was a bright, warm day. Word had leaked out that the Clintons were coming to town, and a large crowd had gathered just down the hill from the cottage. There were nineteen Rodhams crammed into the place, and I was outside with about a dozen staff and security people. After about a half hour the back door opened, and the President, cooped up long enough, came bounding out. He took a quick look around and made a

155

beeline for me and grabbed my hand. "Well, Pat, how're you doing? I'm real glad we got everything worked out."

With that he slapped me on the back and stood there smiling at me. Not bad, my first day on the job and I'm being welcomed by the president of the United States.

"It's a pleasure to be working for your wife, Mr. President."

"I want to go down and say hello to these folks," he said, indicating the crowd.

"All right, just let me get some of your staff to help you work the line."

"Naw, come on, Pat, you can handle it. Let's go."

He flung an arm over my shoulder, and off we went.

Now a lot has been written and spoken about Bill Clinton's charisma, charm, and magnetism, but in order to really understand it, you've got to experience it up close. This was a crowd of ordinary middle-class Americans, and they were blown away by both his star power and his genuine desire to connect with each and every one of them. I swear he has the ability to drain the energy out of anyone whose hand he shakes, absorbing it into his own body. For most politicians this gladhanding is a chore, but Bill Clinton positively lived for it. I've heard Hillary speak of the President's core political strategy: A hand shaken is a vote won. All during his career he's been famous for not leaving an event until he's spent a few moments with *every single person* there.

As he started grabbing outthrust hands, the crowd pressed forward. A woman, about fifty, wearing plaid shorts and a Penn State sweatshirt, grasped his hand and looked up at him. "Don't let them get you down. You're doing a great job!"

"Thank you. I appreciate that," he said, gazing directly into her eyes.

"That Newt Gingrich is full of it. The Republicans will ruin this country if we let them get away with it," she said as she continued to pump his hand.

"I'm doing my best."

"You are the best. And you're going to get reelected. I guarantee it." She was still holding on.

Uh-oh, we've got a lockup here, I thought. If I don't do something quick, she'll hold on to him until the sun sets. At that point I slid close to the President and said to the enthralled lady: "Hey, Penn State! I hear Joe Paterno's got the boys in great shape this year."

She glanced at me distractedly, as if she were coming out of a fog, and the President was finally able to free his hand and move on.

Suddenly my radio crackled: "The President is needed back at the cottage immediately to take a call from Egyptian President Hosni Mubarak."

I leaned in close and said, "You're needed on the phone, sir."

He looked at me, somewhat annoyed, "I don't want to take any telephone calls now, Pat, I'm visiting with these people."

"It's President Mubarak. Should I tell them you'll call him back?"

With that the President stepped back from the crowd, which let out a collective groan. He addressed them in a hoarse shout: "I've got to go take a telephone call from the president of Egypt, but I'm comin' back. Pat, make sure we pick up right where we left off." True to his word, the President returned and wouldn't leave until he had met everyone in the crowd.

This wasn't the first time I'd seen Bill Clinton work his magic on a crowd, but I was about to witness it on a level that even I never imagined.

The overseas trip I'd been waiting for since the first day of the administration, a visit to my ancestral homeland of Ireland, was next on the agenda. The President would be visiting both the republic and the occupied north to drive home the importance he placed on the Irish peace process.

To say I'm attached to Ireland would be like saying Romeo was attached to Juliet. I love everything about it—except that occupying army up north. I was going to be handling the Dublin portion of the visit for Hillary, and Steve Graham, whose family hailed from County Down in the north, was her lead in Belfast.

Dublin was the first part of Ireland to blossom under the country's economic resurgence in the late twentieth century. It's a lively city of cobblestone streets, shops, parks, universities, and neighborhood pubs where singing and storytelling are a way of life. Yet even as it assumed the mantle of a dynamic economic and cultural center, it managed to maintain the feeling of a small European village. Our work there would be of the suitwearing, memo-writing, diplomatic- and protocol-debating sort, but we had some free time that first weekend, so teammate Jack Murray and I drove north to Belfast to visit Steve.

The situation north of the border had changed since my last visit in 1989. The ominous border checkpoints were still there, but now the road detoured around them. Belfast itself was a lot more peaceful. My previous stop had come just after one of the IRA's cease-fires had broken down, and there had been massive numbers of British troops and Royal Ulster Constabulary throughout the downtown area. Everywhere we'd gone troops had pointed guns at us, and on several occasions they'd pulled us over and asked us to provide identification. You could smell the conflict in the air. Not so this time.

Steve and his team were staying at the often bombed Europa Hotel downtown. The area appeared calm, with the only uniformed presence being a meter maid busy ticketing the cars of illegally parked Christmas shoppers. We toured the Falls Road and the Shankhill, two traditional trouble spots in the city, and saw people on the streets and flourishing shops where six years earlier empty storefronts splashed with loyalist or republican graffiti had predominated. We joined Steve and his team for the delivery of a huge Christmas tree to the Belfast city hall. The tree was a fifty-foot pine grown in the United States and somehow flown over by our air force. I had a vision of one of our transport planes with the tree tied precariously on top, the way we'd tied our family tree to the car when I was a kid. I wondered if the crew had sung Christmas carols on the way over. President Clinton was presenting it as a gift to the people of Belfast, and he would be presiding over its lighting in a memorable ceremony at which a child who had lost her father in the struggles pleaded for peace.

As we watched the tree being lowered into place, I said to Steve, "Boy, things are a lot more peaceful around here."

"They look that way, but the troubles are bubbling just under the surface," Steve replied. "I was on a site visit in a working-class Catholic neighborhood yesterday. There was a phone company truck on the corner. Big deal, right? Then the back door opened, and I spotted a half dozen British troops inside. They're still patrolling the neighborhoods; they've just gone undercover."

"Still, telephone company trucks are a lot less intrusive than those ominous gray, heavily armored vehicles they were using on my last visit."

"True. I guess progress comes in small steps," Steve said.

Back in Dublin, our counterparts from the Irish government were friendly and cooperative. In fact, it was the easiest advance I ever did in terms of dealing with the host government.

The Clintons were due to arrive early in the morning. For an advance man, the arrival of Air Force One is like Christmas morning and the Super Bowl rolled into one. If it happens to be on foreign soil, the effect is increased exponentially. After all, this is the most powerful man in the world, flying in on a magnificent blue and white 747 emblazoned with the presidential seal and the words "United States of America." If that foreign soil happens to be the land your forefathers left to come to America, well, the emotion can be almost overwhelming, even for someone as low-key as myself.

It was a typical Irish morning—in other words, overcast, misty, damp, and gray—as I waited expectantly on the tarmac, my nerves keyed high. On the roofs of the nearby terminals I could make out the countersnipers, alert for the slightest hint of trouble. Then Air Force One appeared out of the clouds, the band struck up a formal Irish marching song, and the troops in the honor guard stood ramrod straight. I defy any American not to feel a swell of patriotism at such a moment.

Irish dignitaries in their best formal dress lined one side of the red carpet and were soon joined by their counterparts from the American delegation, who scrambled off the back steps of the plane to take up position for the greeting ceremony. Secret Service agents and Irish police patrolled the area. More than three hundred photographers and journalists crowded the nearby press platform.

The main door of the plane opened, and two air force officers in full dress uniform marched down the front stairs and stood sentry. Then the Clintons appeared. The President was tall and imposing, his gray hair perfectly in place, his blue eyes twinkling. He was wearing an impeccable blue suit, a bright white shirt, and an emerald green tie. Hillary stood at his side, dignified and striking in a finely tailored Kelly green suit, blond hair setting off her radiant blue eyes. Even though I knew these two people well, I was caught up short by what an electrifying first impression they were capable of presenting. The blizzard of camera flashes gave the scene a surreal glow. The band struck up "Hail to the Chief," and the Clintons slowly made their way down the stairs to shake hands with the waiting diplomats.

I scurried over and caught Hillary's eye. She gave me a big smile and a polite nod and went about her official chores.

Our motorcade was lined up on the tarmac: forty vehicles, including two identical bulletproof limousines with their American and presidential flags fluttering. There were two for two reasons: first, to foil any would-be assassins; second, even presidential limousines break down at times. I shadowed Hillary's movements as she made her way down the red carpet and into the waiting car. As soon as she was safely seated inside, I hurried back to the control van and sat next to Anthony Lake, the national security adviser.

We gave the signal, and the motorcade, led by a flying wedge of Irish motorcycle police, pulled out of the airport. The roads had been cleared, and we anticipated a ride of about fifteen minutes to get to Irish President Mary Robinson's house in Phoenix Park, eight miles away.

I knew President Clinton was popular in Ireland, and I had seen people heading toward the motorcade route earlier that morning, but nothing prepared me for what came next. People were lined up at least ten deep on both sides of the road, cheering, screaming, waving American flags, Irish flags, and homemade signs welcoming the Clintons to Ireland. The crowd stretched as far as I could see, an immense, boisterous, joyous outpouring of affection that seemed to take on a life of its own. Fathers held up their babies so they could later boast they'd witnessed President Bill Clinton's first trip to Ireland; teenage girls were near hysteria; old ladies' faces were crinkled with delight. An old gentleman in a wrinkled suit and a weathered scally cap held up a sign that read: WELCOME BILL CLINTON, THE FIRST TRUE IRISH-AMERICAN PRESIDENT.

One reason the Irish were so adoring of President Clinton was his firm stance on peace in Ireland. He had been putting heavy pressure on British Prime Minister John Major to get serious about the issue. Clinton was the first U.S. president to get personally involved and had moved the group working on the Irish peace process from the State Department into the White House. The Irish were grateful for this support and weren't shy about showing it.

My spirits were already soaring, but the sight of all these delirious Irish sent me into the stratosphere. It was as if the island's entire population had come out to greet the Clintons. Tony Lake and I exchanged amazed looks. Just then the motorcade slowed to a crawl, and I instinctively went into high alert. But it was only President Clinton indulging his passion for getting close to the people. He was waving and smiling and making eye contact from inside his car, setting off sequential bursts of frenzy from the crowd as he passed. On her side of the car Hillary's reception was almost as passionate.

Each time it seemed like we were about to come to a complete halt, a terse "Keep moving!" crackled over the radio, the command coming from the Secret Service follow-up vehicle. After about a half dozen slow crawls we heard the Secret Service supervisor bark to the President's limousine, "This is Halfback to Stagecoach. Who's countering my orders to speed up the motorcade?"

"Halfback from Stagecoach, be advised Eagle is issuing the order directly."

Eagle was the President's code name. We weren't going to be moving faster anytime soon. The crowds never thinned along the entire route, and the trip to President Robinsson's took more than an hour.

As we crawled along, I relaxed a little and scanned the faces in the crowd; it seemed as if half of them could be my cousins. After all, my ancestors on both sides of my family had left Ireland for America a century before, their pockets empty but their imaginations full. I couldn't help thinking what a wonderful situation I'd found myself in, how fortunate I was. What would my great-grandfathers have made of it?

Forget my great-grandfathers. A part of *me* could hardly believe it was true. A kid from a small town in Massachusetts, son of a factory worker, didn't even finish college, and here I was in Ireland as a representative of the most powerful nation on earth, accompanying the President, working for the First Lady. Amazing. Some of the kids I'd grown up with were in prison. A lot were in politics. (I guess that tells you something about politics.) I'd made out all right—and then some.

When we got to Phoenix Park, President Robinson showed the Clintons the lamp that she kept burning to welcome home Irish emigrants who found their way back from distant shores. The state of the Irish economy had been such that for a long time the country's major export had been its youth. However, a recent influx of European Union money and some fundamental reforms in the republic's economic policy meant that more and more people were returning each year to be welcomed home by the president's lamp.

That afternoon President Clinton addressed the Dáil, the Irish parliament. I was seated in the distinguished guests' gallery so I could be near the First Lady. As the President began to speak, I looked around and was amazed to see Gerry Adams, the president of Sinn Fein, the political wing of the Irish Republican Army, seated a couple of rows away from me. It was the first time he had ever set foot in the Dáil.

The President spoke passionately of America's belief that the time had come for peace in Ireland. He renewed our pledge of political, economic, and moral support for the peace process and quoted Irish poet Seamus Heaney: ". . . the longed-for tidal wave of justice can rise up, and hope and history rhyme."

This was a significant affirmation of support coming from the leader of a country that had often deferred to Great Britain on Irish matters, and the members of the parliament met his remarks with a prolonged and heartfelt standing ovation.

We left the Dáil and headed to the Bank of Ireland building across the street from the main gate of Trinity College in the heart of downtown, where President Clinton addressed a throng of more than a hundred thousand. It was a truly amazing turnout, and the President didn't disappoint.

The Clintons were staying at the palatial ambassador's residence, also in Phoenix Park. That evening Ambassador Jean Kennedy Smith hosted a small reception for Irish artists. Included was the poet the President had quoted in his speech to the parliament earlier that day, Seamus Heaney, who had just won the Nobel Prize in literature. Heaney was in his sixties with a head that seemed a little large for his body, a mop of unruly gray hair, soulful eyes, and truly prodigious eyebrows. He presented the President with a signed copy of his latest work, which Clinton tucked under his arm.

There was a state dinner at the Dublin Castle that night. It was getting late, and I swung by the presidential suite to see if he and the First Lady were ready. Hillary was all set to go, but the President was still in his undershorts. After our encounter in the Kremlin, I was the picture of nonchalance at finding him in this state of dishabille. He was strutting around with his glasses on, thumbing through the Heaney book, underlining passages with a red pencil, and mumbling, "This is great stuff, really great."

We arrived at the castle a few minutes late, but at least the President was fully dressed. After dinner we were serenaded by an Irish tenor who sang "Danny Boy," often a cliché but in this particular instance powerful and poignant. The President then rose and spoke about what it means to be Irish. He praised the Irish for their commitment to humanitarian efforts worldwide and their hunger for peace at home. Woven seamlessly into his talk were lines from Heaney's poetry. It was an eloquent and moving speech. I was deeply impressed at how quickly he had found just the right Heaney lines to illustrate his points and lift his rhetoric and at how deftly he had inserted them. I know, because I witnessed it with my own eyes, that it was Bill Clinton, not some speechwriter, who knew how to touch a chord with the audience.

By demonstrating his commitment to the peace process so overtly in Belfast and Dublin, President Clinton had sent an unmistakable signal to Prime Minister Major and the Unionists in the north of Ireland that America backed a speedy resolution to the troubles that had plagued the island for so long. It was a significant step toward the Northern Ireland peace accord President Clinton's close friend George Mitchell brokered three years later.

The Dublin wheels-up party was particularly memorable because it was hosted by Guinness, at its St. James's Gate brewery. Some of my Irish friends in Boston had expressed concern about the footing of the Irish economy, claiming that letting me into the brewery was likely to lead to a worldwide Guinness drought.

13

DONOR FEVER

November–December 1995

WE WERE GEARING UP FOR PRESIDENT CLINTON'S REELECTION campaign in the fall of 1995 and were in New York for two fund-raisers and a rally in Times Square. The rally, ostensibly for health care reform but really a kickoff for the campaign, was sponsored by a group of unions and was being put together by Steve Rabinowitz.

Rabinowitz, a great guy, had been Bill Clinton's lead press advance throughout the 1992 campaign. That's a high-burnout job, and legend has it that Rabbi, as he was known, managed to flame out in brilliant fashion. The story goes that he was coordinating for the visit of Pope John Paul II in 1993 when a cardinal inadvertently strayed into a picture he was setting up of the President and the pope. Rabbi turned to the nearest church representative, another high-ranking cardinal, and screamed, "Tell the guy in the red hat to get the fuck out of the picture!" Not long after that Rabbi was defrocked and entered the private sector.

A large stage had been constructed for the rally, and a forty-foot Jumbotron screen was positioned behind it, giving the crowd close-ups of the speakers. Rabbi and the union guys had done a great job turning out a crowd, and the street was shoulder to shoulder for as far as you could see. When Hillary was introduced, the crowd went wild, and she was swept up in their adulation. Our health care proposal may have been on life support in Congress, but it was alive and well in New York City. Hillary, as might be expected, delivered a rousing speech and left the stage as one of those irresistible old Motown hits blared on the sound system.

Backstage Hillary started dancing to the music and swinging her hips. A bunch of us joined her. New York, New York! Just as we were really getting down with our bad selves, a Secret Service agent tapped me on the shoulder and pointed to the Jumbotron. There was the first lady of the United States, forty feet tall and in living color, boogying on the streets of New York with her staff. What to do? We couldn't just stop and slink away. I mean, it's not as if we were making fools of ourselves. No way, my John Travolta imitation is very dignified. Hillary, exhibiting her quick wits and stage presence, smiled and waved to the camera as if the whole thing had been planned, and we retreated to the motorcade with our heads held high.

Our next stop was a fund-raiser at the home of financier Ron Perelman, one of the richest men in the country. F. Scott Fitzgerald said, "The rich are different from you and me." To which Hemingway replied: "Yes, they have more money." I'm afraid I have to come down on Fitzgerald's side, although I would amend it to "the *very* rich." They often seem to think the world exists to serve them, but a lot of them, especially the self-made ones, are socially insecure underneath. President Clinton was something of a genius when it came to hitting these folks up for money. He understood that it was all about status, ego, and access. So he threw glittering fund-raisers that were social events pure and simple, a chance to establish pecking order. Policy? Not tonight, thank you. As for the twenty grand entrance fee? A piddling.

Perelman had a modest forty-room pad on East Sixty-third Street. The party was for about fifty high rollers, who paid at least five grand to have their picture taken with the First Lady. Patricia Duff, Perlman's glamorous wife, greeted us at the door and gave Hillary a (not so) quick tour of the house. After all, the place was about the size of Macy's. We then made our way to the main salon, where Hillary stood and posed for photos with the rich and famous, including Sidney Poitier and Donald Trump. I was amazed to see the man who had such an ego that his name was plastered all over casinos, office towers, and airlines waiting in line like everyone else.

The next fund-raiser was the one I was dreading. It was being held in another vast house, also on the Upper East Side, and included a cocktail reception and dinner for fifty people, followed by a private performance by Johnny Cash and his wife, June Carter Cash. It was during the walk-through for this event that I witnessed a calamitous case of donor fever strike a man who obviously thought his wealth bought him the right to have his own way, even when it came to the President and First Lady.

There were about twenty of us at the walk-through, including the host, the Secret Service, and the New York police. The host was a rotund, florid gentleman in his early fifties, flamboyant enough to play Roger De Bris, the over-the-top theater director, in Mel Brooks's *The Producers.* We all met in a large room on the ground floor to go over such mundane details as arrival points, holding rooms, and bathrooms. No problems. I then began to explain that at an event such as this one the First Lady normally appears after everyone is seated for dinner, spends a few moments chatting with the host, and then speaks and departs. That's when things got weird.

The host listened to my recitation of Hillary's role with growing dismay, his eyes growing larger, his mouth falling open. When I got to the part about her leaving right after she had finished speaking, he went absolutely berserk.

"No, you can't mean that! That will ruin me! Ruin me! Do you know who I am? I'm a big wheel in this town, that's who I am!" he screamed at the top, and I do mean the top, of his lungs. His face bright red, arms waving, spittle flying, he began running around the room in circles, wailing incoherently.

The rest of us stood there, stunned. There was more to come.

Suddenly he stopped and seemed to regain his composure. Apparently he was just waiting for his second wind, because moments later he ripped off his blue blazer with the shiny gold buttons, threw it on the floor, and started jumping up and down on it, screaming over and over: *"Do you know how much I'm contributing? Do you know how much I'm contributing?"*

Out of the corner of my eye I caught the New York police officers slowly easing their hands toward their weapons. This guy was way out of control, and no one knew what to expect next.

Once I got over the shock value of the performance, I thought it was kind of funny. After all, I'd had more experience with donor fever than anyone else present. I knew it responded best to tough love. I walked over to our host and placed a hand firmly on his shoulder. He stopped jumping up and down and started sobbing uncontrollably.

"Calm down, just calm down," I said. "Now let's you and me go out in the hall and discuss this."

I led him out of the room, and when we were alone, I gave him a few minutes to pull himself together. His sobbing subsided to a shocked, shallow whimpering.

"Now you've got to get a grip on yourself here. There's obviously been some sort of misunderstanding. I'll see what I can do about having the First Lady stay a little longer."

He looked up at me with round, red-rimmed eyes—a spoiled child who had just gotten his way—and I saw the method to his madness. "Oh, would you? Would you *really*? Thank you. Thank you *so much*."

When we arrived on the night of the event, I looked around cautiously for our host and was happy to find him fully clothed and behaving himself. Hillary ended up staying, and I must admit that both she and I enjoyed the Cashes' concert.

That close encounter with the craziness that proximity to the presidency can engender was a stark reminder. While I knew our hysterical friend was harmless, his fit had caused real alarm among the Secret Service agents present. Pretty soon the President and First Lady would be out on the campaign trail again, exposing themselves to thousands of strangers daily.

Yes, even though the election was still eleven months off, it was time to fasten our seat belts and strap on our safety helmets. While an election is stressful for all involved, there is nobody it is tougher on than the Secret Service. Gone are the controlled situations where they have the luxury of days and even weeks of preparation. A presidential candidate will change his schedule at the last second, spontaneously plunge into a crowd, subject himself to danger at every turn.

Lew Merletti, the director of the Presidential Protection Division of the Secret Service, decided it would be a good idea for the White House staff to have a thorough understanding of the risks involved. He arranged to have a group of us spend a day at the James J. Rowley Training Center in Beltsville, Maryland. Built in 1975 and named for a former director of the agency, the center is located on a heavily wooded 493-acre campus about twenty miles from the White House. Driving by the landscaped entryway, you might think it was a surburban office park. You'd be wrong. Very wrong.

The Secret Service is a branch of the Treasury Department. It was established in 1865 with the primary mission of safeguarding the United States currency. Protecting the president was added in 1901, after President William McKinley had been assassinated in Buffalo, New York, by anarchist Leon Czolgosz. From time to time there has been talk that the FBI, federal marshals, or some new law enforcement entity might take over, but the simple truth is that no organization on the face of this earth is more skilled at protecting people than the modern Secret Service. We were about to get an up-close and personal look at the training its agents receive.

About fifty of us took part. We were mostly advance staff, but with a smattering of folks from other departments, including Harold Ickes. Our first stop was a large lecture hall. Merletti welcomed us and began by outlining the basic principles of protecting the president and first lady. Much of what he said was known by those of us who spent time on the road, but it was a good tutorial and gave us all a common frame of reference. We learned that agents on presidential detail spend a full 20 percent of their time at Beltsville, honing their skills. Then he moved on to what happens when security fails. The lights were dimmed, a screen was lowered, and film clips were shown.

We watched John Hinkley shoot President Reagan outside the Washington Hilton, Governor George Wallace being shot by Arthur Bremer, and Philippine President Ferdinand Marcos being attacked by a machete-wielding assailant. Merletti then led a discussion of what we'd seen. He ran the clips in slow motion, pointing out how the attacks had unfolded second by second and how the agents had reacted. He also analyzed the responses of nearby staff and asked us to imagine ourselves in a similar situation.

Three things soon became apparent. First, attacks happen very, very quickly. None lasted more than five seconds from start to finish. We also noted the instinctive responses of the Secret Service agents, the product of intense training; these included throwing themselves, without hesitation, between the assassin and the principal. Finally, the staff was often as not more seriously wounded than the principal, most famously, of course, James Brady, President Reagan's press secretary. The sight of the courageous Mr. Brady, with a serious head wound, lying on the ground, his body twitching, was painful to watch, and for someone who spent a lot of time inches from the First Lady, all too close to home.

Next we reviewed the profiles of assassins. I was surprised to learn that they rarely have ideological axes to grind; Hinkley, for instance, had also stalked President Carter. They mostly crave attention and what, to their twisting thinking, is validation. Lou went into detail about several stalkers, including the man who had been arrested at the Nixon funeral, our sweaty friend in the light suit. It was a very scary look at some profoundly disturbed people. It's one thing to have to worry about foreign terrorists or a biological attack, but these homegrown threats are everywhere. They're typically loners and social misfits, although some hold down respectable jobs. The really dangerous ones are very intelligent and tend to travel a lot. Some send letters tipping off their intentions, but the most dangerous are those who cruise below the radar screen. The lengths to which these people would go to harm their victims were incredible. We learned that many wanted to commit suicide by being killed during their attack, a thought that kept coming back to me as we went through the rest of the day's training. I realized very clearly that should I find myself in one of these terrible situations, I would be able to assume nothing about the assailant's responses. He might welcome his own death.

Our next stop was the attack village, the Secret Service's version of the Paramount back lot. There was a hotel, a suburban house, and a commercial street with storefronts, sidewalks, and alleyways.

We walked through a magnetometer (metal detector) and were shown how they're used at presidential events. There was a large and impressive display of confiscated items, including the expected knives, guns, and chains, but also a veterinary hypodermic needle used on horses and a fake can of hair spray with a quarter stick of dynamite inside.

We were then led to the "hotel," which looked like your typical Hyatt or Sheraton, the type of place we stayed at all the time. There was a lobby with a mezzanine level above and an entry portico. We were about to witness a mock deployment of a counterassault team (CAT). These teams travel everywhere with the president, remaining close by but out of sight. Wearing black uniforms with POLICE/SECRET SERVICE stitched on the back and carrying the latest high-tech weaponry, these are the heavy hitters, deployed when massive force is needed ASAP. The last time a CAT saw action was during the first Bush administration, when President Bush visited Panama and a crowd at an outdoor event became unruly. News footage shows the team, weapons drawn, surrounding the president and whisking him to his motorcade for evacuation.

For the purposes of our demonstration I was to play the role of an advance man (a real stretch), and other staffers became the President, the First Lady, and Chelsea. We were working a receiving line in the hotel lobby, shaking hands, when suddenly "terrorists" burst in and began shooting. We all ducked and sought cover. The agents surrounding the First Family shielded them with their bodies. Within seconds another door burst open, and the CAT came in with guns ablaze. They quickly overpowered the terrorists and evacuated the First Family. Although they were firing blanks, the noise of the weapons, the smell of cordite, and the agents' shouts scared the bejesus out of all of us.

We moved outside to the front of the hotel to await the arrival of the presidential motorcade, something all of us had done scores of times. As the limousine pulled to a stop, a sniper shot rang out. With lightning speed, Secret Service agents pushed the First Family back into the limousine, which sped off. Once again everything happened in a matter of seconds. The instructor then asked us where the sniper was hiding. We couldn't even agree on which direction the shot had been fired from, let alone spot the gunman. Suddenly another shot rang out, and the staffer standing next to me was "painted" with a red laser dot. The sniper reported a clean kill. Then he stood up and waved at us—from a clump of bushes a quarter of a mile away. We were amazed at the distance and were told that a trained sniper can take out a subject from a mile away if he has a clear line of sight.

Next we witnessed a truly heart-stopping demonstration. The President and First Lady dropped into a store to do a little shopping. As they came out, a small crowd cheered them, staff milled about, and the President looked as if he were about to start shaking hands. Suddenly sniper shots rang out. Agents pushed the First Couple into their armored limousine. As the limo was speeding away, a large truck suddenly roared into the intersection, and they were trapped. Then terrorists began to rain down fire from nearby rooftops. The CAT appeared and returned fire, taking out most of the terrorists, as the limo driver rammed the truck and opened up a little daylight. Just as they seemed to regain control of the situation, a rocket-propelled grenade was launched at the limousine. The driver managed to speed away with inches to spare, and the grenade hit a vehicle across the street, triggering a massive explosion. The point that there may be sequential attacks was well taken indeed.

At the protective operations driving course a fleet of shiny new Chevy Camaros stood at the ready, and dented and damaged limousines and Chevy Suburbans were scattered about. The instructor explained that the cars are traded in after six months, with only four hundred miles on them. Before we could ask how to pick up one of these bargain mobiles, we were told the cars go through an average of twenty-four sets of tires, their suspensions and brakes are completely shot, and in most cases the engines are on their last legs. Then it was time for the demonstration of how they get that way.

Each instructor loaded three students into a Camaro, and off we went to the track. Now I drive a sports car and have been known to go a mile or two over the speed limit. I consider myself a damn good driver, so I volunteered to sit up front. Mistake. The instructor gunned the car out of a driveway in reverse, turned the wheel sharply and snapped us around 180 degrees, and roared off toward a maze of traffic cones. He slalomed through the pylons at eighty miles an hour, often on two smoking tires. My nonchalance was long gone. I think it's safe to say I was scared stiff. A quick glance at the back seat told me I wasn't alone; my colleagues were a peculiar shade of green, and I was thankful this was taking place *before* lunch. Next came the aptly named panic stops, which made me feel like a human crash dummy. Then we were treated to some 180-degree spins and quick acceleration drills. Finally it was over, and terra firma never felt better.

After a short break Larry Cockell, one of the supervising agents, asked for some volunteers to try a couple of the maneuvers themselves. I hesitated—for about two seconds. After all, how often do you get a chance to demonstrate the fruits of a misspent youth? I slid behind the wheel of one of the three-hundred-horsepower Camaros and was taken out on the course with an instructor by my side to learn the high speed J-turn. The J-turn is what you use when you suddenly come upon, say, a rampaging elephant or stray militia tank in the middle of the road. You slam on the brakes, back up as fast as you can, spin the car around 180 degrees, and speed off in the opposite direction. I knew immediately that it could come in handy when dealing with Boston traffic. Riding in the car with someone else at the controls had been a traumatic experience. Driving it myself was exhilarating.

I listened intently as my instructor ran through the drill. Then he smiled in a way that made me a little nervous. "I just got a radio call," he said. "They want to see which of you staff guys can drive the best. You're not going to let me down, are you?"

"Of course not. I cut my teeth trying to outrun the Massachusetts State Police in a '63 Ford. This is a piece of cake."

At the signal I streaked toward imaginary trouble at over sixty miles an hour. I jammed on the brakes and slid to a stop through a cloud of blue smoke, sending the acrid stench and small hot fragments of burning rubber in the open windows. I jacked the gearshift into reverse and floored the accelerator, one hand on the shift, the other on the steering wheel at the eight o'clock position. At the count of three, racing backward, I abruptly took my foot off the gas pedal, spun the wheel to the four o'clock position, shifted back into drive, and slammed my foot to the floor. The car spun around in a violent but true arc, and I was on my way to daylight.

"Outstanding!" my instructor shouted over the roaring engine.

"Do you think we won?" I shouted back.

"Definitely."

We did. Just don't tell my insurance agent.

Our final stop was the indoor firing range, where we were given a chilling demonstration of the difference between a conventional, or full-metal jacket, bullet and a hollow-point bullet. Two water-filled gallon jugs were strung up. The instructor fired a full-metal jacket round into one jug. The container sprang two leaks. The entry hole was about the size of a dime; the exit hole about the size of a quarter. Water poured out, but the jug was largely intact. The next bullet was a hollow point. The jug exploded, water flew, and all that was left was a shattered mess. The instructor explained that the hollow point mushrooms on impact and has two distinct advantages. First, it provides more stopping power. Unlike in the movies, the bad guy doesn't always drop just because you put a round into him. Many keep on coming, firing away. The hollow point ups the odds that you'll disable your attacker quickly. The other advantage is that it's far less likely to travel through a person and harm someone standing nearby.

As we drove back to the White House on that December afternoon, the talk was about how close danger is each and every time you work around the President and the First Lady. We all knew that we'd be on the road a great deal in the next eleven months, often caught up in the uncontrollable hurly-burly of a presidential election campaign. We were very glad that the Secret Service would be there with us.

14

IT TAKES AN ADVANCE MAN

January 1996

IT TOOK AN ADVANCE MAN TO PROMOTE *IT TAKES A VILLAGE.* THAT was the title of the high-profile book Hillary wrote expounding her belief that we all share a responsibility for the common good. By some remarkable coincidence, the book hit the stores just as the reelection campaign was swinging into gear. Off we went to hawk the tome across the breadth of the land.

Normally a publisher, in this case Simon & Schuster, sends out a couple of people from its publicity department to line up bookstore readings and try to scare up media attention. Well, when Hillary is the scribe, the rules are very different. You're not trying to scare up the media; you're trying to hold them to a manageable number. Getting people to attend an event isn't the problem; dealing with them when they arrive in droves is. Then there are the usual logistical nightmares involved in moving a first lady. In addition, in this case, we wanted the focus to stay squarely on the book and not have each event devolve into an impromptu press conference about the Whitewater investigation or the reelection campaign.

Simon & Schuster wisely realized that it was in over its head. It agreed to hire my crew and me to put together the tour. So my employment round robin continued: For the days that I worked on the book tour, I was off the DNC payroll and the Clinton-Gore '96 payroll and on the Simon & Schuster payroll. I was doing the same job; it was just a question of who was going to pay me for it.

Hillary's book had a special appeal to women, and it was fascinating for me to observe their behavior when they showed up at the bookstores to meet her. While there were women of all ages and from all walks of life, the preponderance of them looked well educated and well-to-do. It was clear from their dress and the briefcases they carried that they had very good jobs. For these women, Hillary was a hero. Many of them were wives, mothers, employees (and often employers), and like Hillary, they were facing the subtle and not so subtle prejudices in our society about the changing role of women. Hillary was a symbol of how far women had come and a reminder of how far they still had to go. As someone pointed out to me during the tour, of the Fortune 500 companies, only one had a female CEO. (I think the figure had skyrocketed to two by 2001.) Out of 100 U.S. senators, 8 were women (today that figure stands at a still-paltry 13). In fact, in the history of the U.S. Senate there have been 1,864 senators, and only 31 of them have been women. Moreover, 9 of those 31 served only a single year as "seat warmers," usually in place of deceased husbands. We say that we support strong women and that there are no more barriers, but many Americans of both sexes still seem threatened by powerful women. Furthermore, while some fields are welcoming to women, others are decidedly not. Oh, by the way, we also want them to look great, stay cool, keep house, take care of the kids, and succeed in the world without letting their ambition become too obvious. I'd like to see a man try to pull off that trick. Hillary's generation, the baby boomers, was in the forefront of redefining women's roles, and its strides were making it easier for the women coming up behind it. Hillary was the most prominent woman of all, a trailblazer and a lightning rod. She had earned her hero status.

Meeting their heroes can have a funny effect on people. It was at a bookstore in Dallas that I witnessed the last word in hero worship. We were at Taylor's Bookstore in a very affluent section of the city. It didn't look like a neighborhood where there'd be a whole lot of Democrats, but issues like choice, the environment, health care, and education were driving many traditionally Republican women into the Democratic ranks, and we ended up with more than two thousand people.

The drill we put together for bookstore events was to have Hillary slip in through a rear door, stand at the back of the store, and make a few very brief remarks to the people waiting in line and the assembled press corps.

Then we ushered the faithful along to shake her hand. After the shake we gave them autopenned copies of the book. Our mantra was: Keep 'em moving.

Kelly Craighead, one of the smartest and toughest women on the Hillary team, rode herd over the line, keeping people flowing through at a pace that Disney World would envy. Kelly always looked out for even the most minute detail of the First Lady's comfort and insisted there be a foam rubber pad for her to stand on, a chair she could rest her back against, and a ready supply of water and hot tea to quench her thirst. We kept a box handy to hold all the gifts people brought, everything ranging from their résumés to fresh-baked pastries, and tried to intercept the offerings before they actually had a chance to hand them to her. We also formed a bucket brigade to take people's bags and backpacks before they got to Hillary and to give them back immediately afterward. With our systems in place and Kelly in charge we managed to get our flow rate up to about twelve people per minute, and if we were really cooking, we could steer a crowd of two thousand through in not much over two hours. I have to confess that although I loved Hillary dearly, I couldn't imagine why someone would wait in line for up to three hours for a five-second encounter, but people did.

At Taylor's Bookstore I noticed a very attractive woman making her way through the line. She was a tall brunette, mid-twenties, wearing a black sweater with red and white stripes. By the time she reached the back of the store, she'd been in line a couple of hours. I could see her excitement growing the closer she got to Hillary, and I expected her to be a gusher, one of those people who open their mouths and unleash torrents of appreciation, affection, adulation. It can be a little off-putting for Hillary, who is, after all, only human—and knows it.

Finally the young woman was next in line, just about vibrating with anticipation. The man in front of her moved away, and she stood face-to-face with Hillary, who held out her hand. Nothing. Hillary smiled. Still nothing. Hillary asked her her name. Nope. The woman just stood there frozen stiff, her mouth hanging open, staring at Hillary with eyes as round as Frisbees. It took a gentle push from Kelly to get our stunned friend to move on.

About an hour later I noticed her in line again. Oh, good, I thought, she's had a chance to compose herself, and now she'll get to shake Hillary's hand and exchange pleasantries and go home happy. The Secret Service had a different take and kept their eyes on her. Could she be a security risk, some nut with a Hillary obsession who would grab the First Lady's arm and sink her teeth into it? You never knew.

Once again I watched the woman's excitement and anticipation grow as she moved toward the head of the line. She'd now devoted almost three hours of her day to this. She finally reached Hillary, stepped forward, and . . . froze like a block of ice, same gaping mouth, same saucer eyes. The poor dear.

I saw plenty of people be overcome with emotion upon meeting Hillary, but our Dallas friend was the only one I ever saw immobilized. It was a powerful reminder of what this woman meant to a sizable portion of the population, and it made me proud of my work for her.

The book tour was creating a lot of favorable publicity, which Hillary needed. There was a constant seesaw between the positive and the negative, between the accomplishments and the abyss. Right now the abyss was named Ken Starr.

Starr was a tall, pasty, sanctimonious attorney who interrupted his morning jogs for impromptu prayer sessions and made a hefty proportion of his income representing tobacco companies. He had been appointed special prosecutor in August 1994 by a panel of three federal judges, one of whom, David Sentelle, was a right-wing Republican ally of Senator Jesse Helms. In fact, Sentelle and Helms had dined together during the selection process. Starr was a known Clinton hater and quickly expanded his investigation from the Whitewater land deal to include the billing practices of the Rose Law Firm, the firing of the White House Travel Office staff, and the suicide of Vincent Foster. All those matters had links to Hillary, and there were whispers that she could be indicted. The whispers escalated to rampant speculation when her former partner at the Rose firm, Webster Hubbell, pleaded guilty to tax evasion and mail fraud in December 1994.

As we planned for another trip to New Hampshire in late January, we learned that Hillary, who had been interviewed by Starr at the White House in April, was to be called before a federal grand jury in Washington the day after the event. It was the first time a first lady had ever been subpoenaed. Naturally, this changed our thinking about the trip since there would now be considerably more media than we had originally anticipated.

Susi Madison, the leader of Girl Scout Troop 659 in Lebanon, New Hampshire, had written to the White House inviting Hillary to meet with her charges. I figured we couldn't go wrong having Hillary appear with cute little tykes who start every meeting with a pledge to serve God and country, be honest and fair, courageous and strong. Madison never expected anything to come of the invitation and was stunned when I called and said the visit was on. She and the girls were thrilled. Another plus was that the troop met in the library of the local junior high school, a traditional New England red-brick building. The whole event was a Norman Rockwell painting come to life, just the image of Hillary we wanted the day before she faced the grand jury.

We allowed for a considerable press area in the library, added more barricades, and recruited local supporters to provide a friendly greeting. I briefed Susi Madison and her girls as best I could, warning them that our national press corps in full howl can be quite a sight to behold.

Hillary was in great spirits when she deplaned at the Lebanon airport. If the impending trip to the grand jury was bothering her, you certainly couldn't tell by her demeanor. When we arrived at the school there was a large crowd of supporters outside. Normally Hillary would have waved and headed right into the building—the Secret Service had drilled into our heads that these impromptu crowds are unpredictable and potentially dangerous—but this time she walked over and began shaking hands. When I saw this, my heart went out to her. Whatever her public face, I think at that particular moment she craved support.

Inside the junior high school we were greeted by the girls of Troop 659, decked out in their green uniforms, and a huge gaggle of media. The girls were adorable; the media, less so. Each of the four major networks and a score of affiliates from across New England had sent crews; in addition, the wire services and newspapers had sent reporters and photographers. The Girl Scouts were outnumbered by better than four to one but showed great aplomb. The situation was almost comical, with the hulking reporters and steely-eyed Secret Service agents bearing down as the little girls in green conducted their solemn business as if it were a normal Scout meeting.

Hillary thanks her staff in Little Rock after the 1992 presidential campaign with Kelly Craighead in attendance.
Photo by Sharon Kennedy

A Russian peddler offers a bearskin for sale at an outdoor Moscow market.

Escorting Chelsea, Hillary, and Colonel Nasir Abbas in Lahore, Pakistan.

Yak attack: An angry yak confronts me in Mongolia. Photo by Jack Murray

Hillary greets a nomadic Mongolian family.

The rejected site in Mongolia for the First Lady's speech on freedom—in front of a mural of Engels, Marx, and Lenin.

Eyeing meat hanging in a Mongolian ger.

Hillary signs a guest book in Istanbul as Chelsea looks on.

Briefing Hillary and Tipper Gore aboard Bright Star, the First Lady's Air Force jet.

The Blairs greet the Clintons in front of #10 Downing Street.

Hillary prepares to go ice skating.

President Clinton and the First Lady lay bricks in Philippi Township, South Africa.

President Nelson Mandela escorts President Clinton, Hillary, and his then-companion Graça Machel on a tour of Robben Island Prison.

Fidel Castro arrives at the Geneva hotel where Hillary was staying.

Residents of Tunisian Village 2626 greet the First Lady.

Pat— Is working for me really that bad? Anyway, thanks for everything — even if you're a little worse for wear!

Hillary

Hillary shares a laugh with her monstrous advance man.

Hillary joins her traveling staff for a photo in Petra, Jordan.

Hillary thanks the Boston Boys at the White House staff party, January 2001 (left to right): *Sharon Kennedy, Melissa Graham, Jack Murray, Hillary, me, and Steve Graham.*

Hillary quickly established a rapport with the girls and put them at ease. They all recited the pledge of allegiance and sang a song together. Then Hillary delivered a brief talk and answered their questions. Most asked about life in the White House and about Chelsea or Socks, the First Family's cat. Then Hillary surprised me for the second time that afternoon when she turned to the press corps and asked if it had any questions. There was a long pause. I wouldn't have believed it if I hadn't seen it, but the big bad media were cowed by those charming, sincere, and innocent young ladies. They asked a polite question or two, but no one followed up or got tough. That was one smart move on Hillary's part.

The staff was on pins and needles all day. Nobody discussed the grand jury appearance, but it was on all our minds. At the airport I gave Hillary a spontaneous hug. "We all love you and stand by you, no matter what happens," I said.

She looked at me and smiled. "Don't worry, Pat, everything is going to be fine."

As the plane ascended, I wondered if she was right. There was no doubt that Starr was a man possessed. He had an absolutely obsessive hatred of the Clintons and, fueled by tens of millions of dollars of taxpayer money, was on the biggest government-sponsored fishing expedition of all time, trying to prove them guilty of some wrongdoing. His zeal was obvious to even the most casual observer. This was a cultural holy war, and the Clintons were the infidels. He didn't just want to help defeat them in the 1996 election; he wanted to *destroy* them. I think his efforts had an unintended consequence: They made Hillary's staff more determined than ever to see her prevail.

I watched television anxiously the next day as she arrived at the courthouse for her testimony. She was wearing a black cape and carried herself with confidence. A couple of hours later she emerged from the courthouse looking none the worse for wear. A huge throng of reporters had the place staked out, and she stepped to a microphone and delivered a statement in steady, measured tones. I was relieved to see that she had held up and felt confident she had been more than a match for Ken Starr and his henchmen.

15

BATTLE OF THE BOSPORUS

March–April 1996

AH, SPRING. IT COULD MEAN ONLY ONE THING, A TRIP TO AN EXOTIC land with Hillary and Chelsea. I relished the adventure, the adrenaline, even the difficulty of doing advance work in a foreign country. It was a challenge, no doubt, but one that carried a whole lot of perks, not the least of which was making sure that two people I cared about had a terrific time together. There was some talk in the White House that Hillary should stay put that spring because of the upcoming election, but she wouldn't hear of it. Spring break with Chelsea was sacrosanct, come elections, special prosecutors, or book tours. This year their trip was to begin with a visit to the American troops stationed in Bosnia, a chance to show gratitude for the difficult mission they were performing.

Bringing attention to the fact that lives were at stake in Bosnia also provided a nice counterpoint to the pettiness of Starr's investigation, which was heating up, with committees in both the Senate and House holding hearings. In the Senate it was the Banking Committee—chaired by Senator Alfonse D'Amato of New York—that was doing the dishonors. Among his star witnesses was a little-known low-level former White House staffer by the name of Linda Tripp.

On the First Lady's itinerary after Bosnia were Greece, to witness the lighting of the Olympic torch, which would then make its way to Atlanta for the Summer Games, and Turkey.

Hillary was eager to visit Turkey. She wanted to show American support for the secular government headed by a Muslim prime minister. She also planned to visit Tansu Çiller, the female former prime minister, who was viewed alternately as a visionary leader or as a thief, depending on which faction held power that month. The trip was to be divided among an official stop in Ankara, the capital, a short side trip to the ancient city of Ephesus, and a religious and cultural stay in Istanbul. Those boundaries were blurred because in Turkey religion equals politics. It's a country constantly struggling to reconcile its strict Muslim fundamentalism with its desire to build a modern secular society. I requested the Istanbul leg of the visit, and my wish was granted.

Istanbul: Even the word conjures up intrigue and splendor. East meets West in a wondrous mix of cultures, architecture, ethnic groups and religions, an exotic playground filled with winding alleys, covered bazaars, spice markets, glamorous casinos, towering cathedrals, glittering mosques, teeming, vibrant, perfumed with a faint scent of danger straight out of a Robert Ludlum novel. All this is set against the blue-green water of the Bosporus Strait, the narrow body of water separating Europe from Asia that has played such a significant role in world history.

The day my advance team arrived was lovely, warm with bright blue skies. My suite at the Hyatt was a delightful surprise, a luxurious four-room affair with a marvelous view and a marble bath the size of a Greenwich Village condo. After a quick nap I set out for a look at the city. The streets were bathed in a late-afternoon sun, and while most people were in Western dress, many women observed the traditional purdah and veiled their faces.

The streets of the old city were punctuated with markets and bazaars, their vendors offering the "deal of a lifetime" on almost anything you could imagine. We were shown leather coats, Persian rugs, "priceless antiquities," velvet paintings, and fresh produce. You could buy a sable coat or a live chicken.

The city's spice market announced itself from blocks away, the intermingled aromas of curry, cardamon, paprika, and a hundred other spices intensifying the closer we got. The market's narrow aisles were so packed with people, food, and enormous piles of spices that it was almost impossible to navigate.

I knew immediately that I would need a lot of help making my way about this labyrinthine metropolis. Fortunately our contact was Chris Stillman, the administrative officer at our consulate. Chris was a tall, lanky guy with a mop of brown hair, a gravelly voice, and an ever-present cigarette that seemed to be a natural extension of his body. He had a lot of nervous energy and appeared to be in constant motion. His eyes took in everything. Chris had been on station three years, and his personality and temperament perfectly suited Istanbul. He was constantly barking into a cell phone in Turkish, cigarette dangling from his lips, while some shady-looking fellow stood by, waiting to speak to him in hushed tones. He could, on a moment's notice, produce virtually anything we needed. As I spent more time with Chris and continued to be awed by his ability to manipulate the many levers of power in the city, it became increasingly clear that as grateful as I was for his help, I didn't want to ask too many questions about how he got things done. He was as mysterious as the city itself, and much more efficient. I wished I could have cloned him for my future travels.

We needed a boat for the First Lady's twilight cruise on the Bosporus, and the White House had given us the names of a couple of prominent citizens who had yachts, but Chris scoffed at their vessels. Within a couple of hours he'd found one that met his standards, and he took me down to a marina to check it out. It was a boat the way the Grand Canyon is a ditch. It had started life as a ship in the Turkish Navy, been converted to a pleasure craft by former President Kemal Atatürk, then bought by a Japanese corporation and renovated for over a hundred million dollars, before being sent back to Istanbul to wow this rather shadowy company's clients. It was, in a word, mind-boggling. It had a five-story elevator, enormous Turkish baths made of white marble, and its very own helipad. It also had enough teak, gold, silver, gilt, china, and crystal to sink a good Democrat's heart. I think even Liberace would have found the joint a little overdone. Chris and I stood in the main lounge, stunned by the opulence.

"Chris, how in the world can we afford to rent this tub? You're talking about the first lady of the United States, not the sultan of Brunei."

"Not to worry, Patrick, the boat and crew are complimentary," Chris said with one of his enigmatic little smiles.

Unfortunately certain members of our intelligence community took a dim view of the yacht's owners, and we had to settle for more modest, but still quite splendid, hospitality from the family of a prominent Turkish businessman.

The First Lady's suite at the Hyatt looked like a landlocked version of the Japanese yacht. It was far and away the most elegant I'd ever seen, with a commanding view of the Bosporus and the city, a grand piano, and a marble platform that rose from the floor at the touch of a button to reveal . . . a television set. The lighting, rugs, fabric, and other details were exquisite. You could easily imagine a potentate of the Ottoman Empire settling right in.

On the day of Hillary's arrival, we began to hear stories from Ankara that the Turkish security people and the Turkish press were very unruly and had jostled the First Lady and Chelsea quite a bit. Chelsea, who rarely complained about anything, was particularly upset. Out at the airport we had set up double barricades to contain the large crowd of rowdy and scruffy-looking Turkish media. We were ready, I hoped, for the onslaught.

Hillary arrived on a small air force jet, not the behemoth 707 she usually used for overseas travel. The smaller plane had been necessary because of a short runway on the side trip she and Chelsea had taken that morning to Ephesus, site of Diana's Temple, one of the so-called Seven Wonders of the World. Our normal routine was disrupted because the crew of the smaller plane, which was to come to a tragic end in less than a week, didn't know who I was and wouldn't let me board to do my briefing. I had to settle for handing Hillary her briefing cards as I escorted her to the motorcade.

As our entourage drove out of the airport, we suddenly heard a deafening roar *right over our heads.* I craned my head out of the window of the lead car and saw a helicopter flying less than ten feet above us, with a cameraman hanging out, taking pictures. This was an extremely dangerous situation. In spite of our screams and gestures, the pilot kept the chopper a few feet above the fast-moving cars. He pulled up only after the Secret Service men brandished their automatic weapons and made it clear they would shoot. And I thought the American media were bad.

It wasn't only the press that was hyperactive. The Turks had laid on so much security and protocol that anytime Hillary moved, sixty people moved with her. A quiet "off the record" dinner at one of Chris Stillman's favorite restaurants entailed a thirty-four-vehicle motorcade. After dinner I joined the First Lady, Chelsea, and a few others in her suite.

"Pat, I could not believe the size of that motorcade. Did you get a count?" Hillary asked.

"Sure did. Thirty-four."

"Thirty-four! And there were only about a dozen of us at dinner. Who *were* they?"

"To tell you the truth, I could account for six vehicles. The other twenty-eight, I have absolutely no idea."

We were all sharing a good laugh at the thought of those twenty-eight vehicles filled with Turks doing who knew what when someone called out for us to come watch a report on the television at the other end of the suite. We knew the town was in the grip of full-blown Hillary mania, but what we saw topped it all. The lead story on the news was a hard-hitting report on Hillary's dinner. The riveting footage featured a close-up of the plate she'd eaten from and the chair she'd sat on. This was followed by a penetrating interview with the waiter who served her. CNN must have been green with envy.

The following morning it was off to former Prime Minister Tansu Çiller's house for breakfast. Çiller was the fifty-year-old mother of two who had gone from an academic career at the University of Connecticut and a professorship in economics at Bosporus University to prime minister of Turkey in a little over two years. That's a meteoric rise by any standard, and it wasn't without controversy. The blond, good-looking Çiller had been accused of everything from ethnic cleansing to collaboration with the Mafia. The fact that she was a woman who dressed in fashionable Western clothes didn't help any either. Like Hillary, she faced criticism no male politician would countenance, such as the charge that she spent over four hundred dollars a month on panty hose. Her allies were wildly supportive of her efforts to modernize the country. Her detractors, almost exclusively male, thought her the devil incarnate. Sounded a bit familiar to me.

Her residence was an impressive mansion right on the Bosporus, featuring an indoor swimming pool and a gilded ballroom. By this time I was getting a little blasé about all the opulence in Istanbul. The house was undergoing a top-to-bottom renovation, and some critics suggested that it was being paid for with ill-gotten gains.

After breakfast we visited the Blue Mosque, one of Istanbul's most picturesque attractions. The mosque isn't blue on the outside; its name comes from the blue Iznik tiles that cover the inside walls. Its majestic domes and minarets, designed to lift the eye to heaven, were impressive.

Our next stop was to have been the Aya Sofya Cathedral, Turkish for Church of Divine Wisdom. If we'd had a little of that wisdom, we probably would've called off the rest of the day.

As the First Lady and Chelsea waited for the motorcade to leave the Blue Mosque, I radioed ahead for a situation report from the cathedral and was told, "Pat, the site is a mess. Don't come!"

This was the first time in my entire advance career I'd heard those words, and I was obviously alarmed. "What the hell is going on over there?" I demanded.

"It's insane. We're swamped. We had the cathedral closed for the First Lady's visit, and everything was fine. Then about fifteen minutes ago the minister of culture showed up and demanded that the good people of Turkey not be kept waiting to see *their* cathedral."

"For Christ's sakes, he's the one who offered to keep the place closed for us in the first place! So what happened?"

"They threw open the doors, and we now have close to a thousand Turks, not to mention busloads of media, inside the cathedral. What a scene!"

It would have been suicidal to take Hillary into that madhouse. I ordered the motorcade held while I called ahead to the Topkapi Palace, where we'd been planning to go after the cathedral, to see what shape that site was in. That was when the Istanbul police official working our delegation, a beady-eyed man in an ill-fitting suit, got out of his car and approached me. "Why you are not moving?" he asked.

I explained the situation at the Aya Sofya Cathedral.

"So what? We go there now. When we get there, I will establish control," he stated emphatically.

"No. We won't go there now. You promised the place would be empty, and it's not. We'll go to the Topkapi Palace now. If your men get the Aya Sofya under control, we'll go there later."

This gentleman definitely was not used to being stood up to. His brow knitted, his jaw clenched, and he unleashed a bitter tirade: "*I* am in charge here, Mr. Halley, not *you*! This is *my* city! Who the hell you think you are!

Mr. Big Shot! Huh, huh? *Mr. Big Shot!* Pheww! You not such a big shot! I am the *police!* You do as I say and go to Aya Sofya *now! Now you go!* Otherwise maybe you go to *Turkish jail!*"

The guy was so fired up that I expected smoke to start coming out of his ears. But I wasn't going to take his threats gently.

"Listen, my friend, I don't care what you say, we are *not* going to Aya Sofya. Period. If you want me to, I'll ask Mrs. Clinton to step out of her limousine, and you can explain to her why you feel the need to place her life in danger."

"Are you calling me a liar?" he screamed.

"I'm saying that we're not going to the Aya Sofya and that we are going to the Topkapi Palace, with or without you. Take it however you wish."

He glared at me, almost vibrating with rage. Then he turned and stormed off.

We went to the palace.

The Topkapi Palace, a sprawling complex built around four courtyards, was home to Ottoman sultans for nearly three centuries. One of its most significant features is the large harem where early sultans kept as many as three hundred concubines. I felt a little funny about taking Hillary to visit a harem, but figured what the hell, she'd already seen Congress in action. We wended our way through the harem's narrow passages, and the visit was going well. I should have known that couldn't last. I got a radio call that a pack of journalists was trying to sneak in through a back door.

I headed outside to check it out and found Kit Menches, the lead Secret Service agent, engaged in a fistfight with a reporter. The Istanbul police just stood by and watched, the only time I had ever, any place in the world, seen "law enforcement" watch a fellow cop get into a jam without rushing to his aid. I jumped into the fight and helped Kit settle the matter.

Later that day we visited the prelate of the Greek Orthodox Church, the highest-ranking clergyman in Istanbul. He was a charming man who granted Hillary and Chelsea a private interview and then bestowed a blessing upon the entire traveling delegation. I appreciated the thought, but it had come a little late.

Our final event was a multidenominational forum at the Islamic Cultural Center. Eight religions were represented, and the discussion of religious tolerance and the role Istanbul has played in religious life through-out the ages was fascinating. Chelsea, who had recently been studying the Koran, played an active role.

When the forum ended, I suggested the clergy pose for a photograph with the First Lady. They agreed, but making the picture proved to be a challenge: There were language differences, each cleric was attended by a handful of assistants, and they had broken up into small groups and were still chatting. Finally I stood on a chair and yelled out: "Okay, I want the members of the clerical council, just the ones with hats, to line up right here. The rest of you folks, *step back!*"

Some of Hillary's staff were flabbergasted that I would address spiritual leaders like that. But it had been a long, hard day, and I wanted to close it out with our only clean picture. It turned out that people who gave spiritual guidance to millions were quite adept at following instruction themselves. We got a great picture.

By the time the motorcade left the hotel for the airport the entire staff was exhausted, physically and emotionally. Little did we know that four days later a terrible tragedy was to take the lives of some of our closest colleagues and friends.

It was just after ten o'clock in the morning on Wednesday, April 3. I was at home, folding clean clothes hot from the dryer and placing them in neat stacks on my bed, preparing for a trip to Los Angeles. I had the radio turned to the BBC broadcast on NPR, but was only half listening, when it announced that a plane carrying Commerce Secretary Ron Brown was missing somewhere over Bosnia.

I went into the living room and turned on CNN. It was showing a map of Bosnia with arrows representing the plane's intended flight pattern and reporting that the plane was now several hours overdue and had dropped off radar screens. As I stood there watching, the phone rang.

"Have you heard?" It was Steve.

"I'm watching CNN."

"Morris West, Teddy Carr, and Lawry Payne were probably on board." All three were close friends.

Within an hour CNN was reporting that the wreckage of the plane, a Boeing 737, had been sighted. It had crashed into a rocky mountainside several miles short of the Dubrovnik airport during a violent storm. All thirty-five people aboard were dead.

By that evening we had details on our three friends. Morris West had gotten on the plane with the secretary but then deplaned just before it took off so that he could use a landline to call ahead and straighten out some details at the next stop. Teddy Carr was in Paris; he had hitched a ride with some of the American business executives who had left before the end of the trip. Teddy was intent on looking up a woman he'd met in Paris on a previous trip, a fact that ultimately saved his life. Lawry Payne, always one to put duty first, had not been as lucky as Teddy or Morris. He died in a fiery crash on St. John's Hill, a mountainside near Dubrovnik, Croatia.

Lawry was an extraordinary person. A successful entrepreneur, tall, handsome, and hyper, he was frugal to the point of being cheap but would give a friend the shirt off his back. He was precise, a perfectionist who drove us all crazy nailing down the details. But once the pressure of a trip was over, he was great fun to be with. Lawry was still searching for the right Jewish girl to marry and have kids with. He was one of the first members of Hillaryland, and he cared deeply about all the things Hillary cared about. All of us who worked with him will always miss him greatly.

I knew the loss of Ron Brown would be an enormous blow to the Clintons. A highly successful attorney, the first African-American to chair the Democratic party, an army veteran and father, he was one of the President's closest allies and most trusted advisers. He was a brilliant political strategist who had been an architect of Clinton's victory. As commerce secretary he was a key player in the cabinet and a dearly loved personal friend. This was a terrible loss.

The air force plane and crew that went down in the crash were the same ones that had carried Hillary and Chelsea to Ephesus and Istanbul a scant seven days earlier.

I headed to Los Angeles.

Hillary was going out West to attend an important fund-raiser and to deliver the keynote address at the state Democratic convention. I went out to LAX and met her plane. She seemed low-key, preoccupied with preparing her speech, so I didn't mention the crash.

Our first stop was at the Beverly Hills home of Sid and Lorraine Sheinberg for a fund-raiser. Sheinberg was an entertainment mogul, and their estate would have felt right at home in Istanbul. Tickets for the dinner were twenty-five grand, and the event was sold out.

This was the same basic deal as that fund-raiser at Ron Perelman's house in New York, but instead of entertaining real estate barons and corporate billionaires, we had Hollywood celebrities and entertainment industry billionaires. The game remained the same: Be seen in the right place with the right people, and show that you can whisper in the appropriate ear. Sheinberg made sure he wasn't upstaged by his famous guests by donating a hundred grand of his personal money to the national Democratic party that day, conveniently timing the arrival of his check so it would be acknowledged by Hillary in front of his guests. His whispers shouted.

My expectations of how the famous guests, who included Danny DeVito and Barbra Streisand, would arrive was based on the Academy Awards TV show, where big limousines pull up to a red carpet and disgorge stars in tuxedos or designer gowns who strut down the carpet under the harsh glare of the spotlights as the paparazzi snap away. In reality it was like a group of friends coming over for dinner, albeit in very fancy cars. DeVito and his wife, Rhea Perlman, showed up in a convertible with him at the wheel, got out, said hello to the agents, cops, and staff milling around outside the house and were greeted at the door by Lorraine Sheinberg. Barbra Streisand got dropped off, but it wasn't a shiny black stretch limo, it was a nondescript sedan, and she was riding in the front seat next to the driver. These folks might have been as rich as the people at the New York fund-raiser, but they seemed a whole lot less pretentious, and I got the sense they were Democrats by conscience, not just convenience.

The state Democratic convention was being held in the Westin Bonaventure Hotel, and Hillary was going to deliver her speech in the main ballroom. The place was jammed with three thousand very excited Democrats. Like New York and Chicago, Los Angeles has an electricity and energy that are contagious. Also, like those two other cities, it has turned into one hell of a Democratic town. Emotions were running high, and there was a palpable buzz as delegates awaited the First Lady.

As always, Hillary came through. She delivered a rousing speech on the importance of education and the need for Democratic leadership on the issue. The crowd was enthralled and went wild when she finished.

I was waiting for her backstage, ready to escort her to the motorcade. She came up and put her arm around me to pull me close. This had never happened before. We walked slowly toward the elevator, not speaking. "Pat, I'm so sorry about Lawry," she said finally.

"He was a hell of a guy, wasn't he? Do you remember the time he booked the advance staff into that hot-sheets motel made up of broken-down railroad cars?"

"Or the time in Tokyo when he took us to the trash plant? He kept apologizing, like it was his idea," Hillary said.

We laughed.

"Well, at least he died at the top of his game, doing what he loved most," I said.

Hillary nodded. When I offered my condolences about Ron Brown, she looked down with tears in her eyes. The strong, confident politician who'd delivered a rousing speech moments earlier was replaced by a woman mourning the loss of a dear friend. I was moved and struck by her obvious need for physical comfort. I put my arms around her. She and I are not very physical people, but right then we both needed a hug.

16

GONE IN SIXTY SECONDS

April–May 1996

IT'S EASY TO GET CAUGHT UP IN THE FUN AND GAMES OF POLITICS, the egos and the intrigue, the power and the pomp. Then something happens to bring it down to where it really belongs, the people. After all, isn't that who our government is supposed to be of, by, and for? And when something really bad happens, a destructive act of nature, shouldn't government be there for those who need help?

On April 21, 1996, at 11:12 P.M., a tornado struck the industrial section of Fort Smith, Arkansas, destroying 35 houses, a number of factories, and the city's sewage treatment plant. Two small children were killed. The twister then crossed the Arkansas River and ripped through neighboring Van Buren, destroying 463 houses and causing major damage to 500 others.

The response of the Federal Emergency Management Agency (FEMA), under the leadership of James Witt, was swift and sure. Within hours rescue workers, food, and medical supplies were on the scene. Temporary housing was arranged. Federally guaranteed loans were made available to homeowners and businesspeople.

As someone born and raised in New England I hadn't had any experience with tornadoes and wasn't sure what to expect when I was sent out to advance the site for a visit from Hillary. In Massachusetts we occasionally get a late-summer hurricane (I was born during a major hurricane;

maybe that explains things), but they always came with plenty of warning and affected large areas. Tornadoes, I learned, come upon a community with virtually no warning and can reduce a house to sticks while leaving its neighbor, not ten feet away, unscathed.

Hillary was going to tour the site of the disaster to console the victims and commend the rescue workers, who had been toiling around the clock. In situations like these, leaders must strike a delicate balance between showing the proper level of support (as President Bush did in visiting the World Trade Center just days after the terrorist attack) and not complicating recovery efforts by diluting focus and draining resources. People take great comfort in seeing their leaders in emotional times, and as the former first lady of Arkansas and now first lady of the United States Hillary was a logical person to reach out to the tornado victims in their time of need.

When I flew into Fort Smith on a small prop plane, I surveyed the scene from the air. It looked like any small American city: a compact old downtown surrounded by suburbs serviced by the generic commercial roads lined with chain stores and restaurants. Everything looked fine to me. Then I noticed a large area near the river that appeared to have been leveled for a construction site. Trees, buildings, roads, and sidewalks were gone. It was as if someone had run a giant lawn mower over a half-mile-wide tract, obliterating everything in its path.

FEMA had set up temporary headquarters in a large warehouse near the center of town. Graham Nance, who was coordinating the agency's response, greeted me and escorted me to his office, where the other members of my advance team were already assembled. Graham, a courtly southern gentleman who wore cowboy boots, had a weather-beaten face and an easy smile. I soon learned that this amiable fellow was in charge of the more than four hundred personnel from twenty federal agencies that were assisting victims of the disaster. He explained that most of his people were part-timers who had come together from around the country. Several of them had worked with him before, cleaning up after floods, fires, hurricanes, and earthquakes. It struck me that this man had seen a lot of pain and suffering in his time and that his steady manner and quiet determination to get results quickly were a response to this.

I was immediately impressed with the professionalism of Graham's team. They had all the necessary facts and figures at their fingertips, and they had no patience with bureaucracy. What was most impressive was the obvious compassion they felt for the victims of the twister. It was clear they were treating them as people who had been through a traumatic experience and not as faceless names on a form. Time and again I saw people being comforted and aided by agents of their government.

This wasn't a time for partisanship, but I couldn't help comparing this FEMA with the agency under Reagan and Bush. Reagan's man got slammed by the General Accounting Office, the government's watchdog, which called the agency "inefficient," "weak," and "dilatory" in a 1988 report. Bush, after letting the agency languish without a director for a whole year, finally appointed a former New Hampshire highway commissioner whose major qualification for running a billion-dollar federal agency seemed to be that his wife was a Republican state representative, who had been an early supporter of his bid for president.

Who can forget the federal government's abysmal response to the devastation of Hurricane Andrew in South Florida in 1992? For days there was no response at all: no food, no water, no housing. Those without friends or relatives to take them in were left to fend for themselves. Disaster relief funds and emergency loans took weeks to arrive. FEMA was AWOL.

Just before Andrew struck, the FEMA administrator reportedly was presented with two damage estimates from which to choose in planning a federal response. The first was done "by the book," relying on estimates from local officials. It concluded that up to 2,000 people could be affected. The other, done by a FEMA disaster analyst named Paul Bryant, employed far more sophisticated tools and suggested the number affected could be as high as 260,000. The administrator chose the lower estimate. Bad call. Andrew left 250,000 Floridians homeless.

Soon T-shirts were seen around Florida that read: "I SURVIVED HURRICANE ANDREW BUT FEMA IS KILLING ME." As the days went by and footage from the scene led the evening news every night, Bush realized that he had a major political problem. Then and only then did he take the highly unusual step of appointing his secretary of transportation, Andrew Card, to oversee federal relief efforts.

By contrast, James Lee Witt was the consummate professional. Sure, he was a good old boy from Wildcat Hollow, Arkansas, given to wearing snakeskin cowboy boots, but he was also the first FEMA director ever to have had experience in emergency management. He had served four years as director of the Arkansas Office of Emergency Services under Governor Bill Clinton.

As governor Clinton had taken disaster relief seriously, and now, under his leadership, the federal government was showing how it ought to be done. In order to plan an appropriate schedule for Hillary's visit, I needed to get a sense of the scope of the damage, so Graham and I set off to survey the area. As we drove through Fort Smith's downtown, I noticed a broken sign here, a shattered plate glass window there. Not a whole lot of damage. Then we turned a corner, and the landscape looked as if the air force had performed a carpet bombing run. Large trees had been torn out by their roots. Factories that had employed hundreds were twisted rubble. Bits of cardboard, clothing, and packing material hung from the few trees and power lines that remained standing. High in one tree I saw a toddler's brightly colored plastic bike. The city's brand-new sewage treatment plant had a gaping hole in its side, shaped like a semitrailer. The twister had picked up the rig and hurled it through the building, destroying both. We moved on to a modest working-class neighborhood, and Graham pointed out the shattered remains of two houses. A five-year-old boy had been killed in one, a two-year-old girl in the other, both felled by debris from the tornado. I'd never seen wholesale destruction like this in my life, and I was unprepared. It really hits you in the gut. I couldn't stop thinking about the two families that had lost their children.

Then we drove across the river into Van Buren to coordinate with Corporal George Cabaniss of the Van Buren Police Department. George was another good ol' boy, three hundred pounds' worth with a drooping mustache and a thick Arkansas drawl. He knew everyone in town, and as he drove around, folks called out or waved. He gave us a running commentary on who they were, what kinds of families they came from, and just what he thought of them. He didn't skimp on the details, and at some point I realized that if I'd been hearing these same remarks from a woman I would have called it gossip. But it was fun, and once I got used to George's thick southern accent I really enjoyed his company.

George took us up a hill to where an affluent neighborhood sat on a bluff overlooking the river. He relayed something much more fascinating than gossip: As the tornado roared across the river from Fort Smith, it slammed into the hundred-foot-high bluff head-on, shearing off the bottom. The top was where the winds were fiercest, and that was what kept going, straight into this neighborhood. Also, because the top was wider, it cut a much broader path of destruction.

We drove past the façades of half-million-dollar houses, but in many cases they were all that were left: façades. Behind them you could see the houses' footprints, bare and forlorn expanses of concrete, often without a speck of debris, as if some giant broom had swept across them. Can you imagine suddenly losing your house, your furniture, your clothes, your records and family albums? All in about two minutes! There were many slabs with no façades, just a doorway or a bathroom sitting there in the open air. If the destruction in Fort Smith had been drastic, in Van Buren it was catastrophic.

George explained that the storm had hit around midnight on a Sunday, when nearly everyone was at home. He believed this was the reason no one had been killed. Anyone out on the street would have been out of luck. In addition, it happened so fast that people didn't have a chance to try to flee; that would have increased their risk. So they took refuge in their bathtubs and closets, the safest places to be. On Monday morning the National Guard arrived and sent out search-and-rescue teams and laid out several hundred body bags. They were truly amazed as the teams came back one by one, each reporting no fatalities.

We stopped at what had been Firehouse Number Three but was now just a wide slab of concrete. The two firefighters on duty had sounded the alarm and then climbed into the fire truck to wait out the storm. The building disappeared from around them, and the truck itself rocked violently. After the tornado passed, Van Buren had two newly religious firefighters. Farther down the road we saw the town water tower, "Van Buren" painted in big bold letters on its side, standing on its last leg.

"What do y'all make of that?" George said, gesturing out the window of the squad car. "Sort of like our very own Leaning Tower of Pisa or some such thang. Maybe we oughta leave it up as a tourist attraction."

"You do, and the next time the wind blows the town's going to lose five more houses," I replied.

I put together a schedule for Hillary that included a tour of the damaged neighborhoods to talk with some of the families who had lost their homes and a discussion about the disaster at one of the still-standing firehouses. This would be where she would convey the President's thanks for the work done by the emergency personnel.

Finding families to meet with the First Lady was a delicate job. It wasn't easy walking up to a couple standing in what was left of their home and asking, in a Boston accent, if they'd mind if we dropped in with the first lady of the United States and about thirty members of the news media. Luckily I had some help. George Cabaniss broke the ice with his folksy manner, and Buddy Young, FEMA's regional director, translated my Yankee dialect.

Buddy was a former Arkansas state trooper who had run Clinton's protection detail when he was governor. There had been a lot of bad publicity about two of Clinton's state trooper bodyguards; several right-wing magazines had published unproved claims that they had aided and abetted alleged Clinton liaisons. I thought it wise to make a discreet inquiry in Washington about how Hillary got along with Buddy. I was informed that they were friends. Whew.

While we were waiting for Hillary's plane to arrive, Buddy and I stopped to get some lunch. Since we both had law enforcement backgrounds, we bonded pretty quickly and got to talking about Buddy's days as Governor Clinton's chief bodyguard. He said Clinton was a pleasure to work for.

"Now that he's President I'm just amazed at how many people are out to get him," Buddy said over coffee. "You wouldn't believe how many people have called me or visited me, claiming to be from this paper or that television station, all wanting the same thing. Some kind of dirt on Bill Clinton. A lot of them use dodges, pretending to be writing about something else, but it all comes back to wanting to tar Bill Clinton."

"What do you think of those two guys from your detail that started Troopergate?" I asked.

"What do I think of them? Not a whole hell of a lot. I think they're liars, plain and simple. I was there. It didn't happen. I think they got their palms crossed to tell that story. I've heard of a lot of people coming down there flashing cash, willing to pay for scandal on Clinton. Hell, let the man do his job. I'll tell you another thing. I think those troopers were using their uniforms and the governor's name to get women for *themselves*. I just wish I'd fired their asses."

When Hillary's plane touched down it was a warm, cloudless day. She seemed a bit nostalgic about returning to the state where she'd been the governor's wife for a dozen years and greeted, by name, not only the officials lined up to welcome her but also the airport ramp workers in their blue uniforms. All seemed genuinely happy to welcome her back. She may have been at the middle of the scandal vortex in Washington and the target of a massive federal investigation, but here in western Arkansas she was an old friend.

Hillary was eager to meet some of the tornado's victims. The first family we visited greeted us at their house, which now consisted solely of a bathroom, the front door, and a fireplace. There was a wife, her husband, and their two young children; they looked like any young family you'd see at a Little League game. Except that they all seemed slightly numb, and the children looked at the media horde with dazed "*Now* what?" expressions on their little faces. Hillary knelt and spoke to them for a minute and then hugged their mother, who looked utterly exhausted. "Are you getting all the help you need?" Hillary asked.

"We are, thank you so much. The response has been just so wonderful. It's made things a whole lot easier to take," the woman answered.

"I'm glad you all made it through. How much warning did you have?"

"About three minutes. My husband's sister called and told us it was heading in our direction. Then Jim stuck his head out the front door."

"The sky was black, and it sounded like a huge freight train was headed straight for us," Jim said.

"We grabbed the kids and ran into the bathroom, and we all huddled down in the tub. My husband pulled a mattress over us. It sounded like the end of the world."

"We could hear the house being ripped apart, it sounded like screams."

"Or maybe it was our screams," the woman said.

It was an emotional day all around, and Hillary was drained by the time it was over. Unlike her husband, who, no matter how much he gave, seemed to *take* even more from his exchanges with ordinary people, Hillary sometimes had trouble shaking off people's problems. The idealist in her had a powerful desire to see things made right, and even though she understood intellectually that can't always happen, I do think it took something out of her to see so much loss.

For me, my experience in Fort Smith and Van Buren was grounding. Even though my job involved a lot of hard work, it was inside the presidential bubble, which, for all the challenges, is a pretty cushy and heady place to be. Seeing the people of these towns who had lost everything in two minutes on a Sunday night put everything in perspective. One of the big reasons President Clinton had won the White House was the perception that George Bush was out of touch with real people and their problems, that his core constituency was the oil companies and other special interests. Bill Clinton had promised to give the people their government back, to be there for the American people. I had just seen proof that he was delivering on that promise.

There was another thing about the experience that struck me as ironic and telling and confirmed something I'd been noticing for a while. For all the antigovernment rhetoric that was filling the air, all the running down of Washington, I never heard of anyone—from a disaster-stricken individual to a cattle rancher to a multimillionaire businessman—who turned down federal largess. The attitude seemed to be: Stay off my back until you have something I want, then give it to me right now! The much-vaunted self-sufficiency went right out the window. So much of the Republican rhetoric decrying regulation and taxation comes from those who are getting enormous tax breaks and benefiting from existing regulations, in many cases from tax codes and regulations written with their input. These people want the government off their backs, even though they're riding on the back of the government to begin with. I never asked any of the people in that affluent neighborhood of Van Buren what their political affiliation was, but I have no doubt many were conservative Republicans. The lesson for me was that the government has a very real place in our lives, and the difference between George Bush's FEMA and Bill Clinton's was as much moral as it was political.

17

MOOSE CALL

August 1996

THE REPUBLICAN NATIONAL CONVENTION WAS IN FULL SWING IN SAN Diego, the Democrats would be roaring into Chicago in two weeks, and I was on a Wyoming mountainside with Hillary and a moose.

The First Family had decided to take a week of summer vacation in Jackson Hole for the second year in a row. There was always competition between Jackson Hole and Martha's Vineyard to play host to the Clintons, and lots of speculation on why they'd choose one over the other. Hillary clearly preferred the Vineyard with its island solitude and cloister of vacationing intellectuals. I think President Clinton may have been slightly more fond of Jackson Hole, at least in part because golf balls travel farther in mountain air. This was a man who would go to great lengths to improve his golf scores.

They were to be guests at the Bar-B-Bar Ranch, a six-hundred-acre spread turned over to them by Max Chapman, a gracious Wall Street financier, so they could have a little peace and quiet in the middle of a very hectic year. The ranch had a commanding view of the Grand Tetons, a six-thousand-square-foot "cabin," plus a guesthouse, gymnasium, putting green, mechanical rock-climbing wall, and private trout stream. It must be nice to be a billionaire.

The ranch was about ten miles north of town, and the only people who were going to stay on the property with the Clintons were the White

House doctor and a military aide. The rest of us gobbled up every available motel room for miles.

Clinton vacations took on one of two very different identities: hunkered down and relaxed or nonstop activity. The previous summer they had buzzed around town and hit every attraction. By the end of the week the poor advance staff had been run ragged and needed a vacation to recover from the vacation. This year, with the convention and then the campaign looming, we were getting a vibe that they wanted something low-key. Still, low-key for the Clintons would be fever pitch for many of the rest of us. I set out to find some possible diversions.

One idea was to take them to a dude ranch for a trail ride and an honest-to-goodness ersatz chuck wagon cookout. One morning about thirty of us from the White House descended on a promising ranch to ride the trails and check it out. The last time I'd been anywhere near a horse—except to bet on one—had been about thirty years earlier. I knew honesty was the best policy here, so I told the ranch hand to saddle me up on the closest thing they had to a donkey. I was given a very attractive horse named Hollywood, which belonged to the actress Cheryl Ladd. Off we went, high in the saddle, for a nice hourlong ride. Everything went well until we turned for home, and old Hollywood, knowing the feedbag awaited, acted as if he were running the Kentucky Derby. My panic-filled screams echoed in the wilds of Wyoming. I'm proud to say that I arrived back at the barn still astride my mount, if only by a little, and I soon knew why cowboys walk bowlegged.

But that wasn't the wildest ride of the day. Our afternoon endeavor was to shoot the rapids in a small rubber raft. I should have known that any activity that required a helmet and a protective vest would be somewhat less than relaxing. Our guides were two experienced park rangers who thought they were cowboys. The only thing they loved more than pushing it to the limit was watching us turn green. We twisted, turned, rose, and fell like a loose sock in a washing machine. By the time I settled into my bunk that night, the combination of the high altitude and physical exertion made me feel as if I'd just spent my first day at the Parris Island boot camp.

The next morning I had a brilliant insight: The First Lady might enjoy an activity that kept her on terra firma. So I scouted out a couple of hikes—nothing too grueling, mind you.

By the time the First Family arrived by helicopter we were fully prepared to keep them entertained for the week. Making our way through the
tiny mountain resort in a presidential motorcade was a little bizarre. We
had orders to keep the disruptions to the town at a minimum, but it still
felt like a scene from one of the *National Lampoon* vacation movies.

As our understated but heavily armed motorcade proceeded inconspicuously through town, gunfire suddenly rang out. The source was
quickly pinpointed: a small cabin set back in the woods. A crack team of
heavily armed Secret Service agents rushed the building and were greeted
by . . . a smiling little old lady who looked as if she'd stepped out of a Hall-
mark card. Except that she was carrying a shotgun. Twenty feet away lay
the bloody carcass of a raccoon that'd had the temerity to sample her vegetable garden. She assured the nice agents that she meant no harm to the
President and sent them on their way.

It turned out that my intuition had been right: This Clinton vacation
fell into the (relatively) tame category, with the First Family relaxing at the
ranch. The President, who was putting the finishing touches on his book
Between Hope and History, spent much of his time writing but nonethe-
less escaped every day to play golf, and Hillary caught up on her reading.
I'd head out to the ranch in the morning, try to get a clue to plans, and see
if I could be of any help. Vacations are tough to advance, because you have
to strike a balance between being available at a moment's notice and being underfoot.

On a typical morning my car would be stopped at the gate and swept
by the bomb team, and then I'd proceed a mile or so up the road to the
garage, where the Secret Service agents were hunkered down, looking like
well-armed tourists. After exchanging the usual greetings/insults, I'd in-
quire if any of the family had been seen yet. Usually the answer was no,
and then they'd ask me to find out what was happening. Next I'd wander
over to the guesthouse, where the senior staff office had been set up, scoop
up any urgent faxes, and head for the main house. There I'd find one of
the stewards and ask him who was up and who was still asleep.

On more than one occasion the stewards were nowhere to be found,
and I'd pussyfoot in, whistling softly to make my presence known. I didn't
want to surprise anyone and scare them out of their wits. Several mornings I found the President sitting at the kitchen table in his robe playing
solitaire. He'd have his half glasses on and would be in an almost trance-

like state of concentration. I'd keep my remarks to the bare minimum and drop off his correspondence. It was almost eerie to see the most gregarious person I'd ever met happily lost in a solitary activity.

When the whole family was up and moving about, I'd try to find an opportune moment to ask Hillary what was on the day's agenda. Most days she told me she intended to remain at the ranch and suggested I go play golf. It wasn't a suggestion she ever had to repeat.

There were three or four times during the week when I had to stop by later in the day to deliver work to the First Lady. I saw the President, Hillary, and Chelsea sitting around the kitchen table, playing hearts; curled up on chairs and couches in the living room, engrossed in books; or lounging around the den, watching videos. They were dressed in jeans and sweats, utterly relaxed, and the bond among the three of them was palpable and touching.

One day I was in the senior staff office when Maggie Williams called from the White House. "Pat, I'm faxing out some copy that has to be approved by the First Lady within the half hour."

"The half hour?"

"Yes, it has to go to the printer in New York."

I hightailed it over to the main house and was told that Hillary and the President were off on a hike. I set out to find them. There was a trail that led from the main house through a pasture, across a small stream, and into the woods. The first thing I spotted were two Secret Service agents. They were tailing the Clintons, but out of view. I passed them and then caught sight of the First Couple, who didn't see me. They were walking hand in hand, enjoying the mountain air. At one point the President said something, and Hillary leaned her head on his shoulder for a moment. They approached the streambed, and he helped her across. It broke my heart to spoil the moment, so I waited until the last possible second and cleared my throat and started whistling.

The President smiled and said, "Honestly, Pat, with all this land out here, couldn't you have found somewhere else to take a hike?"

Several days later Hillary wanted to take a mountain hike. President Clinton was playing golf, and Chelsea was taking a mountain-climbing class. So off she and I went to Signal Mountain, which I'd chosen because you can drive to the top and walk down. The Secret Service agent who drove us up was a resident field agent, essentially a one-man band operating as the lone agent in a remote area, and let's just say he wasn't the brightest bulb. In fact, I'm sure he'd been sent as far away from Washington as possible to limit the damage he could do. At the base of the mountain I pointed out the parking lot where we would emerge from the trail. I'd reconnoitered a couple of days before and knew the exact spot. After my careful instructions, hardly rocket science, he drove us to the summit.

Hillary and I got out, along with two agents from her White House detail. A park ranger had told us that there'd been a bear sighting on the mountain the night before and to be careful. One of the agents brought along a shotgun that he kept hidden in a canvas bag. Hillary and I started down the mountain trail with the agents following about fifty yards behind. Hillary was in a peculiar mood, and I wasn't sure whether she wanted to talk or be left alone. I gave her as much solitude as I could until she initiated conversation, at first just idle chat about how beautiful the views were.

"Did you see Liddy Dole's speech at the convention last night?" she then asked.

"No, I didn't," I admitted. I find watching that many screaming Republicans in one place akin to undergoing a root canal sans novocaine.

"Well, she took the mike and walked down into the crowd, as if she were hosting a talk show."

"Well, when you're as far behind as they are, you have to resort to gimmicks," I said. "At least it's Dole we'll be running against. For a while there I thought we'd be facing Newt Gingrich. It would have been a much nastier race."

"My guess is that Newt's peaked. This was his moment after taking control of the House, and he decided not to run. I still think he's dangerous . . . very dangerous, but his moment has passed."

"How are you holding up?" I asked. "Are you ready to get back on the trail and keep the kind of schedule we did in '92?"

"Yes, I'm ready. There's been a lot going on, and in a strange way I'm kind of looking forward to it. I know it's plenty of hard work and travel, but it seems so focused. How about you? Are you ready? You've been through a lot in the last couple of years too."

I was touched that she was thinking about the people who supported her travels.

"Yeah, I'm itchin' to get going. And by the way, I don't think I've ever adequately thanked you for getting my employment situation straightened out. It's nice having a steady paycheck again. Working for you means a lot to me, and I'm grateful that you'll have me."

"I'm happy to have you, and I'm just sorry that whole mess took so long. That's one of the things that frustrates me, when we almost lose good people because it takes us so long to get anything done."

At times like these, when we fell into an easy rhythm of conversation, observation, and silence, I almost forgot I was with one of the most famous and controversial women in the world. Of course I knew our relationship was a professional one, but it was also a friendship. In these situations there was *nothing* in Hillary's behavior that was arrogant, demanding, or harsh. I'd seen her sharp edges over the years, but hey, she'd seen mine. I often had a hard time reconciling the Hillary I knew with the woman I read about in the media. I knew her as a human being, not as an icon, and I had a tough time imagining someone more interesting, kind, and just plain fun to be with.

People often ask me about her mistakes. She's only human, and I think the mistakes she's been tagged with fall into two categories. The first was attributable to her career as a very skilled lawyer. She'd been trained to keep her cards close to her vest. Sometimes when the political reality called for a more open posture, I think she tended to fall back on her legal training. That got her in trouble in Whitewater, in Travelgate, and with her health care task force. In each of those instances she was ultimately vindicated, but by giving out information painstakingly and often reluctantly, she aided her enemies. In a legal forum that's the way the game is played. In politics sometimes it looks as if you're trying to pull a fast one or hide something, even when you're not. I also think she had a sense that no matter what she said, it would get twisted grotesquely out of shape, so the less ammunition she provided them the better.

The second category of things that landed Hillary in hot water was attributable to her taking more than people thought she had coming, like power, in the case of the health care initiative, or the gifts she took when the Clintons left the White House. My guess, and it's only that, is that she felt they were payback for all the annoyances she had to put up with. I mean, think about it. She had a gang of very powerful people who were out to destroy her and her husband from day one. That gets old after a while. Real old. I can easily see her thinking: "We won the White House, damn it, and I've waited all my life to help steer the ship. They hate Bill and me anyway, so I might as well do what I've always wanted to do and take my lumps. Our friends will support us." As for taking the gifts, which I think was a real mistake, it comes down to a chip on her shoulder. Something along the lines of: "You bastards put me through hell. Spent fifty million dollars trying to put me and Bill in jail. I worked my butt off for eight years when I could have been earning a million a year practicing law. I'm going to take these gifts. I've read the law and know I'm within my rights. So you can all stuff it." She wanted to drive them crazy one last time. And she did.

As we made our way down the mountain, we passed groups of hikers on their way up. I don't think any of them had a clue who the lady in the sunglasses, wide-brimmed hat, and hiking boots was. I also don't know what they made of the two people farther up the trail who had radio wires hanging from their ears and were carrying bags shaped like shotguns.

One group of young hikers bounded up the trail toward us, very excited. I was sure they'd recognized Hillary and were about to shatter our mood. "We just saw a moose and her baby swimming in a pond!" a fresh-faced young woman exulted.

"It was *awesome*," her male companion added.

Within a couple of minutes, Hillary and I saw the small pond, a blue oval glistening against the green pines. We walked quietly, almost tiptoed, to the shore, not wanting to disturb the moose and her baby, but they were nowhere to be seen. We proceeded down the trail, and then suddenly there they were: mother and calf standing in the middle of the trail about twenty yards in front of us. Heading right in our direction. This thing was enormous. I'm talking the size of a good-size motor home. Closing in on us.

"Hey, Hillary! There's the moose!" I said in a very loud voice.

"Be quiet or you'll scare it away!" she said in a stage whisper.

"I'm *trying* to scare it away!"

I knew from my briefing by the park rangers that moose were regarded as more dangerous than bears and had killed more people in the park over the last five years than bears had. They generally leave humans alone unless they think you're trying to harm their young, in which case they'll charge and stomp you to death. That didn't sound like much fun. So I wanted to make very sure we didn't get between this cow and her calf. Fortunately my voice alerted the animal to our presence, and she turned off the trail and into the woods. She passed within a few feet of us, her baby at her side. Moose babies are really cute.

When we got to the base of the mountain, Hillary was in a great mood, humming some tune I didn't recognize. I looked for our motorcade in the parking lot, but it was nowhere in sight.

"They must have gone down to the lodge parking lot. It's just down the hill," I said, and off we went to find them. One of the agents tried his radio but got no reply. When we got to the lodge, there was still no sign of the vehicles. By now we were getting a little concerned. Where were they? I tried to reach the switchboard with my cell phone, but we were out of range. It was never comfortable to lose control of a situation with the First Lady, especially after all our Secret Service training. You develop a healthy level of paranoia, and suddenly a car parked in the shade of a tree, or a man in sunglasses lingering near a soda machine, can look ominous.

We parked Hillary at a picnic table, and one of the agents went off to use a pay phone while the other agent and I stood guard. After several minutes he returned looking very sheepish. It seems that after dropping us off at the summit, the genius resident agent had whipped out a map and proceeded to calculate that we'd emerge *on the other side of the mountain*, where he was still waiting for us to appear.

He came roaring into the parking lot just as the crowd at the lodge began to recognize the lady sitting at the picnic table. The ride home wasn't too pleasant, especially for my hapless friend, who got an earful of my sharp edge.

I was really sad to see the Clintons board their helicopter on the day they left. I felt they had reconnected during their week in the mountains, and they looked rested and fit, a genuinely happy family. I knew that this would be their last quiet moment together for quite some time. The Democratic National Convention was about to start, and then the campaign. Although Clinton was the clear favorite, if there was one thing he'd learned, it was never to take victory for granted, and Hillary would once again be thrown right into the eye of the maelstrom.

The next morning I boarded a plane back east. It was a clear day, and I could see the vast expanses of the West down below. What an amazing country! Soon we would be embarking on that quadrennial exercise in insanity (oh, yes, and democracy) that we call the presidential election. For the next eleven weeks I would be living on adrenaline, my wits, and cold coffee.

I could hardly wait.

18

BACK AT YA, BOB

August–October 1996

THE DEMOCRATIC CONVENTION WAS BEING HELD IN CHICAGO, A TOWN second only to Boston in my heart. Politics there is a blood sport, as it is in Boston, and Chicagoans relish the opportunity to jump into the fray. When you do events in Chicago, there's never a lack of first-class political talent to help out, and you never have to waste time explaining the obvious. The people are sophisticated but friendly, and you can't beat the cheeseburgers at the Billy Goat Tavern.

Hillary's schedule for convention week was a backbreaker, more than forty events between Sunday and Friday. I had the largest advance team ever put together for a first lady, twenty-eight people, many of them novices right out of the Clinton-Gore advance school. Every graduate received a manual he or she could turn to in need. The manuals had hideous Day-Glo red covers and could be spotted from a mile away. Whenever we saw a rookie toting his manual around, it was an immediate tipoff that he didn't know up from down. But I figured that with proper adult supervision we'd be fine.

I spent the week leading up to the convention on a blinding whirl of event walk-throughs. There was one that I'll always remember. Hillary was planning to visit the Robert Taylor Homes, Chicago's largest public housing project, located in a dicey neighborhood. On the morning we arrived for the walk-through, we found ourselves in the middle of what appeared to be a large police raid. About twenty cops surrounded the building, and the place was crawling with police wearing body armor. I pulled up and found our lead Secret Service agent. "What's going on here? Drug bust? Homicide?" I asked.

"No. They're just here to protect you. The Chicago police insisted," he added somewhat sheepishly.

"Great! Here we are trying to establish trust with the people who live here, and you put an invading army between us and them. We're guests of these people! Get rid of these cops. Now!"

The majority of the cops were gone in five minutes, the walk-through went smoothly, and Hillary's visit was a success. The brunt of my little tirade made it back to Secret Service headquarters in Washington, and thereafter agents, who respected our political sensitivity, worked hard at keeping the Chicago police presence to a minimum.

While I was working on the logistics of Hillary's off-site visits, important political events in their own right, much of the rest of her staff was concentrating on presenting her in the best light at the convention itself. Hillary, predictably, was concerned about her speech. The heat was on for a number of reasons, not the least of which was the glowing reaction to Liddy Dole's performance at the Republican Convention and the challenge Bob Dole had laid out in his own speech. Senator Dole, equating the title of Hillary's book *It Takes a Village* with the support of big government, had said, "It doesn't take a village to raise a child; it takes a family to raise a child."

His interpretation was simplistic and misleading, as anyone who had read the book would know. Why did he attack her so specifically in his speech? Did he think she wouldn't notice? Did he somehow think she wouldn't respond? Did he envision her response as shrill and off-putting? Had the Republican Convention taken place after ours, I could see risking such a slam. But with ours following theirs, Senator Dole was only teeing up the ball for Hillary to hit.

Watching her prepare for her speech was a lesson in focus and grit. She asked for input from a wide spectrum of friends and advisers and listened carefully to what they said. She seemed somewhat surprised at the level of specificity the President suggested on policy issues. Instead of a homey soliloquy about what a great guy Bill Clinton was, she was going to deliver a direct call to liberals, Democrats, and women to recall why the Democratic party, and President Bill Clinton in particular, were important in their lives. She was going to take on Senator Dole's notion that "it takes a village" means "it takes a government" and remind people that Bill and Hillary Clinton had been married for twenty-one years and had raised a pretty decent kid.

So Hillary wrote and rewrote her speech, testing every variable. Her determination was palpable, and it was easy to see why she was such a terrific trial lawyer. She practiced her speech so much that she started to lose her voice. Amazingly, this was to be her first time using a TelePrompTer, and she was eager to do it right. Hillary worked with a speech coach at a mock-up of the podium, complete with TelePrompTers and television cameras. When we got back from the convention hall at eleven o'clock on the night before her speech, she told her closest aides to take a break and meet her in the prep room . . . at one in the morning! This is not a lady who leaves things to chance.

The convention was being held at the brand new United Center, home of the Chicago Bulls, who were, at the time, the world champions. The front of the building sported a larger-than-life sculpture of Michael Jordan, his body contorted in one of his trademark leaps to the basket. The stage was set up on one of the basketball sidelines with a monstrous press riser bristling with hundreds of cameras immediately in front and the crowd stretching to the rafters in a bowl shape around it. Standing on the stage, you got the sensation that you could reach out and *touch* each of the fifteen thousand people present. We were the party in power now, and President Clinton hadn't been challenged for the nomination. So unlike 1992, when there were fences to mend, this was one big happy family.

I was standing on the podium when Hillary was introduced. Wave after wave of adulation swept over her. Delegates stood, some on their chairs, and poured out their hearts. Confetti flew, signs waved, and hands clapped rhythmically. Many women had tears in their eyes. It took nearly five minutes to quiet the cheering crowd. I couldn't help thinking it was some small measure of repayment for all she had endured over the past four years. My friend Tom Daschle, then the Senate minority leader, stood next to me, out of the camera shot. He had given up his scheduled slot so that Hillary could speak on time. He was there just to hear her. Hillary has that effect on people.

Hillary drew the audience in by saying she wished they could "be sitting around a kitchen table, just us, talking about our hopes and fears, about our children's future," and she pointed out that she had been advocating on behalf of women and children for more than twenty-five years. She went on to discuss the pressures most working people felt as parents: "Right now there are mothers and fathers just finishing a long day's work. And there are mothers and fathers just going to work, some to their second or third job of the day.

"Right now there are parents worrying: 'What if the baby sitter is sick tomorrow?' Or: 'How can we pay for college this fall?' And right now there are parents despairing about gang members and drug pushers on the corners in their neighborhoods."

She was connecting by reciting the burdens people faced in their everyday lives, burdens the Republicans, with their steadfast gospel of individualism, refused even to acknowledge.

"We all know that raising kids is a full-time job and since most parents work, they are, we are, stretched thin. Just think about what many parents are responsible for on any given day. Packing lunches, dropping kids off at school, going to work, checking to make sure the kids got home from school safely, shopping for groceries, making dinner, doing the laundry, helping with homework, paying the bills, and I didn't even mention taking the dog to the vet."

She reminded folks that parents weren't going it alone, that there were other elements of society all pulling together to maintain community.

"But also right now there are dedicated teachers preparing their lessons for the new school year. There are volunteers tutoring and coaching children. There are doctors and nurses caring for sick children, police officers working to help kids stay out of trouble and off drugs."

She outlined specific policy proposals her husband had championed to improve the lives of working families, such as legislation to make health care coverage transportable, make adoption easier, and improve children's reading skills. It was a gentle reminder that the President cared about people, not big corporations.

Then she closed in for the kill. "For Bill and me, there has been no experience more challenging, more rewarding, and more humbling than raising our daughter."

She delivered the punch line, her voice rising with the mention of each element: "And we have learned that to raise a happy, healthy, and hopeful child it takes a family, it takes teachers, it takes clergy, it takes business people, it takes community leaders, it takes those who protect our health and safety, it takes *all of us*.

"Yes, *it takes a village*."

Pandemonium. The crowd roared its approval with a single throaty voice.

Take that, Bob Dole.

Hillary's mood after the speech was one of relief and euphoria. As we departed by the stairs at the back of the stage, I could feel goose bumps on my arms. Out of the heat and fury of the crowd, the coolness and quiet of backstage seemed like a different world.

"You did an adequate job. I think they approved," I deadpanned, and then broke into a smile.

Hillary smiled back and gave me a high five.

Others gathered around and offered their congratulations. It was Hillary's moment to shine, and shine she did. Then Chelsea appeared, having made her way down from her box, and greeted her mother with a proud hug. My cell phone rang, and it was the President, calling from the train he was taking to the convention, wanting to congratulate her for a virtuoso performance. I handed Hillary the phone, and they chatted for several minutes.

Our evening didn't end there. Chelsea had talked her mother into taking her to the *George* magazine party, the hottest ticket in town. As we pulled up at the School of the Arts Institute on South Michigan Avenue, John F. Kennedy, Jr., came rushing out to greet his star guests. Our largely female staff appeared *instantly*. Kennedy was wearing a dark suit with a white shirt and patterned silk tie, a white handkerchief in his breast pocket. He looked every bit the movie star handsome heartthrob he was.

"Hello, Mrs. Clinton. Welcome to the party. I'm so glad you could come," he said, extending a perfectly manicured hand.

Hillary shook it and said: "We're delighted to be here. Your party is the biggest event in town. If I didn't come, neither Chelsea nor my staff would ever speak to me again."

After a few moments inside it became clear that the party was going to be a zoo, too crowded for Hillary to enjoy.

Chelsea, who was dressed in a beige suit and matching heels, had already caught sight of some of the celebrities in a crowd that included Oprah Winfrey, Bianca Jagger, and Kevin Costner. This was the place to be. "Mom, please let me stay," she begged. She picked a good moment to make her request. Hillary nodded and smiled, and mother and daughter shared a parting hug.

The rest of us returned to the hotel like a conquering army and repaired to the presidential suite. Hillary passed out glasses, opened a bottle of champagne, and poured. "Here's to all of you in deep appreciation for your hard work. I most certainly couldn't have done it without you. You're the best," she toasted.

Kelly ordered some fantastic desserts from room service, and eight of us sat around and relived the evening. At one point the phone rang.

"Oh, hello, Mr. President," Hillary said. "Nothing special, just sitting around, drinking champagne and eating éclairs with the gang. . . . Our daughter? I left her with John Kennedy, Jr."

We could all hear the President's "Oh, mah Gawd!" booming over the receiver and roared with laughter.

"Don't worry, she has about eight thousand chaperones," Hillary said.

We sat around until well after midnight, telling stories and laughing. We worked together as a tight-knit, well-oiled team and there was an easy camaraderie among us. Of course Hillary was the sun around which we all revolved, but it was never just about *her*. She made sure of that. That magical night, from the triumph of Hillary's speech to the affectionate relaxation with the team, is a memory I shall always treasure.

The rest of the convention went smoothly. The only fly in the ointment came on the last day. Just twelve hours before the President's speech the *New York Post*, with a blaring front-page headline, recounted a story from the tabloid *Star* about pollster and Clinton adviser Dick Morris. A two-hundred-dollar-an-hour call girl who had had several sessions with the married Morris had been paid by the tabloid to lure him out to his hotel balcony during one of their trysts, and incriminating pictures had been taken with a long-distance lens. It was a blatant attempt to tarnish the President's triumphant week and link him with unseemly behavior. We were always waiting for the other shoe to drop with President Clinton, and now it had. Literally. Apparently Mr. Morris had quite a thing for toes.

With the convention behind us it was time to focus on our opponent, the irascible senator from Kansas Bob Dole, and the upcoming presidential debates. Dole was a curmudgeonly sort, a disabled World War II veteran a generation older than Bill Clinton. He was a man who had paid his political dues, and the Republican party had rewarded him with its nomination. A fierce partisan in the Senate, he was known for his blistering rhetoric, sharp wit, and animus to President George H.W. Bush and indeed the entire Bush family, whom Dole, a self-made man, regarded as elitists who had had everything handed to them. In one memorable exchange on *NBC News* the night of the 1988 New Hampshire primary for the Republican nomination, Dole was asked if he had anything to say to the vice president, who was beaming into the broadcast from his victory party. Instead of congratulating him on his win, Dole furrowed his brow, narrowed his eyes, and snarled: "Tell him to stop lying about my record." Again, when Bush prevailed against Dukakis in November of that year, Dole's reaction, duly noted in a front-page story of the *New York Times*, was to castigate Bush for not doing enough to support Senate candidates in swing states. I saw Dole on *Larry King Live* on election night 2000 right after Florida had been called erroneously for Gore, and he could barely contain his glee.

In an apt metaphor for his chances against Clinton, Dole had taken a tumble through the railing and off the stage at a California rally early in the campaign. The incident was caught on film and replayed endlessly on television. It was painful to watch his humiliation—the proud old warrior losing his footing, eyes wide, his mouth flying open in shock as he fell sideways, disappearing from view before a stunned audience—but for some reason it was a pain I was able to endure.

The fall was just one of his problems, and the Dole forces were having little luck making any headway in the campaign. Dole belonged to a generation that was losing its power, and every time he stressed his service in World War II, obviously intended to point out the fact that Clinton hadn't gone to Vietnam, it only reinforced the perception that the guy was old and out of touch with the boomers. He had also made what many considered a blunder by naming former Representative and Cabinet member

Jack Kemp as his running mate. Kemp was proving to be a halfhearted campaigner and a boring speaker, unable to hew to message. Finally, the economy was in a sustained boom, crime was down, the deficit was disappearing, and the American people had taken Bill Clinton to their hearts. Even those who couldn't find room in their hearts for the lovable scoundrel were appreciative of his Herculean work ethic and the results it was achieving.

Unable to gain traction on the campaign trail, the presidential debates became a do-or-die forum for Bob Dole. Dole needed to wound Clinton, and a face-to-face confrontation offered him his best shot.

A presidential debate is the ultimate high-stakes event, the Super Bowl or World Series of politics. Lose a debate, and you can blow an election. The media cover the debates like a blanket, the American public is completely focused on the candidates, and the pressure on them is as intense as it gets. There's so much adrenaline and tension in the air that you can get dizzy. Everyone is pumped and hyper and has his or her two cents' worth to offer the candidate. The poor candidate is trying to absorb the advice, remember a score of stock answers, stay cool, look and sound presidential, dope out his opponent, and, most important, make that elusive, intangible connection with the American people. No wonder most of them end up bouncing off the walls.

Presidential debates usually fall into one of two distinct categories: boring (which we hoped for, given our big lead) and historic (usually because one of the candidates screws up in a big way).

The first Clinton-Dole debate was held on Sunday, October 6, at the Bushnell Theater in Hartford, Connecticut. The White House sent in an all-star advance team, but we had only two days to prepare. A clear premium was being placed on getting the job done right to preserve the President's lead. An abundance of senior White House aides was floating around, hoping somehow to be helpful, and one of our tasks was to keep them out of the Clintons' hair without bruising any egos. It was a matter of maintaining a low profile and keeping people as loose as possible.

The Clintons arrived separately on the morning of the debate. Hillary was tight-lipped and tense. Their accommodations were in the Hastings Hotel, little more than a dormitory for people coming to town to do business with Hartford's insurance companies, and were somewhat makeshift. Make that very makeshift. The "presidential suite" consisted of five spartan rooms that didn't even connect. We'd taken the doors off the rooms and put a pipe and drape curtain in the hallway to serve as an entrance.

When Hillary saw the arrangement, she hit the roof and demanded that we move to another hotel immediately. She calmed down only when we explained that we'd scoured the city high and low and found nothing better available on such short notice. Moreover, with all the electronic equipment we'd set up for communications and speech preparation it would be physically impossible to move anyway.

Hillary is the ultimate pragmatist, and it took her about five seconds to accept the inevitable. She immediately set to work making adjustments to the layout that she thought would help her husband focus. Since I usually worked with her alone, this was one of the few times that I saw firsthand how fiercely protective and supportive of her husband she was.

After a brief welcoming rally the President retreated to a function room at the hotel to work on his opening and closing remarks, take questions from our "moderator," and spar with our "Senator Dole." We'd recreated the debate set as accurately as possible and had television cameras and monitors in the room to videotape the performance. Hillary sat in on the session and offered her moral support and political advice. Afterward they headed upstairs to get ready to go to the hall.

As debate time approached, I went up to make sure everything was on track. I found Bruce Lindsey, Harold Ickes, Leon Panetta, and Erskine Bowles inside the blue curtain that served as a door, pacing up and down the hall as if they all suffered from the same anxiety disorder. These were the White House heavyweights, the inner circle.

Hillary emerged from the bedroom. "Boy, you guys look uptight. Just relax, the President is doing fine. As a matter of fact, he's practicing his opening remarks in the shower," she said.

The thought of the great orator sudsing up, waving a bar of soap while reciting his lines, was enough to break some of the tension. Lindsey, Ickes, and Panetta laughed, and even the ever-dour Bowles managed a tight smile. About fifteen minutes later President Clinton appeared looking like a movie star, geared up but cool, and we got in the motorcade for the short ride to the hall.

In situations with this much at stake every little nuance of placement, podium height, lighting, dress, makeup, etc. takes on enormous importance. One of the biggest battles of the weekend had been over seating. The debates were run by a nonpartisan commission, and both campaigns had asked for three times as many seats as we were ultimately given. We naturally wanted to control all the seats up front so we could place recognizable and friendly faces in them, while the commission wanted to save some of that prime real estate for the people they'd hit up for money to fund the event. Both camps had agreed that the wives would sit on opposite sides of the auditorium, each across from her husband's podium so she could maintain eye contact with her spouse.

The burning question then became: Who would occupy the choice positions near Hillary and Liddy? These folks were sure to be seen regularly on camera, so each was picked for a clear political or strategic reason. I spent a couple of hours working on the decision with Maggie Williams and two political staffers. We wanted diversity of age, race, and geography. Hillary would be flanked by Chelsea on her right and Bill Daley, a Chicago attorney who was about to become secretary of commerce, on her left. Wellington Webb, the African-American mayor of Denver, sat behind Hillary. Walter and Selma Kay, an elderly Jewish couple from New York who were friends and large contributors, and Senator Ted Kennedy and his wife, Vicky, were nearby.

The Dole campaign, as it often did, went for a less than subtle swipe at the President. It seated Billy Dale, fired as the director of the White House Travel Office and the subject of one of the Clinton "scandals," near Liddy Dole. If they thought this move would shake the President, they were sadly mistaken: He'd never laid eyes on Billy Dale, and he, like most of America, had no idea who the guy sitting near Liddy was.

The hall was packed, and there was a large crowd outside. This was one of the few times when both candidates would be in the same place, and there were two of everything: press corps, motorcades, Secret Service details, and sets of staffers. Each side wanted to impress the other, not to mention the VIP-laden crowd and the millions of folks watching from home. It was almost comical how all of us preened and looked our spit-shined best. To outside observers we must have seemed like the most self-obsessed people in the world.

Backstage President Clinton had his makeup touched up and then took off the white paper bib that shielded his suit while it was applied. He glanced in the mirror and stood up. Hillary moved close and straightened his tie ever so slightly. They exchanged glances but did not touch. Television makeup is cruel that way.

"Good luck, Bill. I know you'll do fine," Hillary said as Mort Engelberg, his advance man, came to the door to escort him to the stage.

The President smiled but didn't say a word. He reached out and squeezed Hillary's hand with both of his.

Both Clintons now had their game faces on. Any nervousness they had displayed earlier was replaced by a cool professional calmness. This was the chosen arena of their lives, and they were as comfortable as one can possibly be in such shark-infested waters.

Hillary and I remained in the holding room, a drab concrete space with exposed plumbing and thick black electrical wires running through it. There was less than five minutes until airtime, and she had already been made up by Bruce Grayson and had her hair done by Cristophe Schatteman. Bruce and Cristophe were her personal favorites and flew in from L.A. for major events.

"Pat, I want to be sure Mrs. Dole is seated before I go upstairs to the theater," Hillary said matter-of-factly.

"Yes, ma'am, I'll see to it," I replied. This was the "all-business" Hillary, and it was no time for one of my wisecracks.

I walked up the flight of stairs and stood on my tiptoes to see inside the window of the red upholstered door leading to the auditorium. I could make out the stage with its deep blue carpet and large gold American eagle. With about four minutes remaining until we went live, both candidates were standing silently behind their podiums studying briefing cards. The moderator, Jim Lehrer, sat in a chair at the front of the stage with his back to me. There was a low buzz from the crowd. All our people, including Chelsea, were seated. Only Hillary's chair remained empty. I looked across the aisle. Liddy's seat was also empty. I went back downstairs to fill Hillary in on the details.

A second scouting trip a minute later yielded the same result: still no sign of Liddy Dole.

Less than three minutes to go, and things were getting dicey. The show was going live on national TV at nine o'clock sharp, whether we were seated or not. I didn't relish the thought of our traipsing in after the debate was on the air.

I was on my way up the stairs for the third time when I heard the audience, at least most of them, applauding. I cracked open the door to see Liddy Dole wave to the crowd and take her seat. Finally.

I sprinted down the stairs and nearly ran headlong into Hillary, who had started up, wanting to be in position to move quickly when the time came. I gave her the high sign and opened the door for her. She swept into the room and strode confidently to her seat to a warm ovation from the crowd. At least most of them.

Hillary one, Liddy nothing. We had our first win of the night.

The debate went very much as we had hoped. President Clinton outlined the many things he'd done to improve the lives of the average American. "Four years ago you took me on faith. Now there's a record: ten and a half million new jobs, rising incomes, falling crime rates and welfare rolls, a strong America at peace."

Bob Dole, well, he was Bob Dole. Stiff, diffident, almost angry. This guy just didn't come across well on television. He started by recounting his war wounds and talking about his recovery in a Chicago hospital after the war. He didn't do much to dispel the notion that his time had come . . . and gone.

As was always the case with Clinton, there was that nagging apprehension that some wild accusation would be made and tip things upside down. It had happened in the 1992 race with the Gennifer Flowers and draft-dodging charges, and we always knew that the possibility of another calamity lurked in the dark, just around the corner. If Dole had any dirt, this would be the place to hit us with it.

Fortunately there were no surprises from the Dole camp except a rather strange appeal at the end when the senator said he was directing his closing remarks to young people and asked them to support him. In a misguided effort to show how up-to-date he was, he invited youngsters to "Tap into my homepage," and recited its address—in tones that sounded like a prisoner of war stating his name, rank, and serial number. "That's WWW-dot-DoleKemp '96." Big pause. "Dot-org."

It only served to accentuate his age and discomfort with new technology. It was all a little sad because Bob Dole *was* a self-made man, and you got the sense that he had some real backbone. It would have been a lot sadder if he hadn't been such a hatchet man for most of his career, not to mention a water boy for the special interests. His favorite means of transportation was the Archer Daniels Midland company plane, and he was often referred to in Washington as the senator from ADM.

The postdebate handshake is somewhat of a tradition but unscripted. As the two candidates made their closing statements, I moved into position to escort Hillary and Chelsea to the stage. The President went first, followed by Senator Dole. When Dole finished, the hall erupted in applause, and as the candidates crossed the stage and shook hands, their respective families came up and joined them. I was leading Hillary up when Robin Dole, Senator Dole's daughter from his first marriage, maybe thinking I was a long-lost Clinton child, tried to engage me in a handshake—right at center stage in front of the cameras. I slipped by her and out of the shot as politely as I could, but I felt bad because she looked puzzled and hurt by my brushoff.

Hillary and Chelsea flew back to Washington right after the debate. It was a school night for Chelsea. The President stayed overnight in Hartford, and when I got back to the hotel, he was, predictably, relieved and animated. He was holding court in the senior staff lounge and didn't look as if he were going to run out of steam anytime soon, but I was tired and called it a night. It was still a long road to November, and I had learned long ago not to try to keep up with the Clintons.

19

PLAY IT AGAIN, SAM

October–November 1996

WE HAD REACHED THE HOMESTRETCH OF THE CAMPAIGN, AND IT WAS looking good. Dole was obviously struggling. I was continually amused by the ineptitude of his campaign. In the end most Americans vote their pocketbooks, and the economy was in the middle of its largest expansion in history. Clinton had delivered on his 1992 pledge to get the country moving. Dole meanwhile was having a hard time getting out from the shadow, the very large shadow, of the monumentally unpopular Newt Gingrich.

In fact, the most dramatic moment of Dole's campaign had happened almost six months earlier, in May, when he unexpectedly resigned his Senate seat. He did so to prove to skeptical Republicans that his heart was really in the race, that he wasn't just being offered up as a sacrificial lamb that would retreat to the sinecure of the clubby Senate once the race was over. His biggest campaign pledge was a 15 percent across-the-board tax cut, which was accompanied by the usual Republican rhetoric about the need to shrink the government, and served only as a reminder that it was the Republicans who had shut down the federal government to the ire of voters of all stripes.

In the closing days of the campaign a desperate Dole turned to attacking the President's integrity and suggested Clinton's fund-raising, the most successful in Democratic party history (but still meager compared with that of the Republicans), was "unethical."

I wouldn't say the Clinton campaign was coasting during the final weeks—the President was actually working like a dog—but there was a pervasive and building confidence. None of the personal attacks was sticking, and there was a growing sense that even Americans who didn't particularly like Clinton personally were happy with the job he was doing and were going to vote for him. The President himself was looking for a big win, hoping to enter his second term with a strong mandate. He dearly wanted to get over 50 percent of the vote. After his victory in the three-way race against George Bush and Ross Perot in 1992, when he won 43 percent of the vote, some Republicans questioned his mandate because he hadn't hit that magic 50 percent mark. (These same people are strangely quiet on the subject of young Bush's mandate.)

My final event before November 5 was both thrilling and eye-opening. It was a get out the vote rally at Florida Agriculture and Mechanical University, a largely African-American school in Tallahassee. Florida A&M has had some great football teams over the years, but it has been over-shadowed by the team across town, the Florida State University Seminoles. No one, however, outshines its band, the world-famous Florida A&M Marching 100, which has performed all over the world and is renowned for its musicianship, precision drills, and over-the-top spirit.

I was thrilled at the prospect of using these showstoppers at a Hillary Clinton event. The band's director, Dr. Julian White, and I quickly built a program around their talents.

The Tallahassee rally was part of the Clinton campaign's all-out push to put Florida in the Democratic column for the first time since Jimmy Carter had carried it in 1976. The state, its population swelled by immigrants from Latin America and transplants from the Northeast and Midwest, had been trending Democratic during the nineties. Winning it would be a real blow to the GOP's southern strategy, the linchpin of its successes in electing Reagan twice and Bush once. The leaders of the Florida Democratic party all were going to speak at our rally. They included Governor Lawton Chiles, Lieutenant Governor Buddy McKay, Attorney General Bob Butterworth, and Insurance Commissioner (now Senator) Bill Nelson.

It was homecoming weekend at FSU, and Tallahassee was jam-packed with alumni in town to witness the big football game. The streets were clogged with cars and pickup trucks sporting Seminole flags, bumper stickers, pennants, and in some cases whole custom paint jobs that made them look like rolling football helmets. Tallahassee is one of those weird cities that nobody's from. The two big colleges and the legislature (it's the state capital) with its attendant aides, lobbyists, and journalists mean there are always a lot of people in town, but they're all from someplace else.

As I worked on the rally, I was faced with a disturbing truth for which I wasn't prepared: Tallahassee, Florida, in 1996 was a very segregated city. When I suggested we try to draw students from the Florida State campus, none of the people at A&M, FSU, or the Clinton-Gore headquarters seemed to think it would work. FSU was the "white" campus, A&M was the "black" campus, and the two just didn't mix. Despite a concerted effort on my part to reach out to the FSU College Democrats, its women's organizations, and any other progressive campus groups I could identify, in the end only a handful of FSU students ventured onto the A&M campus for our rally.

One night, after a long day of preparations, we all were sitting around on the half-built stage. There was my all-white team from the Clinton campaign and a group of A&M students, including Gene Waters, the president of the student government. Everyone had been getting along famously, and we were caught up in the excitement of the rally.

"Let's knock off and go out to CiCi's for pizza and beer," I said.

My team voiced their approval, but the response from Gene and the other students was muted. "Pat, you all go ahead. We're going to Gumby's," Gene said.

I was puzzled and thought perhaps he didn't realize I was inviting them to join us. "Why don't you guys come along with us? It's on Clinton-Gore."

"No, we're going to our own place," Gene replied.

"Well, we'll be happy to tag along there," I said.

"That might not be a great idea, Pat. I think you'd be a lot better off at CiCi's."

That's when I realized that whites and blacks didn't socialize openly in Tallahassee and that Gene and his friends didn't think they'd be welcomed in a "white" establishment. I dropped the subject, and we went our separate ways. The exchange cast a pall over our meal and brought home to me how deep-seated the racial divide still is in parts of our country.

When you worked for the Clintons, it was often possible to forget about that divide. Both the campaign and the administration were fully integrated, and the blacks, Latinos, and Asians brought aboard were top-notch, not just tokens. Far from it. From Ron Brown to the lowest-level political operative in campaign backwaters, people got hired, fired, and promoted on the basis of performance. That hadn't always been the case in other Democratic campaigns I'd been involved with, in which the minority staffers had been regarded as a "protected class," held to different standards. The liberal Democrats were scared stiff of the bad publicity they'd get if they didn't have minorities in top slots and were terrified of what could happen if they dared fire one. That well-intended but flawed protectionism bred resentment. And so, ironically, there was often more racial tension. With the Clintons, race was never the issue, and pretty soon you forgot about it. We all were there to do a job. End of story.

Since the Florida A&M rally was on Halloween, I decided a little comic relief was in order and bought a Richard Nixon mask. When Hillary's plane landed, I waited to board until she was in the rest room. She emerged to find Tricky Dick in her seat, flashing his trademark V sign. "I am not a crook," I croaked.

"Now that's what I call scary," Hillary said with a laugh.

Unlike the end of the 1992 race, when Hillary had run herself into the ground, she seemed rested, vibrant, and full of energy. She'd been shuttling all around the country campaigning for her husband and fellow Democrats but seemed to have hit a comfortable stride. That's what a healthy lead in the polls will do for you.

I was eager to get everyone over to the campus because I'd arranged an entrance that I immodestly thought would have made P. T. Barnum proud. It was a beautiful fall day under the Florida sunshine. The Florida A&M Marching 100, resplendent in their bright white uniforms with green and orange trim and tall hats, marched onto the campus quad, playing "76 Trombones." The large, exuberant crowd roared its approval. Suddenly the band, still playing furiously, split in two to reveal Governor Lawton Chiles and the First Lady. The crowd went wild. To deafening cheers, two tall drum majors in plumed hats marched back through the band, and each offered an arm to the honored guests, who were led down the center of the band by their high-stepping escorts. It appeared as if the band had conjured up these beloved figures. The excitement built with each step, and both the Governor and Hillary were elated by their grand entrance.

Lawton Chiles then delivered a knockout speech. Chiles, who died in 1998, was a fascinating figure and superb politician. A three-term U.S. senator before being elected governor in 1991, he softened his considerable wiles with a warm, folksy manner that connected emotionally with voters. One of his proudest accomplishments was defeating Jeb Bush in 1994. Although Chiles was the incumbent, Bush was the favorite to win and was leading in the polls before the final debate. In that memorable encounter, Chiles pulled out all of his tricks, turned in a masterful performance, and blew away his opponent. He delivered one of the more colorful lines of American politics when he regarded the younger Bush, furrowed his brow, drew up his lanky frame, and proclaimed: "The old he-coon walks just before the light of day." Translation: "The crafty old veteran will strike at the right time." He did. He closed the gap in the final days and won reelection.

Hillary gave her get out there and vote speech, a robust podium-thumping riff that made folks want to run out to vote right then and there. This was far removed from her calm, cerebral policy speeches; it was pure fire and brimstone. The crowd ate it up.

Despite Bob Dole's bizarre ninety-six-hour closing odyssey, in which he flew around the country desperately seeking votes, our polls were holding. The Dole trip was a sad last-ditch attempt by a man who had been striving his entire adult life to capture the holy grail of politics. As the clock ran out, it became increasingly clear to him that he wasn't going to win, but he was determined, old warrior that he was, to go down fighting. Perhaps the most memorable aspect of the trip was the sight of him aboard his campaign bus, clad in a satin jacket, trying to do a hip rendition of the old rock and roll song "Rock Around the Clock." By that point he was exhausted, his voice was spent, and all he could do was hold the microphone close to his mouth and croak: "Rock! Rock! Rock!" As with his other attempts to appear youthful and "with it," you could almost smell his desperation. The tour also included an advance man's worst nightmare: a 3:30 A.M. rally in New Jersey that nobody attended. And I do mean *nobody*. Dole and the press pool deplaned to find an empty tarmac—well, except for the police detailed to contain the "crowd." Talk about whistling past the graveyard.

With victory all but assured the most pressing issues seemed to be the size of our margin and what kinds of gains we would make in Congress.

After a brief stop in Boston for some clean clothes, I was off to Little Rock for election day. Hillary was completing a last-minute swing through targeted congressional districts and was going to meet the President in Cleveland. After several more rallies, culminating in Bill Clinton's last-ever campaign event as a candidate, in Sioux Falls, South Dakota, they were to arrive together in Little Rock at about 4:00 A.M.

I was waiting in the predawn chill on the tarmac at Little Rock Airport for the Clintons to arrive. A crowd of a few hundred people had gathered, and the mood was one of exhausted jubilation. These were diehard Clintonites, come to cheer home their man from Hope. The sound system blared Chuck Berry's "Good Golly Miss Molly," and I swept Molly Buford, one of Hillary's scheduling staff, inside the rope line, and we danced. As Air Force One made its final approach, many in the crowd waved sparklers, giving the scene a dreamlike quality.

A roar went up as the Clintons emerged, arms around each other, waved, and made their way slowly down the steps. Despite everyone's fatigue, the mood was upbeat and homey. The President was intent on shaking every last hand. Hillary, after making a quick pass at the rope line, was content to chat with a small group of us. "I think I joined the President just in time. Things were getting a little weird on that plane," she said.

"Weird? What do you mean?" I asked.

"Too many tired men in one place. They were getting silly. The press had watched the video *Fargo* eight times running," she recounted with a chuckle.

"What did you do?"

"I confiscated it before they could watch it a ninth time. I didn't want the President held responsible if anyone ended up in a wood chipper."

"How did they react?"

"They were gentle as lambs. A couple even thanked me. That's when I knew they'd been pushed beyond their limit."

"A docile press corps? That *is* weird."

The motorcade into town was like the procession of an ancient king returning to the homeland after a successful battle. We reached the Excelsior Hotel, where we all were staying, and the Clintons bade us a weary good night, even though the sky was light and in New England the voting had already begun. There was an almost eerie satisfaction in knowing that we had entered the final news cycle and had escaped with our hides intact.

Election day in Little Rock was beautiful, in the fifties with bright sunshine. Our original plan was to have the Clintons vote early so we could provide pictures to the morning shows and noon news. They usually voted at Little Rock's old train station, now an office complex, but they understandably decided to sleep in, and at ten-thirty I went up to their suite on the eighteenth floor.

The suite had double doors opening into a large living room with a wall of windows overlooking the Arkansas River. Hillary was up and dressed, sitting on a couch talking to Maggie Williams. She looked rested and chipper.

"Morning, Hillary, Maggie," I said. "I hope I'm not interrupting."

"Good morning, Pat. No, I have an appointment with the optometrist this afternoon, and Maggie is helping me decide what kind of reading glasses to buy."

"She doesn't want to look like a grandmother," Maggie said.

"And rhinestones are out," Hillary added.

Hillary and Maggie had an easy relationship with each other. It seemed as much personal as professional. They genuinely liked each other. Maggie had been with her since the early days of the first campaign, and Hillary counted on her to keeping things running smoothly in the chaotic Clinton White House. Maggie, the consummate professional, didn't disappoint. Hillary was saddened when Maggie left midway through the second term to get married and take a position as president of a large public affairs firm, but they remained close friends.

Kirk Hanlin, one of the President's advance men, came in. Kirk was tall and thin and spoke with a hint of the small Missouri town he hailed from.

"There's a new voting system in Arkansas this year, Mrs. Clinton. I have a sample ballot here for you to look at," he said as he produced a large yellow document.

Hillary took the ballot and studied it. Kirk began pacing, waiting impatiently. Finally the door to the bedroom opened and William Jefferson Clinton appeared. He was resplendent in a blue suit, a crisp white shirt, and a striped tie. He rubbed his hands together briskly. "Morning, all."

"There's a new ballot this year, Mr. President," Kirk said, handing him another sample.

The President donned his reading half glasses and moved closer to the picture window for better light. "Hey Hillary, look at this," he exclaimed. "There are *a lot* of people running for president. I may have to rethink my vote."

As the laughter died down, he and Hillary began a spirited discussion of how they would vote in the state and local races. Some candidates received the Clinton thumbs-up of "he's a great guy"; others were remembered for slights real or imagined and given an unequivocal thumbs-down. I couldn't help thinking that this exchange between the First Lady and the most powerful man in the world was no different from those taking place around millions of kitchen tables across the country that morning.

Chelsea, a typical teenager who loved to sleep, was the last to appear. She emerged dressed and ready to go, but I'm not convinced she was actually awake.

At the old train station the President put his arm around his daughter, and she joined him in the voting booth, just as she had on every election day of her life. This was a bittersweet moment because in the next election she would be casting her own ballot.

From the polling place we went to Senator David Pryor's house for a luncheon celebrating his retirement from the Senate. The house was in the Clintons' old Little Rock neighborhood and was overflowing with well-wishers. I was struck by how the city's ruling class seemed to have a different perspective on victory the second time around. There was satisfaction and the warmth of friendship, but there was also the unmistakable and unspoken knowledge that some who had shared the joys of victory in '92 were no longer there to partake. Vince Foster had committed suicide,

Web Hubbell and Jim McDougal were deeply entangled in federal investigations, and more than one person at the party had been hauled before a grand jury. These folks were the movers and shakers of Arkansas, and like movers and shakers everywhere, they got a little uneasy when anyone started looking too close. It was great that their friend and former governor Bill Clinton was president, but they could have done nicely without all the feds crawling around town sniffing out the minutiae of every two-bit business deal they'd ever made.

Hillary left the luncheon early, and she, her Secret Service agent, and I hopped in a van and went to see Dr. Danny Thomason, television producer Harry Thomason's brother and her optometrist, at his shop. Danny was quite a character. Known to one and all as Dr. Danny, he was a Baptist Sunday school teacher, mainstay of the choir, and never at a lack for words. He'd known Hillary almost as long as Bill had and greeted her with a bear hug. His shop was soon a swirl of activity as word spread that Hillary was there, and people began leaving the beauty parlor, bookstore, and other nearby businesses to stop in to wish her well.

Hillary laid out her criteria for the new glasses. "They've got to be stylish, but not flashy. I don't want to look matronly, and no cracks from you, Dr. Danny."

"Me! Why, Hillary, you're so young and beautiful it doesn't matter what we put on your face. You make the glasses, not the other way around." He then pulled a pair of silver wire-framed spectacles from his display case.

"I bet you say that to every woman who walks in here."

"I do not. Only to first ladies. Cross my heart."

Hillary tried on the glasses, looked in the mirror, and crinkled her nose. "How soon can you have these ready?"

"Oh, sometime this afternoon. I'll deliver them myself."

"Okay, sold."

Once Hillary disentangled herself from all the well-wishers, we went to Doe's Eat Place, a famous Little Rock barbecue restaurant, to meet Hillaryland for lunch. Patti Solis Doyle, Hillary's scheduler and confidant, had arranged a table on the back terrace. She was there, along with Dorothy Rodham, Maggie Williams, Kelly Craighead, deputy chief of staff Melanne Verveer, press secretary Marsha Berry, assistant press secretary Neel Lattimore, former press secretary Lisa Caputo, personal assistant

Capricia Marshall, speechwriter Lisa Muscatine, and Sara Grote and Julie Hopper, who worked for Patti.

As I surveyed the group, it struck me that we all had been with Hillary since day one, four long years through thick and thin. Of her entire staff, only Lisa Caputo had gone on to other things, accepting a once-in-a-lifetime offer to become an executive vice-president for CBS. The President had been through three chiefs of staff, two press secretaries, two secretaries of defense, two treasury secretaries, and a whole bunch of staff. Yet Hillary, who was very deliberate when she chose the people around her, inspired great loyalty. The fact that we all were still with her, and still enjoyed her company, was a great testament to that.

Spirits were high, and the gossip and stories began to fly. As we sipped our second pitcher of iced tea, I knew the time was finally right to come clean. I told Hillary the whole gruesome truth about my naked night in the hallways and lobby of the Hotel Okura in Tokyo. As usual the story got raucous laughter out of everyone, including Dorothy, who was a rather proper Presbyterian lady but a terrific sport.

"Pat, I cannot believe I haven't heard this story until now. You must inspire real loyalty," Hillary said.

"I think fear might be more accurate," I said.

"It's a good thing the press never got wind of it," she added.

"Amen to that," I said, and never have three words been more deeply felt.

Danny Thomason arrived bearing Hillary's new glasses, which she modeled for all assembled. Danny then dived right into the food and the gossip.

Hillary spent the rest of the afternoon driving herself around Little Rock, with just her Secret Service agent as her passenger. It's not easy to get behind the wheel of a car when you're the First Lady, and I think she treasured the chance to take a self-guided tour down memory lane. Little Rock was her adopted home, the place she had moved to when she married her law school sweetheart. Her parents had followed her, and her daughter had been born and raised there. She knew by then that she was going to be First Lady for another four years and that she and her husband would probably never live in Little Rock again. Hillary is the last person to dwell in the past, but she's also quite emotional and feels things deeply. I imagine she spent that warm, sunny November afternoon revisiting the places that meant the most to her, taking stock of where she was, and preparing for the next phase of her life.

I took a catnap back at the hotel and then had a couple of soggy room service cheeseburgers for dinner. By then it was after eight and the polls were closing around the country. Although my room was on the ninth floor, I could hear the resounding cheers from down in the lobby each time CNN projected another state for Clinton. My thrill and relief were bolstered by the news that my friend John Tierney had been elected to Congress from Massachusetts on his second try. As I got dressed and prepared to join the Clintons, I turned on the television and watched the crowd swell outside the Old Statehouse, where Clinton would be claiming victory.

The mood in the President's suite was jubilant. Folks who normally had the weight of the world on their shoulders were carrying on like a bunch of kids. Harold Ickes and George Stephanopoulos were wrestling over the television remote, and Erskine Bowles actually had his tie loosened.

At about 10:00 P.M. we got word that Senator Dole was on the phone. The President went to take the call.

It was official. We had done it. Although no one mentioned it, there was a slight undercurrent of disappointment that the margin wasn't greater. Yes, he had beaten Dole 49 percent to 41 percent, but he had missed that magic 50 percent mark by a whisker and had lost three states he'd carried in 1992: Colorado, Georgia, and Montana. He had, however, won Florida, a big prize.

It's hard to overstate the excitement, joy, and relief that reelection brings. A president and his staff spend every waking moment of the first term worrying about that next election. Every decision is made, and every action is taken, with an eye toward how it will play at the ballot box. Will you be sent packing, as Ford, Carter, and Bush were, or will you get the opportunity to burnish your legacy and drive history for the better part of a decade? No Democrat had been elected to a second term since Franklin Delano Roosevelt in 1944. Also, for us this victory was all the sweeter because of the nadir we'd faced after the 1994 midterm election. Bill Clinton had been beaten and left for dead a scant two years ago, and his comeback had been one of the most startling turnabouts in American political history.

The crowd at the Old Statehouse was being serenaded by a Memphis gospel choir that sang "Oh Happy Day" and by Tony Bennett, a great Democrat, who crooned "The Best Is Yet to Come." It was a crisp, clear night bathed in bright moonlight. The President, Hillary, and Chelsea strode onstage arm in arm, right into the adulation of the crowd. I took up position stage left. As President Clinton concluded his remarks, the sky lit up with fireworks. I felt the moment achieved that delicate balance between cutloose celebration and presidential dignity.

The parties began in the presidential holding room at the back end of the Old Statehouse, where White House stewards served up champagne. At one point Dorothy Rodham approached me. "Patrick, I almost didn't recognize you with your clothes on," she said.

"That's the last time I tell *you* a secret."

"I sincerely doubt that it's a secret any longer," she said with that Rodham twinkle in her eye.

Each time the television broke in with an updated vote count the President and Vice President would elbow their way to the front of the crowd and watch intently—sometimes leaning in to exchange a word or two—like two young stockbrokers watching the Dow Jones ticker.

From there it was back to the Excelsior and a succession of parties that lasted until dawn. There is something just a little surreal about walking into a ballroom crowded with cheering revelers at 3:30 A.M., long after sensible people have gone to bed.

But then whoever said political junkies were sensible people?

20

SPEECHLESS

November 1997–January 1998

THE CLINTONS WERE GOING DOWN UNDER TO AUSTRALIA TO ATTEND the annual Asia-Pacific Economic Cooperation (APEC) meeting, and I was sent to do Hillary's advance. I left two days after the election, in a state of pleasant exhaustion. I'd always wanted to visit Australia and was thrilled to be given the chance. I knew from my encounters with Australians during my travels elsewhere that they were some of the friendliest and most entertaining folks in the world, and I was truly happy that I was going to be among them. Little did I know that I'd be reduced to a yacht-chasing mass of sweaty panic when I lost Hillary's very important speech.

At the time of our trip Australia was undergoing a change in political leadership with the new Conservative government of Prime Minister John Howard taking power. He had defeated Paul Keating's Labor party soundly in the March elections, owing in no small part to the country's 9 percent unemployment rate. It was the first time in thirteen years Howard's party had been in the majority, and it was busy in Canberra, the nation's capital, cleaning house and taking names.

As soon as my team and I arrived in Sydney, we took a walk along the harbor and ended up at The Rocks, an old cobblestoned warehouse district now gussied up. We stopped for dinner, and I was shocked to see kangaroo on the menu.

"You actually serve kangaroo?" I asked our waitress.

She shot me an appraising look. "Yeah. Of course, mate, what's wrong with that?"

"The kangaroo is your national emblem. You'd get thrown in jail for eating an eagle in the United States."

"I can't say I've ever had eagle, but our roo is damn good. You ought to try it."

It was delicious. However, I was relieved to learn the kangaroo was in plentiful supply and, like the ostrich, was being bred specifically for human consumption.

Hillary's schedule wasn't terribly complicated, the high point being an address on women's issues that she was to deliver at the world-famous Sydney Opera House. This should have been a very easy trip, but I quickly found that the phenomenon I'd experienced in other former British colonies stood true here. Although the people were very friendly, the government officials were pompous and overbearing. I don't know what it is about the former colonies, but their bureaucrats seem to have retained the worst traits of their former rulers. Or maybe they just have chips on their shoulders from having been colonists. Most egregious was the government's liaison for the visit, a staff member from the prime minister's office. I went to visit him at his office to discuss the details of Hillary's opera house speech. I found a pinch-faced little man with bushy eyebrows and bad breath.

"Mr. Halley, the First Lady's program has already been decided, and the invitations have been sent out," he informed me in a very condescending manner.

"I see. And what exactly is her program, if you don't mind my asking, and may I see a copy of the invitation list?"

Those eyebrows shot up in disbelief. How dare I make such an impertinent request? "I represent Prime Minister Howard," he said, dragging out the last three words with an air of finality.

"Great. And I represent the first lady of the United States," I said, dragging out "United" and "States." "And I want to see her program and know just who has been invited to hear her speak."

"Well, Mr. Halley, I don't have that information *right here on my desk.*"

You'd have thought I was asking him to produce a singing wallaby.

"I can wait," I said. Then I admired the view out the window, humming softly. I'd played enough poker to know when someone was bluffing.

"Yes, well, that's all very well and good, isn't it? I, however, *cannot* wait. I have a very busy schedule this morning."

"All right then, I'll make you a deal. I'll just go ahead and plan the program with the First Lady's office back in Washington and my contacts here in Sydney. We'll also come up with a guest list and get it to you as soon as possible so you can send out the invitations. Sound good?"

There was a long pause, during which the fellow looked as if he were sucking on a particularly sour lemon. "I suppose we may proceed in that manner," he finally choked out.

Then, like the actor in a scene out of *The Three Faces of the Deputy Secretary,* he switched personalities. He gave me a wide, cheery smile, stood up, heartily shook my hand, and showed me to the door. "It has been *such* a pleasure, Mr. Halley. Do call on me anytime. No request is too small."

My difficulties with the prime minister's staff paled in comparison with the yacht-related calamity, which befell me shortly after the Clintons arrived. Prime Minister Howard and his wife, Janette, were hosting the obligatory moonlight cruise for the President, First Lady, and assorted high-ranking officials and multimillionaires. The boat was the *Aussie One,* a posh little vessel, the pride of Matilda Cruises, and reputed to be the largest catamaran in the Southern Hemisphere. We launched from the Fleet Steps next to the Sydney Opera House. I went along as Hillary's "body person," available to take care of any need that might arise. It usually boiled down to demanding tasks like coat holding. Sure enough, Hillary gave me her purse to hold during dinner. I was seated in the aft part of the main compartment and set it down at my feet. She remained seated throughout the cruise, so there wasn't anything for me to do but stretch my legs on deck from time to time and chat with my friends from the Secret Service.

After several hours of cruising Sydney Harbor, we put back into shore. When our motorcade arrived back at the hotel, I got out of the control van and approached the presidential limousine to escort the First Lady to her suite. The door opened. Hillary stepped out and waved her purse at me. *"Patrick, where is my speech?"*

I was totally mystified. She hadn't spoken to the crowd on the boat, so I didn't know what speech she was talking about.

"What speech?" I asked in a tiny voice.

"The speech I'm delivering tomorrow. It was tucked in the outside pocket of my purse, and now it's gone!"

Uh-oh.

"Go find my speech *right now.*"

"Yes, ma'am."

I flew back into the van. "Back to the dock. *Fast!*"

As we screeched to a halt at the dock, my heart sank, and my panic soared. The *Aussie One,* still filled with its component of partying Australians, was sailing away. I leaped out of the van, ran down the dock, and grabbed the nearest sailor. *"Where are they going?"*

"Walsh Bay. Pier Four."

I raced back to the car and barked the address at my driver. We flew through the streets of Sydney, squealing tires on every turn. Hillary's speech, which was purported to have a strongly feminist tone, was getting a tremendous amount of publicity, anticipation was high, and it was going to be televised nationally. I shuddered to imagine her mood if the text appeared in the morning papers before she delivered it. I also shuddered to imagine my mood as one of the suddenly unemployed.

We roared up to the dock, which was lined with limousines. I jumped out of the van, ran up to the nearest guard, and flashed my credentials. "Listen, I have to get back on that boat *as soon as it arrives.*"

Unlike the deputy secretary, this chap responded immediately and let me through. Just then the boat appeared, coming around the bend in the cool night air. I jumped from the dock onto the gangway, dodging the passengers lined up to disembark. I got some startled looks from the prime minister and his bodyguards as I blew past them and started crawling around on the floor of the main cabin near where I'd been sitting. There it lay, under a banquet table, looking more beautiful than the Treasure of the Sierra Madre, eight folded sheets of white typing paper. Oh, rapture! I clutched it to my breast as if it were a recovered fumble in the last thirty seconds of a tied-up Super Bowl and raced back to the van.

It was almost midnight by the time I got back to the hotel. I approached the Secret Service agent posted outside the presidential suite. "Are they up?"

"I don't know. Nobody's come in or out for about an hour," he answered in a loud whisper.

Up or not, I was going to deliver the damn speech, so I boldly opened the door and walked in. Hillary was playing the piano and immediately stopped. "Pat, you startled me," she said, an edge in her voice.

I held up the speech in triumph.

She took the pages from me and looked them over. "You're a great advance man, Pat, but a lousy purse holder."

As I muttered an apology, the President appeared in the bedroom doorway and said, in a voice that sounded almost as relieved as I felt, "Boy, Pat, am I glad you found that speech."

That Australian trip was one of many times I traveled with both Clintons, and I never tired of watching their teamwork. They really did have a yin-yang relationship. They were finely tuned to each other's moods, and when one was down, the other always seemed able to pick up the slack. The Clintons' remarkable ability to carry one another, and the potential consequences of their both being down at the same time, was on display shortly after my return from Australia. After a relaxing holiday season in which I was able to get some much needed rest, I was summoned to Washington to help coordinate Hillary's participation in the 1997 inaugural. That duty included accompanying the Clintons to all fifteen balls held on inauguration night, January 20, 1997.

It was past eight o'clock, we were already running an hour late, the First Couple were due to hit the fifteen balls, and they hadn't even emerged from the family quarters yet. Their stony-faced staff and security detail was loitering around the map room and the back hallway of the White House. We were fading fast. It had been a long day, with the inaugural parade, the swearing in, and the inaugural address. Making history can be exhausting. Plus we were all dressed in constricting black tie and looked like a flock of pooped penguins. Andrew Friendly, the President's trip director, was red-eyed and grumpy. Ralph Alswang, the official photographer, was slumped over in a chair, sound asleep.

Suddenly the bell sounded to signal that the Clintons were on the move. We all sprang into action; the place looked like a firehouse after the alarm as everyone grabbed gear and dashed for the motorcade. Secret Service agents in tuxedos with ominous bulges under their jackets, military aides in their finest dress uniforms toting the "football" (the box with the codes to launch a nuclear war), White House medical unit doctors with their equipment bags, and communications specialists with radios and satellite phones all piled into the twenty vehicles that were to take us on our odyssey.

The President, as always, looked elegant. He wore a black tuxedo and, although clearly tired, exuded the confidence of a man who has just been given a new four-year lease on the best piece of real estate in the world. Hillary was, in a word, stunning. Her gold Oscar de la Renta gown was covered by a flowing gold cape and set off by buff-colored gloves and a miniature gold purse.

"You look magnificent," I told her.

"Thank you, Pat. I feel like death warmed over," she said with a wry smile and a little roll of her eyes. I knew what the eye roll referred to: The Clintons were playing host to about fifteen relatives, so the residence was jam-packed, noisy, and full of the inevitable tensions that arise when in-laws collide.

It was 8:30 P.M. when we set off through the streets of Washington, lights flashing and sirens blaring, on our way to celebrate the first reelection of a Democratic president in almost fifty years. The original schedule projected a 3:45 A.M. return to the White House, and with the late start and Clinton's well-deserved reputation for tardiness, most of us figured that sunup would find us showing up at cavernous halls populated by a few lingering drunks.

Our first event, at the Shoreham Hotel, was billed as "A Salute to Heroes," and the crowd was almost exclusively veterans, including many Medal of Honor recipients. The briefing for the event was less than perfect. Instead of a ball with people dancing where it would be acceptable to wave and say a few words, this was a sit-down dinner with a head table. They expected the President to deliver a speech, not dance for them. Since this little fact had been overlooked, both he and Hillary had to speak extemporaneously. They managed to acquit themselves well, but it was hardly the smooth start we wanted for such a grueling evening. As we left the event, the President's dark side appeared, and he snapped at Andrew. "That was a major embarrassment," he growled. "Are the other balls going to be this screwed up?"

Hillary's mood matched the President's words, and we walked to the motorcade in tense silence. Things were going from bad to worse, and if they didn't turn around, it would be obvious to all the partygoers—not to mention the media—that the Clintons were just going through the motions.

This was supposed to be a happy occasion, a time to forget Ken Starr, his investigation, and all the other Clinton haters, put aside our differences with the Republican-controlled Congress, and kick up our heels and do a little celebrating. There would be plenty of time in the future to fight those battles, and fight them we would, but tonight we were among friends.

The second ball was at the Air and Space Museum of the Smithsonian Institution. The atrium was decked out in red, white, and blue, and the party was in full swing when we got there. Massachusetts, where President Clinton had gotten a higher percentage of the vote than anywhere else and where many of his big donors lived, was among the states celebrating. The crowd was wildly enthusiastic and gave the Clintons a thunderous ovation. It went slightly better here, with the President even managing a tight smile, but it was clear to anyone who knew them well that the First Couple was phoning it in.

As we entered ball number three, at the cavernous Pension Building, an imposing structure located on F Street, between Fourth and Fifth streets, the President headed for the rest room. Hillary was alone in the holding room, and I ventured in to see if I could cheer her up. "At this rate your second term will be up before we get to all fifteen balls," I said. That fell flat, but I plunged onward. "Hey, did you hear that Newt Gingrich's ego is so out of control that he's going to introduce a bill to change some state names? He wants Newt York, Newt Jersey, and Newt Mexico." A slight smirk.

"And I hear he's gonna join Rush Limbaugh and Pat Buchanan to form a new singing group: the Three Gasbags." A titter.

"Look, Hillary, I know you're exhausted, and I feel bad for you. But relax. Let's have some fun. We'll get through this a lot better that way."

She smiled wanly. I could see that she was trying to rally what little was left of her energy.

The still-grumbling President appeared, and I whirled around and addressed him. "And you!" I said pointing directly at him. "Cheer up. You just got four more years as the most powerful man on earth, so stop acting like someone shot your dog."

He glared at me for a second and then burst into laughter. He and

Hillary hugged, and the two of them headed out onto the stage to the sound of "Ruffles and Flourishes" and wave after wave of applause. Both of them threw back their shoulders and gained an inch in height, broke into huge smiles, and began to pick out familiar faces in the crowd, pointing and mouthing greetings. Soon they were down front grasping outstretched hands. The President threw back his head and laughed.

The Isley Brothers were the headline performers, and they broke into their classic hit "Let's Fall in Love." The President grabbed Hillary's hand, and they started to dance. Pretty soon the whole hall joined them. I watched as they moved offstage: Would they stop dancing? No! They boogied down the corridor and right out into the night. We were home free.

These two thoroughbreds had hit their stride, and the balls began to flash by like posts on the track. The drill was the same at each stop: a few words from Hillary, who would introduce the President, a heartfelt thank-you from him, a quick dance, and a lot of hearty waving to the crowd as we made our way out. As we left each ball, the President would call out, "How many is that, Pat?"

"Six down and nine to go!" I'd shout back.

As we were leaving our sixth or seventh ball, President Clinton stopped to grab a bottle of apple juice and a cookie from one of his stewards. I took the opportunity to swipe a cold bottle of water. Hillary took one look at us standing there slaking our thirst and cried: "Come on, you can drink as we walk. Let's keep moving, boys!"

The Clintons were in such a groove that, miracle of miracles, we actually made up the lost time. Then we got to the Washington Convention Center, a huge modern facility a few blocks from the White House and the site of three balls. We got through the first ball with the now familiar talk-dance-wave routine and headed for the Arkansas Ball, probably the biggest one of the night, after which the official photographs would be taken. But first we had to make a pit stop. The First Lady's hair and makeup people had come to the center and set up shop in a back corridor. Just as Hillary sat in the chair and they got to work, the Marine Band, moving from one ball to the next as quickly as a band in red military tuxedos can, rushed by to get in place for "Ruffles and Flourishes," immediately followed by the press pool, twenty weary souls carting cameras, sound booms, and aluminum stepladders, who were equally eager to get to the Arkansas Ball and set up their cameras. I quickly stepped in front of Hillary so that the press couldn't get a photo of her being touched up. Suddenly the President joined me, leaning in close like a fellow football player in a huddle, and we stood shoulder to shoulder, effectively blocking the media's view. This made me part of the only presidential cover-up of which I have any knowledge.

The Arkansas Ball was wild, noisy, and raucous. President Clinton was clearly excited to be back among his fellow Razorbacks, and he, Hillary, and Chelsea, who was making the rounds of the balls separately with a small group of her friends, danced up a storm to Sheryl Crow's singing. They stayed longer than they had at any other ball, and I had to use my best "Come on, Mr. President, your wife is waiting" wiles to tear him away. As we finally headed out, he put one arm around Hillary and the other around me, and we made our way to the motorcade.

There were three stops left, and the Clintons breezed through them with grace, ease, and great good fun. As we were entering the Washington Hilton, the site of the final ball, we ran into Vice President Gore, Tipper, and their entourage on their way out.

The Vice President was clearly giddy and called out in a hokey southern accent: "I do declare! It's President Clinton! Say, Mr. President, I'm from Hot Springs, and I've voted for you so many damn times I've plum lost count!"

The President and Hillary broke up, and the Clintons and the Gores shared exhausted hugs. We were all a bit silly by now, laughing at almost everything and aiming to make it into the record books for the most presidential inaugural balls attended in the least amount of time. We figured it ranked right up there with the fastest mile.

We walked back into the White House at 1:40 A.M., a full two hours ahead of schedule.

"What a relief. I never thought we'd make it," I said to Andrew Friendly as we trudged through the back door of the West Wing. "I'll bet everyone's happy."

Andrew regarded me with a tired smile. "Everyone but Chelsea. She was betting on her father running late. She's still out partying."

21

LIONS, TORIES, AND
OTHER ANNOYANCES

March–May 1997

THE CALL I'D BEEN DREADING CAME FROM CRAIG SMITH, THE WHITE house political director, on the morning of the last Friday in February. I was at home in Boston, drinking a cup of coffee and reading the morning paper. "Pat, you can probably guess why I'm calling," Craig said.

"To tell me the President's named me ambassador to Ireland? Yeah, I think I can guess."

Republicans in Congress had been conducting an investigation into possible fund-raising abuses by the Democratic party, and it had come to light in early February that some White House employees, including me, were being paid by the party. I thought I was safe after several staffers had been let go and I hadn't been one of them. Then Colorado Governor Ray Romer, the party's national chairman, appeared on ABC's *This Week,* and was asked if he still had White House employees on the DNC payroll. Certainly not, he replied. Sam Donaldson smirked and waved a document in front of his face. There were three names on it, mine and two other advance people. Uh-oh. It was the following Friday that Craig called.

"We're going to announce at the daily press briefing, about an hour from now, that the three of you are being terminated," Craig said, not sugarcoating the pill.

"I understand."

"We'll pay you for another thirty days, and we're also going to try to find you another job, within the government."

Great. So I was about to be unemployed. Again.

I couldn't believe this was happening. After all, my job wasn't costing the taxpayers a dime. I was paid by the party. Past White Houses, Republican and Democrat alike, had done the same thing, having a couple of party advance people who could do official, political, or even personal trips for the president and first lady without running afoul of any ethics laws. It made sense. But President Clinton's good intentions had gotten him in trouble. His 25 percent cut in the budget for presidential staff was too deep, and managers everywhere in the White House were desperate for more personnel. They turned to the party to fund a few positions, thus creating a whole raft of higher-echelon people being paid by the Democratic party. They had "hard passes," which let them roam the grounds unescorted, they attended meetings at which classified information was discussed, and they carried out official government business. The problem was, they didn't go through any sorts of background check, face drug tests, or file ethics disclosure forms. So an attempt to get the job done and save the taxpayers money was twisted by the opposition to look like something sinister.

You might think, after Clinton had been reelected by a large margin, that the Republicans would have backed off from their relentless campaign of petty harassment and personal destruction and let the man do his job. Well, that's not the way the Republican right operates. If anything its obsessive hatred of him seemed to intensify. In magazine articles, on talk radio, on television, and in Congress Republicans ratcheted up their level of vitriol. Moreover, since they, through Speaker Gingrich and Senate Majority Leader Trent Lott, controlled both houses of Congress, they had the ability to call for special prosecutors and the votes to open congressional investigations at will.

Investigate they did. Agriculture Secretary Mike Espy, Interior Secretary Bruce Babbitt, Housing and Urban Development Secretary Henry Cisneros, and Labor Secretary Alexis Herman all were investigated by independent counsels. They even investigated Eli Segal, who ran the government volunteer service program, not to mention Ron Brown, who was dead! No matter was too small, no transgression too minor to escape the attention of these scandal-hungry bloodhounds.

The Republicans' modus operandi for years had been to destroy their opponents or, that failing, to scare people into thinking that Democrats were somehow less than good Americans. "George McGovern will grow marijuana in the Rose Garden." "Jimmy Carter is soft-minded, and his family is downright weird." "Walter Mondale is in the tank to big labor. Elect him, and the bosses will run the country." "Mike Dukakis is a pacifist midget in a tank. And what kind of name is *Dukakis* anyway?" The implication in all these characterizations was: *They're not like us,* nice white people who don't raise our voices. I've seen it time and again throughout my adult life. The Republicans don't stand *for* things; their energy and motivation come from being *against* people and programs. They need an enemy to thrive. And more often than not their whispering campaigns and appeals to people's fears and prejudices succeed.

That's why Bill Clinton scared the living daylights out of them. He seemed bulletproof. No scandal seemed capable of stopping him, people admired his work ethic, and tens of millions of Americans took him to their hearts as a lovable rogue. "But he sleeps around, and besides, he's *white trash,*" the Republicans whispered. It was a cultural holy war, and the self-proclaimed defenders of the so-called American way of life saw him as the devil incarnate and were desperate to drive a stake through his heart.

One of the more depressing aspects of this vendetta was the way moderate Republicans rolled over and played dead. The truth is when you play hardball, you often win. Moderate Republicans, many of them thoughtful and principled individuals, were browbeaten into submission by the likes of Gingrich, Tom DeLay, and Lott. As Clinton's second term began, the Republican party was turning into an organized hate machine, throwing its vast resources into a single goal: destroying the democratically elected President of the United States. Take a look at the amount of legislation that was passed during Clinton's second term. It's relatively small; most of the administration's considerable accomplishments were gained unilaterally through executive order and cabinet-level initiatives. The Republican leader in Congress didn't have the slightest interest in working with President Clinton.

Of course, their most powerful ally was Special Prosecutor Kenneth Starr. Starr, who had close ties to the whole network of Clinton haters, was a fanatic, a man possessed. He was determined with every fiber of his being to bring down President Clinton. His original mandate was to investigate Whitewater, an Arkansas real estate development that the Clintons had been involved with dating back to 1978. But he continually extended his reach, spending tens of millions of dollars of taxpayer money to hire more attorneys and staff to investigate as many Clinton allies as possible. They did bring some people down, but there is not a single administration in American history that could survive that level of scrutiny unscathed.

One of the remarkable things about the Clintons was how relatively unaffected they were by all this. That of course only further inflamed their enemies. They both felt that they had jobs to do, and they weren't going to allow themselves to be distracted any more than absolutely necessary. That brings me to another point: The Clinton administration *worked*. It got things done and delivered results, just about the across the board, for the American people. It was made very clear to all of us that this was what it was all about. So while the Republicans were having their mad tea party, we were getting on with things and, more often than not, having a great time along the way.

Of course *I* was now unemployed. Back in limbo and feeling a distinct sense of déjà vu all over again: If I wanted to continue to do advance for Hillary, I needed a government job that paid well, came with an understanding boss, and allowed me to be a no-show a lot of the time. That sort of job doesn't grow on trees.

Meanwhile Hillary and Chelsea were preparing to leave for Africa on their annual spring break jaunt, and I got a call from the advance office asking me if I would do the Victoria Falls, Zimbabwe, leg of the trip. There was just one catch: It was a gratis gig. With a twist: I was still on my thirty-day severance from the DNC, and the White House wasn't using any DNC employees. That put me in the bizarre position of being paid if I stayed home and did nothing and not being paid if I did my job and went to Africa. Hello, Africa.

The Victoria Falls, in western Zimbabwe at the Zambia border, is one of the seven natural wonders of the world. They were originally called Mosi-oa-tunya, "smoking thunder," by the Kololo tribe, but when British explorer David Livingstone came upon them in 1865 and "discovered" something local people had known about for centuries, he claimed them in the name of his queen. The falls are a spectacular sight, like five Niagara

Falls placed end to end. The spray rises a thousand feet in the air and creates the continent's only rain forest as it falls to earth in the Victoria Falls National Park.

The airport in Victoria Falls was clean and relatively modern, and the embassy had arranged air-conditioned vehicles for us. The road into town was wide and paved, and our hotel was luxurious, with well-tended gardens.

Lest my young team get the wrong impression about Africa, I thought I should show them that the way we were living was the exception. "Driver, could you show us the neighborhood where you live?" I asked.

"Certainly."

He turned off the paved road about a mile outside the center of town, and we bumped and slid along a muddy pockmarked trail for another half mile before coming to a group of shanties crowded together. They were made of corrugated metal and scraps of wood; some had straw hatching for roofs; one was an abandoned school bus. The only electricity in the area was a solitary streetlight, and few, if any, of the shacks had indoor plumbing. My charges, some of whom were African-American, were wide-eyed.

"I wanted you to see this, because this is how the people here live. Remember that this week when you're dealing with the staff at our hotel, the merchants, tour operators, and anyone else. Not everybody lives in an air-conditioned hotel."

We were staying at the Victoria Falls Hotel, a throwback to the days of British imperialism, built in the Victorian style, with heavy red leather chairs in the lobby and silent black servants in white coats and gloves. You could easily imagine a sweaty Sydney Greenstreet and a seamy Peter Lorre meeting in a dark corner of the bar to hatch a sinister plot involving crown jewels, corrupt government officials, and a beautiful fallen woman. This impression was reinforced when our government contact turned out to be the local spy, Charles Mukwamba, director of the Victoria Falls branch of the Zimbabwean Central Intelligence Organization. Mukwamba, who was completely forthcoming about what agency he worked for, was a roly-poly fellow in his mid-thirties with darting eyes, a deep voice, and a curiously high-pitched laugh. He made the mistake of trying to add to his intelligence about our methods of protection by approaching us in the hotel bar after dinner and offering to buy drinks. He wasn't nearly as shrewd as he thought as he was; his efforts were obvious and easily parried. After a few rounds of drinks I started buying, and he started talking. By the end of the night I could have run the entire Zimbabwean intelligence operation myself. Hey, I did need a job.

Since this was a pleasure trip for Hillary, I had some free time leading up to her arrival, and I used some of it to take two safaris, the first in the Zambezi National Park, the second in the Hwange National Park. Virtually all the animals are nocturnal, and since many will curl up and go to sleep at night if their bellies are full, the best time to go is at dusk, when they're just beginning their rounds.

At the Zambezi Park we embarked in two open Land Rovers and by the time we hit peak viewing hours were deep in the park. Our view of the countryside as the hot sub-Saharan sun settled into the horizon was stunning. Wide expanses of grassland were laced with small streams and dotted with occasional scrub brush, and that was where we encountered most of the animals. Our guide was named Clever, and he lived up to his name by delivering us to superb viewing spots. We saw giraffes, impalas, baboons, zebras, waterbucks, vervet monkeys, elephants, and lions. I'd been to the zoo, but this was something else altogether.

The animals were used to the Land Rovers and came quite near. Their calculation went something like this: "Land Rovers don't taste good, so I shouldn't eat them. No Land Rover has ever attacked me or my friends, so I shouldn't be afraid of them." Clever managed to get us very close to a bull elephant, which we followed as he began to move away. After a couple of minutes the elephant had had enough. He turned, raised his trunk, and let out a piercing trumpet call that scared the hell out of us and made Clever laugh. I found it hard to laugh at something that was three times the size of our truck, ten feet away, and clearly pissed off.

A perturbed pachyderm was nothing compared with my encounter with the king of the jungle. We came across a pride of four lions playing less than ten feet from our vehicle, and I scooted over and leaned out of the truck to try to take a picture of the nearest lion, which looked up and made eye contact with me. Suddenly he let loose a bloodcurdling roar, causing me to jump back and reach for the guide's rifle. Again Clever only laughed and told me I had nothing to worry about. I did my not worrying from the far side of the Land Rover.

Hillary's first stop in Zimbabwe was in Harare, the capital, where she was felled by the flu. I figured she would probably use her day in Victoria Falls to recuperate, so I kept the arrival ceremony to an absolute minimum. The only thing we were on the hook to do was go to the falls and make a photo, so the traveling media would have something to show for the day. There's a path that runs along the rim of the falls, and from the first two vantage points you can view them without getting soaked. If you go beyond that, you end up looking like a drowned rat. I told Hillary she could do as little walking as she wished. Once she saw the beginning of the path she was intrigued and rallied her legendary energy. She and Chelsea ended up walking the entire length of the falls, at the end of which they were rewarded by the sight of a perfect rainbow.

Newly invigorated by her walk, the First Lady took a swim in the hotel pool, went shopping, cruised the Zambezi River at sunset, and took in a native dance show. The woman put her young and athletic traveling staff to shame, displaying a resilience and stamina none of them could match despite constant workouts.

Beautiful as the trip was, I found myself plagued by financial anxiety. I made a decision about my future and asked to speak to the First Lady alone in her suite at the hotel. "As you probably know, I've been taken off the DNC payroll," I told her. "This is the second time I've been bounced around like this, and I've got to have a paycheck to survive. I've decided to move on and wanted to let you know why."

She focused her blue eyes on me like a laser. "Pat, the President and I deeply appreciate everything you've done for us, and we want you to stay on board. Don't worry, we'll work out the employment thing somehow."

It turns out the circus is a lot harder to quit than it is to join.

Even though I was still unemployed, in late May I agreed to work on a quick visit to London that the Clintons were making to show their support for Tony Blair, the newly elected Labor prime minister, who was making the tradition-loving Tories apoplectic with his cry of "Cool Britannia." Blair was Britain's answer to Bill Clinton. Young, bright, dynamic, charming, he'd ended sixteen years of Conservative party rule.

Of course there may have been another reason for the Clintons' wanting to create some positive press. On May 18, ABC News reported that John Bates, a deputy to Ken Starr, had told a federal judge in St. Louis: "We certainly are investigating individuals, and those individuals, including Mrs. Clinton, could be indicted." Then, on May 27, the Supreme Court had ruled that Paula Jones could pursue her sexual harassment suit, which was being financed by wealthy Clinton enemies, against the President. It seemed as if the Clinton haters were getting the breaks and their efforts were gathering steam.

Not only was Tony Blair in many ways the British equivalent of Bill Clinton, but his wife, Cherie, mirrored Hillary. She was young, attractive, and a highly successful lawyer in her own right, a woman of strong opinions not inclined to play the role of subservient spouse. Also, like Hillary, she was a dedicated mother. The Blairs had three young children and had decided to live in 11 Downing Street, a residence traditionally occupied by the chancellor of the exchequer, Britain's version of the secretary of the treasury. Even this move set them apart from the hidebound traditions of their Tory predecessors and reinforced their carefully cultivated image as new leaders for a new Britain.

When it came to negotiating the details of a presidential visit, the British had a well-deserved reputation for being difficult. They fought us every step of the way on issues of minor importance, and I couldn't help thinking that they still hadn't quite gotten over being eclipsed by a former colony and were grasping at an elusive sense of superiority on their home shores. They challenged us about the size of our motorcade, the types of communications equipment we could use, and the number of guns they would allow our Secret Service agents to carry. One argument, about which security force would occupy the critical front right seat of the presidential limousine, went all the way to the chief of staff level of the two governments.

In fairness, there were two distinctly different attitudes about our visit, one by the Blair staff members at 10 Downing Street, who were cordial and cooperative, and the other by the Foreign Office's Inward Visits Section, a group dominated by Tory appointees who had little use for the new prime minister and even less use for us. At one meeting a stern and erect young woman from the section approached me. There was no doubt who her role model was: Margaret Thatcher.

"Mr. Halley, I have a request," she said in tones that made it clear she actually considered it an order. "Mrs. Blair's sister Lyndsey Booth would like to accompany your First Lady and Mrs. Blair in the First Lady's limousine."

"Did this request come from the prime minister's staff?" I asked.

"It most certainly did," she assured me emphatically.

"Well, we can probably accommodate Ms. Booth," I said.

The woman raised her chin and walked off without another word.

Mini Maggie should have been a little bit nicer to me, and she might have gotten her way. But I found her so off-putting that I called Roz Preston, Mrs. Blair's chief of staff, to make sure the request was legitimate.

"Patrick, that idea certainly did *not* come from Mrs. Blair. What you've just witnessed is what we call Tory interference. The Foreign Office doesn't want the first ladies to spend any time alone together. Hillary is very popular over here, and they have an absolute phobia that some of it will rub off on Mrs. Blair," Roz explained.

Our negotiating session with the prime minister's staff took place in his study at 10 Downing Street. We passed through a security checkpoint at the end of Downing Street and parked in the courtyard across from the entrance. As I approached the famous black door, with its peacock feather transom and wrought iron lantern hanging above, I felt proud to tread the same path as Winston Churchill and Eamon De Valera, the Irish president who had negotiated independence for the Irish Republic. The inside of the place was standard-issue British stately: high ceilings, chandeliers, polished wood, plush carpets. A creaky stairway lined with portraits of previous prime ministers led us to the second floor, where Blair's study was located. It was a comfortable room with high windows overlooking the precisely tended grounds. It was more of a working space than the name implied and was dominated by a large conference table.

The first thing we did was lay out the basics. The trip was going to be under twelve hours long and had been designated a "Guest of Government Visit," as opposed to a state visit, which meant a lot less pomp and circumstance and thankfully left the royal family out of the picture. The queen's representatives had passed word that she'd be willing to have the President and/or the First Lady in for tea at Buckingham Palace, but the Clintons had been there, done that. This visit was about the Blairs.

One of the most important things we wanted was a picture of the Clintons and the Blairs outside No. 10, to show the two world leaders in a familiar setting, after which President Clinton and Prime Minister Blair would have a working lunch inside while the first ladies had lunch next door. Then Hillary and Cherie would go to the Globe Theatre and try to sit still during a performance of *Henry V.* The President meanwhile would address the British cabinet and hold a joint press conference with the prime minister. We then had a block of time for informal off-the-record activities.

The agenda for the meeting between the President and prime minister was limited to a discussion of NATO expansion, Northern Ireland, Bosnia, Hong Kong (which was to pass from British rule in less than two months), Iraq, Iran, air service between our two countries, nuclear matters, Libya, and the Lockerbee bombing. Just your average lunch chat—if your name happened to be Bill Clinton.

Immediately after our cordial session with the Blair staff, we had a much larger meeting with representatives of the Foreign Office. This was held in the Map Room, a huge conference room on the second floor of the Foreign Office Building a few steps from 10 Downing Street. The walls were covered with gigantic maps of what used to be the British Empire. There were only a few remnants left, mostly obscure islands nobody in his right mind would want in the first place. The Foreign Office seemed to choose this setting for its ability to recall the power and majesty of Britannia. I saw it as a reminder of how its status had diminished over the past hundred years.

This meeting was chock-full of flush-faced British bureaucrats with insufferable attitudes. First to speak was the head of the North American Department. He was so old and stiff I was afraid if he stood still too long, someone might water him along with the potted plants.

"I'm afraid I must start by pointing out that on previous state visits, the behavior of the American support staff has left rather a lot to be desired. Might I remind you: *You* are visitors in *our* country. I must *insist* in the *strongest* possible terms that you respect *our* protocols. Specifically, your communications and security personnel will not be allowed to *run all about the place* during the visit. Is that *perfectly* clear?"

It was difficult to take this very undiplomatic outburst seriously, so we just nodded and got on with the work at hand.

If my sensibilities hadn't been offended enough already, an incident the next evening certainly did the trick. I was returning from dinner and decided to drop into an Irish pub near the hotel. Tom McCarthy and a couple of other Secret Service agents were there with some of their counterparts from the Metropolitan Police Department, and I joined them at their table.

Tom introduced me to the liaison from the Marylebone District, which is headquartered across the street from our hotel.

The bloke, clearly inebriated, was around forty, about six feet tall with black hair and a prominent chin. As he shook my hand, he said, "Oh, you're that Catholic bastard from Boston. I hate Catholics."

Tom hadn't mentioned anything but my name, so I was taken aback by his knowledge of my hometown and religion, not to mention his crudeness.

"Now how would you know that about me?" I inquired. "Have you been reading my dossier?"

He looked a bit embarrassed by his slip of the tongue, which tipped his hand on who was reading what about whom, but continued right on with his insults. "I just know you're a no-good Fenian bastard," he said, referring to the long-extinct secret society made up of Irish citizens and American sympathizers dedicated to achieving Irish independence. The Fenians hadn't been around since the 1850s, but the Irish Republican Army and Sinn Fein are their direct descendants.

No one had ever called me a Fenian bastard before, but he wasn't done yet. His goal was obviously to goad me into a fistfight. "I hate the bloody Irish. Little people with grubby hands, always looking for a handout." He weaved a bit unsteadily but kept his eyes locked on mine, his challenge clear. "Especially the Catholics. Looking to bloody Rome for everything."

With this he leaned closer, and I could see my friends getting ready to step between us. It wasn't easy, but I refused to take his bait. The last thing Hillary needed was those kinds of headlines. Instead I said: "I was wondering, Sir, if your family history includes some overly familiar cousins."

His mouth hung open, and I seized the opportunity to leave before his alcohol-soaked brain had the chance to process what I'd just said.

Despite the unhelpful behavior of some of our British friends, our advance planning went well, and we readied ourselves for the Clintons' arrival. The weather the day of the visit was excellent. Hillary and the

President got off the plane, shook hands with the official greeters, and climbed into our truncated motorcade for the ride to the prime minister's residence. I didn't have a chance to chat with Hillary, but I watched her closely for any sign that the announcement by Starr's office was bothering her. She seemed comfortable and composed, as much at ease as she was on any foreign trip.

We were able to make the traditional picture in front of 10 Downing Street with no trouble. The first ladies then went into No. 11 for lunch. It was a small gathering of five women: Hillary, Cherie, Lyndsey Booth, Melanne Verveer, and Roz Preston.

"We're still in the process of settling in, as you can see. I apologize for the bare walls and rather impersonal feeling of the place. You'll have to come back after we've made it a proper home," Cherie Blair said.

Once the ladies were seated I made myself scarce and saw that the traveling staff got fed, though I popped my head back in to check on things periodically. Hillary and Cherie Blair seemed to get along quite well and spent a lot of time discussing the pressures that public life put on families. Mrs. Blair was particularly interested in the steps Hillary had taken to protect Chelsea from publicity and how they could be applied to her children.

After making it through the first three acts of *Henry V* at the Globe, we returned to Downing Street. As we approached, I called Jeff Eller, the President's lead, on the radio and he informed me that the President and prime minister were still holding their press conference in the garden behind No. 10. Because of Ken Starr's announcement, we didn't want Hillary to be subjected to any questions. As she got out of her limousine, she turned to me. "Pat, what should I do?"

"Why don't you slip inside and watch the rest of the press conference on television?" I suggested.

Mrs. Blair agreed, and we entered No. 10.

"To tell you the truth, I don't actually know if there *are* any televisions in here," Cherie Blair said. She turned to one of her husband's staff. "Are there?"

"Yes, ma'am, there's one in the prime minister's office."

So that's where we headed, and I sat with the two wives as their husbands appeared on the global stage.

The day ended with the Clintons and Blairs enjoying a four-hour dinner together. These were four people who definitely weren't faking it for the cameras. By the time the dinner broke up at ten-thirty we all were exhausted and just wanted to get the Clintons to the airport and on their way back to the United States. Our motorcades, under the supervision of the diabolical Foreign Office, had been a mess all day, but what happened next was the worst, and most potentially dangerous, example of bad planning I'd ever seen.

As we drove onto the Tower Bridge over the Thames, the gate near the center of the bridge closed, signaling that the center section was about to be raised to allow a ship to pass through. The presidential limousine was suddenly trapped between two cars, unable to move either forward or back. It looked like a terrorist setup, and I felt my short hairs stand up. I expected to hear gunfire at any second, and I don't think I drew a breath for the next several minutes. Secret Service agents jumped from their vehicles and surrounded the limousine. Fortunately there was no gunfire, the ship passed under the bridge, and we continued on our way.

It was the first time in history that a presidential motorcade had been stopped by a suspension bridge, and it wasn't just any bridge, it was the one Londoners call Gladys, a universal symbol of the British Empire, or what's left of it. Gladys provided a fitting end to the amateur work done by the British Foreign Office. The foul-up was front-page headlines in the following day's newspapers.

As I watched Air Force One take off from Heathrow, I knew the Clintons were flying back to a city filled with people intent on exposing their every weakness, in the hopes of decreasing their awesome political strength. The American people had spoken, but the Clintons' enemies felt that they answered to a higher power.

22

OF TANGOS AND TEAPOTS

October–November 1997

IT WAS A STRANGE FEELING TO BE LEADING A LARGE ADVANCE TEAM overseas, representing the White House, being chauffeured around foreign capitals in a Mercedes, holding meetings with high-level government officials, all while I was on the dole.

Luckily, my months of voluntary servitude finally came to an end in late July 1997, when I was appointed special assistant to the regional administrator for the General Services Administration's New England region (try saying that three times quickly). The job passed muster in three important ways: I could stay in Boston, the pay was decent, and I could advance the First Lady. After three months of my lying low in my new position, my first advance came through in early October: Buenos Aires, no less. I felt like a kid let out of school. Hillary's mission on this trip was to deliver one of her trademark speeches calling for the empowerment of women.

It took almost fifteen hours to fly from Boston to Buenos Aires, but we were still in the same time zone when we arrived, and that seemed unreal. Usually when you're that far from home, you're dealing with massive jet lag, not to mention trying to figure out when to sleep, eat, and call the office. In Buenos Aires I was raring to go.

I quickly realized that Argentines are an organized people. Usually the size of our advance contingent intimidated our hosts. Time and again I'd been to meetings where we'd show up with fifty or more people only to find one or two perplexed reps from the host government. The level of knowledge our people want about medical facilities, radio frequencies, riot control, electrical power, etc. is usually well beyond their purview. Not so in Argentina. At our first meeting in Buenos Aires, sixty-five Argentines showed up!

We wanted to use the venerable Teatro Colón for Hillary's address, but our counterparts argued that we could never fill it. I assured them that it wouldn't be a problem, and they reluctantly gave us the go-ahead. Opened in 1908, the Colón is one of the world's greatest halls, a gilt and rococo confection; its stage has been graced by Caruso, Stravinsky, Callas, and Pavarotti. It was a powerfully symbolic venue for what was being touted as a major speech, and I knew that with minimal effort we could generate enough interest among college students, women's groups, and expatriate Americans to assure a sellout. My team spent the next several days using all our familiar tricks to build a crowd.

We then found ourselves with some time on our hands and decided a boat trip over to Uruguay was in order. That was when I found out that there was still a little south of the border leeway in the much-vaunted Argentine attention to rules and organization.

Off we went to buy our tickets. However, the people at the ticket office downtown informed us that since we were traveling on government passports, we would need visas to enter Uruguay. People traveling on ordinary tourist passports didn't.

Since I always carried my tourist passport with me just in case, I was okay. So was one other member of my team, Huma Abedin, who was on her first trip and had not yet been issued a government passport. The rest of the team didn't want to hassle with getting the visas, so the two of us set off. We got to the dock, purchased our tickets, and presented our passports to a customs official.

He waved Huma through, but as he leafed through my passport, a puzzled look came over his face, and he said in somewhat broken English, "Señor, you have no Argentina stamp in your passport. How did you arrive in our country?"

"Oh, I used my other passport," I said without thinking.

"Your *other* passport!" he said, his voice rising. "This is highly unusual!"

No doubt thinking he'd caught a high-level American spy trying to abscond with some of his country's secrets by way of a slow boat to Colonia, Uruguay, he reached for his pistol.

"No, wait. You see, I work for the White House and carry *two* passports, one for my official travel, which is the one I used to enter Argentina, and then this one, which I carry, well, you know, just in case something like this comes up."

He narrowed his eyes; my convoluted explanation was just another nail in my coffin. "I think the police will want to talk to you," he said ominously.

"I demand to speak to your supervisor," I said in desperation.

His boss was summoned, and I again explained my situation, this time producing government identification. The boss was an older fellow with a large stomach who didn't seem to appreciate having his siesta interrupted. He studied my passport and my identification for a long time, but it didn't look to me as if his eyes were fully focused. "Okay, let him through," he said finally.

"No. There is no entry stamp on this passport. He cannot leave the country," Junior said, puffing up his chest.

The boss just stood there silently for a long minute. Then he reached down and picked up the other fellow's date stamp. He wheeled the date mechanism backward, opened my passport, and gave it a whack. He then wheeled the date forward and passed the stamp and passport to Junior. Junior opened the passport as if for the fist time, stamped it, and handed it back to me. "Have a wonderful trip," he said with a big smile.

I took the resolution of this international incident as a good omen. Had I known what was transpiring in a secret meeting back in Washington, I wouldn't have.

The Clintons arrived in Buenos Aires as the sun was setting on a nice spring day—in mid-October. While we're raking leaves and hunkering down for winter in the United States, the Argentineans are planting gardens and shopping for bathing suits. Little did we know that as the President and the First Lady were shaking hands with the elite of Argentina, Linda Tripp was meeting at an apartment in Washington with a reporter from *Newsweek* to relate tales of a "friend" of hers named Monica Lewinsky who claimed she'd had an affair with President Clinton.

But the Lewinsky scandal wasn't on our radar screen yet. At this point we were focused on preparations for Hillary's speech. She planned to issue a call to the women of Central and South America to become more politically active in promoting education, economic opportunity, health care, and legal protections. It was going to be a hard-hitting speech in which she would point out that no nation could possibly succeed in a global economy if half its people were categorically denied the right to use their God-given promise.

By the day of the speech the anticipation in Buenos Aires was palpable. Hillary's event was being talked about on radio and television, written about in the newspapers, and debated in restaurants and sidewalk cafés.

Not surprisingly, the Teatro Colón was packed, including the nosebleed seats in the upper balconies. The crowd was almost exclusively female, many of them college students. Onstage, in front of a thick velvet drape, was a comfortable living room setting. Hillary's entrance caused pandemonium and ignited a rhythmic chant of "Hill-a-ree! Hill-a-ree!"

After a brief introduction Hillary got to the meat of her speech, occasionally thumping the podium to emphasize a point. ". . . I would like to talk about voices, powerful voices, the voices of women in this country and my country, throughout our hemisphere and our world, and what we can do to make all of our voices heard. To have our voices heard about our shared commitment to advancing the cause of women's rights, advancing the cause of democracy, and making it clear that the two are inseparable."

After her speech Hillary met backstage with representatives of the Grandmothers of the Plaza de Mayo, an organization of women who were working to locate the children of the "disappeared," political opponents of the military regime who were murdered during Argentina's so-called dirty war of the 1970s. When the military deposed Isabel Perón, the widow of the legendary Argentine president, it went on a killing spree to eliminate its opposition. At least nine thousand people went missing, and virtually all are presumed dead. It had recently been revealed that many of the dead had been tortured and that a favorite means of killing had been to fly out over the ocean, blindfold the victim, and then throw him or her out of the plane. Many of the disappeared had been young parents, leaving the Grandmothers of the Plaza de Mayo to raise the children. The Grandmothers were intent on locating their offspring or at least learning about their fate.

Hillary was very moved by the stories these women related and promised to speak to the American ambassador and have the embassy offer whatever assistance it could. Of course just the fact that the first lady of the United States had met with these women and mentioned them in her speech gave them an enormous political boost in their homeland. Believe me, it's not something Barbara Bush or Nancy Reagan would have done.

The state dinner that night was, at least to a blasé veteran like me, the same old same old. You know, spectacular setting, unbelievable food, incredible wine, beautiful women, powerful men, exciting entertainment. I could barely stay awake. But what followed, ah, now that was worth staying up for.

On the way back to the hotel the Clintons suddenly decided they wanted to . . . tango. And so we changed directions and headed to the hottest tango club in town. It was in the nightclub district, in a long, low-slung building with a modest sign. The inside was dark and smoky, and the stage was bathed in a cool blue spotlight. The place was already in full swing, sexy and stirring, but as the Clintons entered, a buzz rippled through the crowd, and the excitement level soared.

We sat at a group of small tables, and the show began. The performers burned up the floor, sensuous, provocative, smoldering with passion. I thought of Rita Hayworth and those wildly romantic movies set in South America. The dancers were clearly playing to the Clintons, and it wasn't long before one of the female dancers coaxed the President into joining her. To the rhythmic clapping of the crowd, he started slowly, but before long he got the hang of it and managed to acquit himself quite admirably—for a gringo.

Hillary's speech received wide play across South and Central America. Her stature was growing around the world, and she was deluged with invitations to speak. With barely a day back in Boston to unpack and repack, I went from a tango to a teapot—from Buenos Aires to Belfast.

Bombs were still going off, and former Senator George Mitchell was gamely trying to hammer out what came to be known as the Good Friday Agreement, when Hillary agreed to travel to Belfast to make a speech and accept an award for her peacemaking efforts.

The University of Ulster had initiated a lecture series on the peace process and had named one of the addresses in honor of Joyce McCarten, a working-class Catholic mother from the Shankhill section of Belfast, who had died in 1996. Joyce was a brave and passionate woman who had seen enough senseless killing. Determined to keep another generation of Belfast's sons and daughters from getting caught up in the cycle of violence, she had gone out into her neighborhood and organized local mothers to begin a dialogue between themselves and Protestant mothers. She had become a symbol for all the Irish, and then for all the world, of the power that ordinary women have.

Hillary had met McCarten when she visited Belfast in December 1995. They had sat in a small neighborhood restaurant called Ye Olde Lamplighter on Lower Ormeau Road, drunk tea, nibbled cookies, and talked about their shared dream of peace in Ireland. At one point Hillary remarked to Joyce how nice and warm the teapot kept the tea, much better than the pots she had back at the White House. When they said good-bye, Joyce gave Hillary the teapot. It was ordinary-looking, made of thick stainless steel with a wooden handle. In all the years I worked for Hillary, I never saw a gift she treasured more. She brought it back to Washington and used it regularly.

In her speech, devoted to her hopes for a peaceful and prosperous Ireland, Hillary spoke of Joyce McCarten, of what her life had meant to Ireland and to the world. Then, to laughter and applause, she produced the teapot, which had been transported back across the Atlantic with a care the crown jewels would envy. She spoke of how the teapot, and the tea she brewed in it, gave her comfort and strength and made her feel connected not only to Joyce McCarten but to women all over the world who were working to make their neighborhoods, and nations, better places. She then used it as a metaphor for the peace process: "I thought often about the troubles here as I have thought about Joyce McCarten and the women I met as I have fixed myself a pot of tea. I don't know whether a Catholic or a Protestant made this teapot. I don't know whether a Catholic or a Protestant sold this teapot. I only know that this teapot serves me very well. And that this teapot stands for all those conversations around those thousands of kitchen tables where mothers and fathers look at one another with despair because they cannot imagine that the future will be any better for their children. But this teapot is also on the kitchen table where mothers and fathers look at one another and say, we have to do better. We cannot permit this to go on. We have to take a stand for our children."

Looking back at that speech, I see a sad irony, because Hillary's personal peace was about to be shattered in a way none of us could have possibly imagined.

23

ON THIN ICE

January–February 1998

SWITZERLAND IS A NEUTRAL COUNTRY, SO I WAS LUCKY I WAS THERE when war broke out.

The *Washington Post* had reported back in June 1997 that Special Prosecutor Starr had begun investigating President Clinton's personal life. Those of us who'd been around through the campaigns and earlier scandals knew what that meant, the possibility of more "bimbo eruptions." But that was all in his past, right? More rehash of the shenanigans he'd been accused of before he became President. Sure, a replay of all the squalid details and accusations wouldn't help, but hey, it was all in a past that was becoming more distant every day. He'd faced the voters twice since the allegations, winning both times.

On January 19, 1998, the bomb hit. The "other shoe" we'd always dreaded came hurling out of the sky and caught us square on the noggin. The Internet columnist Matt Drudge reported on his Web site that *Newsweek* was holding a story about President Clinton's being sexually involved with a twenty-one-year-old White House intern. The report didn't skimp on details and even gave her name, Monica Lewinsky. The mainstream media picked up the report the next day, and all hell broke loose.

This wasn't some recycled tale from the Arkansas days. This was current, in the White House, and devastating. The Republicans had been working for six years to destroy President Clinton. Had he handed them the ammunition needed to do the job?

I was dismayed by the news. If true, it was very stupid behavior on the President's part. On the other hand, sex between two consenting adults is their business. Period. But my primary concerns were for Hillary. This was an enormous blow to her on every level, and I knew that she wouldn't take it sitting down. Her every instinct is to fight back when she or her husband is attacked. She didn't disappoint. The following morning she went on the *Today* show, denied the allegation, and blamed it on a "vast right-wing conspiracy" of President Clinton's enemies.

Still, beneath her bravado this had to hurt and hurt badly. It was a nightmare come true for any woman, let alone one in Hillary's position, where privacy is nonexistent, where every humiliation and lurid detail are trumpeted on the evening news.

I was in Zurich advancing a trip for Hillary. In the days that followed I spent every spare minute watching CNN as the story mushroomed. On the twenty-sixth of January, President Clinton declared forcefully, during a routine White House announcement, "I did not have sexual relations with that woman . . . Miss Lewinsky."

The following night he was due to deliver the State of the Union address to Congress, the Supreme Court, and the nation. The country and the world were riveted. How could he show his face in public? Would he mention the scandal that was spreading like wildfire, consuming all the political and cultural oxygen? I wasn't about to miss this performance and braved the six-hour time difference to watch his speech from my hotel suite at three o'clock in the morning. There was a shot of Hillary in the gallery, looking serious and composed. I wondered what was going on behind her careful façade.

The President entered the hall to a standing ovation, although several Republicans were boycotting the speech and Tom DeLay sat there sneering. President Clinton then delivered a breathtaking performance. He was at the peak of his powers, confident and articulate, doing what the Republicans feared and hated most: connecting with the American people. He ignored the scandal and turned the country's focus to its *real* problems, declaring that we must "save Social Security first." Even his enemies were impressed. It was as if he had thrown a bucket of cold water on the flames of Ken Starr's prurient obsessions. Sadly, the respite was short-lived, and within days talk of impeachment had begun.

Four days after the State of the Union, Hillary arrived in Switzerland. Given all the craziness in Washington, I had no idea what to expect. Would she be drained by the swirling controversy? Would the seamy details leaking out hour by hour dampen her spirit, sap her energy?

It was overcast and cold when she landed, the silver sky hinting a storm might lurk in the near future. How fitting.

As usual I went aboard her plane to welcome her and do a quick briefing on our upcoming activities. She was in the main cabin, fresh, bright-eyed, and ready to go. The scandal was the big pink elephant in the middle of the room, but like any employee in any job, I wasn't about to ask the boss how the marriage was holding up. "My, you look fresh. You must have gotten some sleep on the way over here," I said.

"Yes, I did," she answered with a smile. "I managed a few solid hours, not my usual catnaps. I'm ready to go. Is it cold out? Will I need my heavy coat?"

This was game day Hillary, focused, sharp, eager to get about the day's business. But was it all show? After all, no one can take the kind of news, not to mention news coverage, she was absorbing and be completely unaffected. Then it dawned on me. Her way of dealing with the crisis was to live in the present. To put what happened yesterday and what might happen tomorrow in a different compartment of the mind and to concentrate on the here and now. She was all business, and I responded in kind.

We had scheduled a walking tour of Lucerne, a beautiful Alpine village. I knew how much Hillary loved to walk, and I wanted to do everything I possibly could to make this trip easy and enjoyable for her. Unfortunately the number of reporters who usually accompany us had grown exponentially since the Lewinsky scandal broke, and there was a continuous barrage of shouted questions. Some of the questions were very crass, and Hillary ignored them as best she could, but more than once I saw her flinch.

After our walking tour we left the media mob behind and boarded a paddle wheel steamboat. An hour later we put into Brunnen. The small town, with its rosy-cheeked lederhosen-wearing citizens, its oompah band, its meadows, and its cuckoo clock houses, made me feel as if we'd landed in the middle of a cough drop commercial. Several thousand enthusiastic people lined the dock and the streets to greet Hillary. I had no idea she was that popular in Switzerland, and I could tell the reception buoyed her spirits.

In spite of my professional resolve, the day was difficult for me. I felt as if I were walking a tightrope. I was very protective of Hillary and worried about her in a way I never had been before, but I knew it was hardly my place to express my concerns and certainly not without her initiating the conversation. So I acted as if it were just another trip. I joshed occasionally and tried to be solicitous without seeming overly anxious.

That afternoon Hillary gave a speech at the University of Zurich. It was upstairs in the largest lecture hall, and more than two thousand people crowded the auditorium while more listened downstairs in an overflow area. Perhaps the most remarkable thing about her performance was how routine it was. While Ken Starr leaked lurid details about her husband's behavior and the talk shows and tabloids raised intimate questions about her marriage, Hillary was standing before a large academic audience, apparently unfazed, going on with her life.

Later that evening, after a long day of speeches, handshaking, and diplomatic courtesy calls, Hillary decided to go ice-skating. I led her up the hill to the hotel's outdoor rink. It was clear and cold, and as we approached, we heard the laughter of some of our traveling staffers, already doing their best to work off the jet lag with a little exercise. Hillary is a great ice skater and had brought her own skates. We laced up, and she held my arm as we wobbled down the wooden ramp to the rink. We skated together for a while, and then she began to look a little tired. "Would you like to take a rest?" I asked.

Hillary nodded, and I led her to a bench near the rink; it was set off by itself and afforded some semblance of privacy. We sat in silence for a couple of minutes as she caught her breath. I think she welcomed the physical fatigue. We watched the others skaters, skating to Mozart, the rink bathed in soft light. She seemed at peace, though I sensed that she wanted to talk.

"If you don't mind my asking, how are you doing?" I said.

"I've had better weeks."

"Are you going to be okay?"

After a moment she nodded. "This is a tough business. I've always known there are people out to destroy us, and this is just one more attempt. We can't let them get us down. That's only playing into their hands. We'll get through this, but it's going to get ugly."

"Are you ready for it?" I asked gently.

She paused and looked up the sky; I wondered what she was thinking. Then she looked at me. "I'm ready. And I honestly don't take it personally. These people are out to get us because of what we stand for and what we're trying to do. And that's why we can't let them win."

"No, we can't."

"You know what they say?"

"What?"

"When the going gets tough, the tough go skating. Come on."

With that, she grabbed my hand and led me back out to the rink.

24

MY LIFE AS A SPY

March–May 1998

IT WAS GOING TO BE MY SECOND ST. PATRICK'S DAY IN A ROW SPENT IN Africa, where, believe it or not, the day just isn't a big deal. There are no parades, the rivers are not dyed green, and no one gets so drunk he throws up on his shoes. Oh, well, I guess spending time with one of the seminal figures of the twentieth century was some consolation.

Cape Town was the last stop on President Clinton's tour of the African continent. He had adopted a policy of increased U.S. engagement with Africa and was only the second sitting U.S. president to visit Africa, having been preceded by Jimmy Carter, who had toured Lagos, Nigeria, and Liberia in March 1978. Clinton's visit attracted enormous attention, abundant enthusiasm, and massive crowds. Hillary was eager to show him some of the things she'd seen on her own trip to Africa the year before, including cooperative housing being built by local women in one of the townships. We would also pay respects to President Nelson Mandela and return to the Robben Island prison where he had first been held as a political prisoner.

This was almost two months after I had sat beside her at the skating rink in Zurich. Starr's office continued to leak like a sieve, and the scandal gripped the country. Most people fell into one of two camps: "What does this have to do with his job as president?" or "He has demeaned the presidency and should resign or be impeached." Passions were white hot on both sides; the nation was in the middle of a high-stakes battle the likes of which it had rarely seen before. Starr and the Republicans smelled blood in the water. They thought they finally had the goods on President Clinton and were counting on a national sense of revulsion against his behavior to become so strong that he would be unable to govern and would be forced to resign. Instead something remarkable happened. His poll numbers remained steady and even rose. Perhaps the most heartening development during this whole sad and sordid period was that the American people never deserted the president they had elected.

I think there were three primary reasons for President Clinton's continued popularity. First of all, he was doing a good job. Second, he is a man of enormous personal appeal. Third, the country was way ahead of the Republicans on matters of private behavior. There was a real cultural disconnection between the moralizing of the Republicans in Washington and what was going on out in the real world. Popular culture had been treating sex with honesty and humor for years. The Republicans were apoplectic that the American people could look at President Clinton's alleged adultery and say, "So what?" Although Starr and the Republicans denied it until they were blue in the face, it was the adultery per se for which they thought President Clinton should be driven from office. Many of these men—there wasn't a single woman leading the charge—were self-proclaimed evangelical Christians, and those who weren't were adopting the holier than thou mien of the true believers.

I'd been receiving regular updates from friends in the White House on what the mood was like there. The news was surprisingly good. Of course the scandal was consuming a lot of time and energy, but the Clintons were determined to keep on course. And they were. The White House was announcing a steady stream of initiatives and directives on issues ranging from land use to school uniforms to saving national historic treasures. The President was thick into the peace processes in Ireland and the Middle East and was highly engaged in foreign affairs around the globe. He was working with Congress as best he could, and both the President and First Lady were traveling and speaking around the country and hosting state dinners at home.

Still, I was looking forward to spending time with Hillary to see how she was doing. I felt very strongly that part of my role during this period was to provide her with a means of escape and to ensure that her travels were trouble-free. I wanted her to have a chance to focus on the things that were really important to her—and to have some fun. South Africa certainly offered ample opportunities for both.

Cape Town is a very cosmopolitan city, and the coastline around it was as beautiful as any I'd seen, with deep blue waters crashing against a craggy shoreline. Then there were the penguins. I didn't associate the African continent, home to lions and giraffes, with the little birds in tuxedos. But there they were, in vast numbers.

One of the people from the State Department working with us on the visit was April Gillespie, the former U.S. ambassador to Iraq. In some quarters Gillespie was blamed for starting the Persian Gulf War because of a comment she had made to Saddam Hussein after he told her at a meeting on July 25, 1990, that he intended to invade Kuwait in January of the following year. Gillespie was blond, in her fifties, and talkative. A group of us had dinner with her at a charming countryside restaurant while we were preparing for the Clintons' visit and she was not at all reluctant to discuss her days in the gulf.

"Saddam had a very active household. Something was always going on there. One of his sons is totally out of control, and we heard stories that he had shot a household servant for not pressing his shirt correctly. So Saddam wasn't the only loose cannon in the family," she told us.

I was interested to find out how she felt about being blamed for starting the Gulf War and couldn't think of a delicate way to broach the topic, so I barged right into it. "April, I've read that some people say you were responsible for giving Saddam the go-ahead on Kuwait. Does that bother you?"

"What bothers me is that I was set up. You'd think I told Saddam to go ahead and roll his tanks into Kuwait. They make it sound like he asked my permission and I didn't say no. Anyone who knows how he operates knows it just didn't happen like that. Saddam doesn't ask permission; he does what he wants. And he says a lot of outrageous things. Lots of them are just bluff and bluster. So when he said in the middle of one of his monologues that he was going into Kuwait and paused and looked at me, I told him we didn't have a position on that, meaning I hadn't been instructed or authorized by the State Department to say yes or no. As soon as I got home, I called Washington, and the matter got top-level attention, all the way up to Jim Baker. I did my job. I did what I was trained to do."

She paused and took a sip from her wineglass.

"The Bush White House and the State Department had instant notice and knew exactly what was going on. They knew what Hussein had said and how I'd replied. If they wanted to send him a firm message to stay out of Kuwait, they had ample opportunity. They didn't. So to look back after the fact and blame me is just a matter of political convenience."

The Clintons arrived in the dark of night, well after one o'clock in the morning, following a five-and-a-half-hour flight from Uganda. I only had the chance to say a quick hello to Hillary, who looked as if she'd been sleeping.

The next morning we set out for the Victoria Mxenge Housing, in the Philippi township about fifteen miles outside Cape Town. There were black townships outside all of South Africa's major cities; they were home to the cooks, maids, groundskeepers, and nannies who worked in town. The conditions were desperate. I'd seen poverty everyplace in the world, including the United States, but I'd never seen anything like Philippi. There were tens of thousands of people living on top of one another in huts made of cardboard and scraps of wood and metal. There was no running water, sewerage, or electricity, and the dust could choke a horse.

During her visit to the Mxenge homes the previous spring, the First Lady had cut the ribbon at a housing project being built by local women. At that time 18 simple cinder-block houses had been constructed. This year there were 104, a new community center, and 44 more houses planned or already under construction. The women had purchased a second plot of land where they planned to build 230 more houses.

The project was named for Victoria Mxenge, a lawyer who had struggled against apartheid and had been assassinated for her efforts. It was run entirely by women, and the average cost of a house was about twenty-four hundred dollars.

The houses were small, square, and functional. Compared with the nearby shanties, they were palatial. Wearing my panama hat to ward off the intense heat and bright sun, I led the Clintons through the project's dusty streets. As the township's population and the American media watched, the President and First Lady, instructed each step of the way by two women in yellow dresses and colorful headwraps, laid bricks and smoothed in cement with a trowel. We had planned for them to lay only one brick each, but they got going and put in a half dozen. Was the

President honing his job skills in case things didn't work out back in Washington?

After a quick stop to change clothes we went to the Tuynhuys, President Mandela's official office and residence, for the formal arrival ceremony. As the presidential limousine pulled to a stop at the edge of the red carpet, Nelson Mandela and his companion, Graca Machel, stepped forward to greet them. President Mandela was tall, proud, and surprisingly vigorous for a man of seventy-nine years. His trademark warm, wide smile appeared, and he grasped President Clinton's hand and placed his arm on his shoulder. Then the two of them walked past an honor guard, about half of whom were white. I wondered what Mandela was feeling; only eight years earlier these same troops were serving a nation that had held him captive for twenty-seven years. He'd gone from prisoner to president, and now the army answered to him.

The state dinner was held at a vineyard about sixty miles outside Cape Town, and the guests included the usual mix of politicians, businesspeople, and celebrities. Among them was another familiar figure, Bishop Desmond Tutu. We all were crowded into a big white tent on the lawn, and despite repeated attempts by the South African staff, guests were slow to take their seats. Then Bishop Tutu took the microphone. "This is Desmond Tutu speaking. If you don't sit down right now, I'm going to tell God!" People took their seats.

Not long after the meal was served there was a brief thunderstorm and the power went out. We were plunged into darkness. Had Bishop Tutu brought this upon us? I ended up standing behind the Clintons with a flashlight so they could see their food until I was mercifully replaced by candelabra.

The next day we flew by helicopter to Robben Island to visit the jail where President Mandela had been held as a political prisoner for eighteen years of his captivity. I had read Mandela's book *Long Walk to Freedom* just before leaving on this trip, and it gave me goose bumps to walk through the halls of the prison and to see the cell where he spent so many years, with the man himself as the tour guide.

In his book Mandela describes his childhood in the countryside, his training as a lawyer and amateur boxer, and the incredible persecution he and his people faced. The brutally repressive government had led this iron-willed intellectual and humanitarian to become a freedom fighter and landed him on the notorious list of banned men, to be arrested on sight. After a kangaroo court trial he'd been locked up, eventually arriving on Robben Island, where he was assigned a cell so small that when he lay down, he stretched from one wall to the other. He was forty-six years old and sentenced for life.

Once again I found myself wondering about his emotions as we visited first the granite quarry where he had been forced to work in the blinding sunlight so long that his eyesight had been permanently damaged and then his cellblock. There's something inherently eerie about an abandoned prison; it's almost as if you can hear the spirits of its former inhabitants calling to you. Did Mandela hear those spirits?

While I waited outside in the courtyard, Mandela led the Clintons down the cinder-block corridor to his tiny cell. Then the two men walked into the cell, and Clinton, perhaps trying to get a sense of what Mandela's perspective on the world had been, walked to the window and grasped the bars with both hands, looking out. It was a chilling sight to see my president peering out from behind those bars. This man's political opponents wanted to strip him of power and perhaps put him in jail, and here he was looking out from the very room that had held the body but never the spirit of one of the great men of our times.

Moments later they emerged into the fresh air of the courtyard, where they were serenaded by a school choir. President Clinton reached out and embraced Hillary, draping an arm over her shoulder as she clung to his waist. Had they heard the spirits? Were they seeking each other's physical comfort after such a close encounter with the blunt end of political power, such a stark reminder of what your enemies can do to you?

Perhaps the spirits were simply a product of my imagination, but I was very moved by the whole experience.

Six weeks later, on a trip to Switzerland, I went from the exalted to the profane, or at least to the thorn in our side. Of course, this thorn was also one of the twentieth century's seminal figures. It was early May, and I was in Geneva advancing Hillary's visit to the World Health Organization, where she was going to receive an award for her work promoting the well-being of women and children around the world. This was her fourth trip abroad in as many months. Sometimes it feels good to get out of town.

When I arrived at the Intercontinental Hotel, I was amazed at the level of security. The parking lot behind the hotel looked like a military base: tents, mobile command trailers, a squad of armored vehicles, several helicopters. I tracked down the hotel manager.

"I appreciate all the security, but don't you think it's a little excessive?" I asked.

"Oh, no. We're hosting another distinguished guest in addition to the First Lady," he informed me.

"No kidding, who?"

"Fidel Castro."

"Fidel Castro?"

"Fidel Castro."

Fidel Castro!

This was the first I, or anyone else on my very large team, had heard of this. I immediately called the White House. It was the first it'd heard of it too. Its response naturally was complete panic. "Get the First Lady the hell out of that hotel" was its message in a nutshell. "No can do" was my equally succinct response. The WHO meeting and the fiftieth anniversary meeting of the World Trade Organization later that week had combined to suck up every hotel room within a hundred miles. We were stuck at the Intercontinental with Fidel.

My next instructions came straight from the National Security Council: Hillary and Fidel must never, *ever* cross paths. That sounds pretty straightforward, doesn't it? Except for one huge wrinkle: We never communicated with the Cuban government. *Ever.* So I couldn't call them up and say, "Hey, when is old Fidel going to be coming and going? And by the way, when and where is he going to be eating, and walking, and getting a manicure?" I mean it wouldn't do for Hillary to be eating lunch at some nice restaurant and have a bottle of wine sent over by the bearded gentleman in the army fatigues two tables over.

Enter Patrick Halley, international man of intrigue.

I got very cozy with the hotel staff and found out the times that Castro's people had requested that the elevators be held. Then I had my Secret Service people ask the Swiss police if they could ask the Cuban advance people when they wanted roads closed for motorcade movements. Little by little I was able to piece together Castro's schedule pretty well—except for his initial arrival time, which kept changing.

The day before Hillary was due I was walking through the hotel lobby when there was a sudden commotion. Security people I didn't recognize—but they sure looked Cuban—materialized out of nowhere and cordoned off the crowd. Except they screwed up and roped people *in* instead of out. I was one of those people. Trapped. The buzz in the lobby grew, and by craning my neck, I just caught a glimpse of Castro getting out of his limousine. He and his entourage proceeded into the lobby, and there I was, a sitting duck, face-to-face with the Cuban dictator, scourge of nine U.S. presidents, the man who had brought communism to the Western Hemisphere.

Beard neatly trimmed, he was dressed in pressed green army fatigues, collar open, army hat perched on his head. He strode across the lobby purposefully—*right in my direction.* I did what any polite person would have done under the circumstances. I stuck out my hand. We shook. Then he moved on.

Well, at least I had his arrival time nailed down.

Hillary arrived in good spirits, and of course I never mentioned the ugliness unfolding in Washington. Most of her schedule revolved around her WHO speech, which Castro was due to attend. That meant we had to make sure they didn't get close enough to end up in the same picture. I put Paul Rivera, a very resourceful member of my team, on "Fidel watch" and told him to use whatever means were necessary to keep the bearded one away from our gal. It turned out to be easy. Castro sat and listened politely throughout Mrs. Clinton's speech and then went on his dictatorial way.

Hillary left and flew to Birmingham, England. I went back to the hotel to pack, only to receive an urgent message that I should stay in Geneva. The President had decided at the last minute to attend the WTO session, and Hillary was coming back to meet him. It seemed as if neither one of them was finding Washington too hospitable.

In fact, the evidence was piling up that the President *did* have sex with that woman. Miss Lewinsky. There was talk of a blue dress from the Gap with a telltale stain on it. Of hanky-panky in the Oval Office. The country's fever was spiking. At the center of the storm were two increasingly beleaguered people.

25

EVEN COWGIRLS GET THE BLUES

September 1998

HILLARY HAD THE THOUSAND-YARD STARE SOLDIERS GET WHEN THEY'VE been in battle too long: vacant and focused in the far distance. There were dark circles under her eyes, and her skin looked drawn. She moved slowly and exhibited no interest in her surroundings. I'd seen her tired after long overseas flights before, but this was different. This depressed and withdrawn woman who had just arrived in Ireland was a Hillary I had never seen.

Two weeks earlier, on August 17, President Clinton, after spending the afternoon testifying before a federal grand jury, addressed the nation and admitted that he'd had an inappropriate and "wrong" relationship with Monica Lewinsky. "I know that my public comments and my silence about this matter gave a false impression. I misled people, including even my wife. I deeply regret that."

He went on to express his desire to mend fences and recover his family's privacy: "Now this matter is between me, and the two people I love the most—my wife and our daughter—and our God. But it is private, and I intend to reclaim my family life for my family. It's nobody's business but ours. Even Presidents have private lives."

If the President thought this statement would satisfy the vultures on the Republican right, he was wrong. They had brought Clinton to his knees and were winding up to deliver what they hoped would be the knockout punch, Ken Starr's report to Congress.

My thoughts were with Hillary. It would be hard to imagine a more brutal or public humiliation. I was up in Boston, but I knew from conversations with colleagues in the White House that a grim bunker mentality had descended over the place.

So I was relieved when I was called to advance a hastily arranged trip to Ireland for the Clintons. Few places in the world offered a warmer welcome. The Irish people are renowned for giving folks in trouble the space and solace they need to come to grips with things.

They arrived at Dublin International Airport late on the night of September 3, during a rainstorm. Hillary stayed aboard the airplane until the last possible moment, then did a perfunctory handshake with the welcoming officials and ducked into the limousine. I held an umbrella over her head but didn't even have a chance to say hello.

The first time I got a good look at her, and registered what bad shape she was in, was when we arrived at the ambassador's residence in Phoenix Park, which was where the Clintons were staying.

"Welcome back to Ireland," I said gently. "We don't have anything on the schedule until late tomorrow morning, so I'll stay out of your way. Just let me know if you feel like doing anything."

"Thanks, Pat," she said, her voice as drained as her countenance. "What I really need is some rest."

"Yes, ma'am. Why don't you go on upstairs? I'll see that everything gets brought up."

She turned and walked slowly up the stairs.

The next morning I went out to the ambassador's residence a few hours early, to see if there was anything I could do. I found an unusual level of activity: presidential aides silently scurrying around, all of them looking as if they'd just seen a particularly terrifying ghost. Their fear and anxiety were palpable. The Clintons were sequestered in their suite, and from time to time one of their aides would be summoned to join them.

"What's going on here?" I asked Marsha Berry, Hillary's director of communications.

"Senator Joe Lieberman made a speech on the Senate floor yesterday afternoon. He really laid into the President on Lewinsky. It was brutal."

Until then no prominent Democrat had publicly chastised Clinton. The unspoken questions that hung in the hushed air of the ambassador's residence were: Is this the beginning of the end? Would congressional support for the President evaporate?

Lieberman's remarks had indeed been cutting. He condemned the President's actions and said: "Such behavior is not only inappropriate, it is immoral and it is harmful." He went on to say that President Clinton had "compromised his moral authority" and was deserving of "public rebuke and accountability." When he finished, Democratic Senators Bob Kerrey of Nebraska and Daniel Patrick Moynihan of New York endorsed his criticisms.

The very fact that it was Joe Lieberman leading the charge was troubling. The Clintons were very close to Lieberman. Their relationship dated back to the 1970s, when, as students at Yale Law School, they had worked on his campaign for the state legislature. Would this rebuke by a close friend signal to other Democrats that the time had come to abandon Bill Clinton?

It took some time, but Hillary finally appeared from the upstairs bedroom suite. She was wearing a navy blue suit, with a single strand of pearls. She looked a little shellshocked, as if she hadn't gotten much sleep, but she had obviously made an enormous effort to pull herself together. I was very glad we were in Ireland, where the overwhelming sentiment was one of disbelief that we Americans could make such a big deal of such a private matter. After all, the reasoning went, the man was a magnificent president, young and vital, loved and revered in Ireland and indeed around the world. Why are you hounding the poor man for his very human mistake when your country is in such excellent shape?

Hillary paid a brief visit to Trinity College to view the Book of Kells and then joined President Clinton and some prominent Dubliners for a luncheon at the Royal College of Surgeons. Afterward she did what millions of women do when they're facing a crisis: She went shopping.

Now Hillary likes to shop. I can't think of a single country we visited where she didn't fit in a little shopping if she had any time at all. But this was clearly shopping as therapy. I mean we hit the House of Ireland like a tornado. She stocked up on enough Irish linen and crystal to furnish a mansion on Washington's embassy row *and* a large house in, say, suburban New York. Then she insisted we return personally to pick up her purchases once they'd been wrapped. We came back to one of Dublin's busiest intersections at five o'clock, just as people were pouring out of their offices, and we quickly attracted a large crowd that watched with fascination as we carried out box after box after box, stuffing them into every available space in the motorcade. Hillary remained in the limousine, surrounded by her purchases. We were one box away from having to strap stuff to the roof.

That evening the Clintons hosted a small party at the ambassador's residence to thank the embassy staff for the work they'd done to coordinate the trip. To everyone's star-struck delight, U2 showed up. The band's lead singer, Bono, is incredibly popular in Ireland, one of the country's most famous, and highest paid, citizens. His soulful music and tireless efforts on behalf of the world's have-nots have earned him a special place in Irish society, which greatly values humanitarian efforts.

The whole band, and wives and girlfriends, were on hand. I escorted them into the library and got them settled as the President and First Lady finished shaking hands with embassy employees on the back lawn. When the Clintons came inside and saw the large gaggle of staff, mostly female, lurking just outside the library door, the President laughed and said, "Hey, Hillary, look at all these people standing around. What do you suppose they could possibly want?" Without waiting for an answer he added, "Why don't you all come on in with me? I'm sure they won't mind."

The cluster of staffers gleefully squeezed into the library. The President took a seat on the couch, and Hillary sat in a chair off to the side. She had perked up some, but she still wasn't hitting on all cylinders. The President was his usual gregarious self. Bono, dressed in black slacks and a black sports coat over a white satin T-shirt, presented him with an antique leather bound two-volume set of books on Irish history. "You know, President Clinton, I'm really happy we had a chance to see you today. Because I want to thank you personally for everything you're doing to bring peace to Ireland. A lot of politicians give it lip service, but you've done more than any other political leader to get both sides to take this seriously. What you're doing here, in the Middle East, and God knows where else to bring us peace is truly remarkable, and I just want you to know we appreciate your efforts."

On that up note the Clintons departed the sanctuary of Ireland for the more turbulent waters of home.

Six days later Ken Starr delivered his final report to Congress. It was 445 pages long, came with thirty-six boxes of supporting documents, and contained, according to a report leaked to the *New York Times*, "graphic depictions of sexual encounters." The scandal-hungry media and Clinton's league of enemies howled for its public release. Two days later the Republican-controlled House Judiciary Committee obliged. The report wallowed in every salacious detail of Clinton's liaisons with Monica Lewinsky, as if their trysts had been high crimes against humanity. It revealed as much about Mr. Starr as it did about President Clinton.

Fortunately the Republicans didn't know when to stop, and they overplayed their hand. Ten days later, they released President Clinton's videotaped testimony to the grand jury investigating whether or not he had lied during his sworn testimony in the Paula Jones case. If his televised statement admitting to having sex with Monica Lewinsky had been painful to watch, this was torture. The President was pale, sweaty, squirming, backed into a corner by investigators from Starr's office intent on trapping him in a lie. They won the battle but lost the war. The American people, including many Republicans, were repulsed by the video and the killer tactics of Ken Starr. Sympathy for President Clinton soared; his poll numbers rose once again—and never fell during the whole ordeal of impeachment.

Hillary's poll numbers were even higher than the President's. Two things seemed to be working in her favor. Some people sympathized with her as a woman wronged, and others admired her for standing by her husband. The Democratic party quickly realized that it had a potent weapon on its hands in the upcoming midterm elections, and she was deployed to campaign in as many close races as possible. A Democratic takeover of the House would almost certainly mean that impeachment would fail.

Hillary threw herself into the campaign for all she was worth, making speeches in district after district. About a month after the Starr report was released, we were in Allentown, Pennsylvania. It was Halloween, and I continued my holiday tradition of greeting the First Lady wearing a mask that made me appear even scarier than usual. This time it was a green monster of no particular pedigree. Hillary stepped out of her limousine, took one look, and burst out laughing. Then she had her picture taken with the monster. A week later I received a copy inscribed: "Pat—Is working for me really that bad? Anyway, thanks for everything—even if you're a little worse for wear!"

Sadly, despite Hillary's best efforts, the Democrats came up just short. Although they picked up five seats in this off-year election—the first time since 1934 that the party that controlled the White House had done so—they were still six seats short of a majority. On Tuesday, December 8, 1998, the House Judiciary Committee began hearings on four articles of impeachment against William Jefferson Clinton, the forty-second president of the United States.

Then the chickens came home to roost.

Shortly after the midterm election Speaker of the House Newt Gingrich resigned from Congress, ostensibly because of the losses his party had suffered. The real reason, however, was common knowledge in Washington. The whole time Gingrich had been trying to bring down President Clinton for an adulterous affair, he was having one himself. His relationship with Callista Bisek, a thirty-three-year-old congressional aide, was ending his second marriage. His hypocrisy was about to be unmasked, so he gave up a position of enormous power, one that he had dreamed of occupying for all his adult life and that had put him third in line for the presidency, rather than jeopardize his crusade against President Clinton.

In the end Newt was a victim of the very environment he had created. No one had done more to personalize politics and lower public discourse to the level of supermarket tabloids. He learned, a bit too late, that the politics of personal destruction cuts both ways.

Gingrich was hardly the only hypocrite among the Republican leadership. The House Judiciary Committee's impeachment hearings were presided over by Henry Hyde of Illinois, a somewhat Dickensian figure in his early seventies. He was tall with thick white hair and sharp features and a bulky body that made his movements appear awkward and halting. A self-proclaimed devout Catholic, Hyde was in perpetual high umbrage over the President's behavior. That is until it was revealed that he had carried on an affair with Cherie Snodgrass, a married mother of three young children, from 1965 to 1969, bringing about the end of her marriage. Hyde, who had been in his mid-forties at the time, called it a youthful indiscretion and demanded the FBI investigate to determine who had been the source of the story.

Gingrich and Hyde weren't the only moral crusaders unmasked. Far from it. Bob Livingston, the Louisiana Republican who was in line to replace Newt as speaker, suddenly announced, on the day the House began to debate the articles of impeachment, that he was stepping down because he had "occasionally strayed from his marriage." Turns out those occasional strays were more like frequent journeys.

Two of the nuttier members of the House, both right-wing extremists and strident Clinton critics, had their closets opened as well. Georgia Representative Bob Barr, a family values fanatic and the first to call for Clinton's impeachment, had, according to a story in the *Washington Post* on February 10, 1998, "enlivened a Leukemia Society luncheon by—as one local Georgia newspaper put it—'licking whipped cream from the chests of two buxom women.'" Barr, sponsor of the Defense of Marriage Act, was on his third wife. One ex-spouse, Gail, divulged that the vociferously antiabortion Barr had actually driven her to a clinic and paid for her abortion. Indiana Representative Dan Burton, who had called Clinton a scumbag in a meeting with the editorial board of the *Indianapolis Star* and had taunted the Clintons after the Vince Foster tragedy—even going so far as to "assassinate" pumpkins on his property in an attempt to recreate the Foster "murder"—revealed that he had fathered a child out of wedlock in the 1980s.

Then there was Republican Representative Helen Chenoweth, the Idaho firebrand. This militia-friendly extremist admitted to a six-year adulterous affair with a married associate. J. C. Watts of Oklahoma, the only African-American Republican in the House, who had once referred to certain black political leaders as welfare pimps, revealed he had fathered a child out of wedlock in 1976.

Topping it all off was David Schippers, the majority's lead counsel on the Judiciary Committee. Shippers was an old Hyde crony from Chicago, another oh-so-devout Catholic who wore a small cross on his lapel. Bearded, sanctimonious, with the self-conscious baritone of a bad actor, the guy couldn't open his mouth without invoking everyone from his friend who flew bombing missions over Europe in World War II to Lizzie Borden to God. His outrage was blistering; the fate of the nation hung in the balance! Allowing the President to get away with this would have a devastating effect on the honor and respect due the United States. The independence of the three branches of government was at stake. We could have tyranny! In a perfect ending to the Schippers saga, he too was revealed to be involved in a long-term extramarital affair. Documents filed in a court suit divulged Schippers had carried on an adulterous affair for *twenty-five years* with Nancy Ruggero, his office manager.

I found it telling that these deeply religious men never once mentioned the word "forgiveness" during the proceedings. That was left to courageous Republican Representative Amo Houghton of New York, who, in an op-ed piece in the *New York Times* explaining why he was breaking ranks with his party to vote against impeachment, ended with three simple words: "I forgive him."

I did two trips for the First Lady during this period, but perhaps most telling of her composure was a tour she took of Beach Camp in the Gaza Strip, the largest and most crowded of the Palestinian refugee camps, in an area controlled by the Hammas terrorist group. As its name suggests, Beach Camp is located on the water, a couple of miles from the center of Gaza City. Hillary insisted, to the dismay of our embassy in Tel Aviv, that she wanted to visit the camp and see for herself the conditions under which the Palestinian women and children refugees lived. We broke away from the President's traveling group and drove into the camp. The streets were narrow and dusty with squat one- and two-story houses piled hard against one another. Laundry hung on clotheslines, and people crowded the street to get a look at our motorcade. Nobody in Gaza lives in luxury, but even in such an economically challenged city these surroundings were bleak. Hillary visited a group of women involved in a microcredit program, where the loan of a hundred dollars or so helped them start cottage-based businesses. The women told her that because of the difficulty they and their husbands faced getting across the border to menial jobs in Israel, these tiny enterprises, making knitted goods and simple jewelry, were often all that stood between them and starvation.

As she had in other countries where she had visited microcredit programs, Hillary listened with rapt attention and discussed the women's hopes and dreams.

Later that afternoon at the Shawa Center, where the Palestinian National Congress was meeting to ratify a deal with Israel to swap land for peace, we had a few moments to spare, and I had a chance to chat with Hillary backstage. "Beach Camp was pretty amazing, wasn't it?" I said.

"Yes, it was. I'm amazed at how women we've seen all over the world are able to carry on under such bleak circumstances if they're given even the slightest chance. These microcredit programs are worth their weight in gold. It really puts things in perspective when you see how little it takes to keep their hope alive."

That hopeful, persevering attitude was typical of Hillary throughout the impeachment mess. She of course knew how serious the situation was, and she had been personally devastated, but she didn't let it dampen her intellectual curiosity or her commitment to supporting the struggles of women and children around the world.

The Hillary I saw on these trips was a far cry from the emotionally drained woman who had deplaned in Dublin almost four months earlier. It seemed as if she had found a way to move past the worst of her pain. She pulled herself together and went out and made public appearances at a time when most people would just have stayed at home and pulled the bedcovers up over their heads. She had a remarkable ability to use her intellectual prowess to put things in perspective. It wasn't a cold, calculating denial of the facts by any means. It was a very human and courageous desire to move on and to salvage what was good in a twenty-five-year partnership.

I'd been with her when she'd visited Mother Teresa's orphanage in the slums of New Delhi, where girl children had been abandoned because of their gender, and Pakistan, where young brides had been burned to death because their dowries were too small. We'd been to countries where girls were genitally mutilated to rob them of sexual pleasure and temptation. Then there was Beach Camp and other places where women were more subtly devalued, kept from education, health care, and participation in the political and economic systems.

Hillary really believed in the politics of meaning she'd first discussed in her speech in Austin, Texas, the day her father died. She believed in the global emancipation of women. She held resolutely to the notion that life should have a broader, common meaning and that those privileged enough to have wealth, power, and public support had an obligation to improve the lives of those less fortunate. Her determination to work for her beliefs made the impeachment saga look insignificant.

I think there were two other reasons she was able to move past all that had happened. One was her daughter. She adored Chelsea and was fiercely protective of her. She was determined to hold the family together for her and to set an example of how to respond to a terrible situation. The final reason, deeply personal, was her faith. Hillary is a regular churchgoer, and I believe she has developed a strong relationship with her God. I think this is where she found a large measure of solace and strength.

On December 12 the Judiciary Committee voted 21–16, along straight party lines, to forward four articles of impeachment to the full House for a vote. (Republican Lindsey Graham voted no on one of the articles.)

There was, however, some real suspense about whether or not the full House would impeach the President. There were two dozen or so moderate Republicans, mostly from the Northeast, who represented districts where Clinton was popular. Since the Republicans held only a twenty-two-seat edge in the House, if twelve of the moderates voted against the articles of impeachment and the Democrats held ranks, they would fail.

The days that followed were tense ones, characterized by a sense of unreality. Was this really going to happen? Were these people really going to put the country through all this division and trauma over an extramarital affair?

The Republicans argued that Clinton's "crime" was much worse than that of Henry Hyde, David Schippers, or Newt Gingrich because he lied under oath. True, he lied under oath—about his *sex life*. Boy, that's a real threat to the Republic, isn't it?

As the Republican leadership strong-armed the wavering moderates, it was like a watching a version of *Alice in Wonderland* directed by Alfred Hitchcock: completely absurd but still scary as hell.

On December 19, 1998, I sat at home in Boston and watched as the House of Representatives, for only the second time in history, voted to impeach the president of the United States. They debated for several hours and then approved two of the four articles. Article One, charging him with perjury before the grand jury, was approved 228–206, with 5 Republicans voting against it, offset by 5 Democrats who voted for. Article Two, alleging perjury in the Paula Jones case, was rejected 205–229, with 28 Republicans against and the same 5 Democrats in favor. Article Three, regarding obstruction of justice in the Jones case, was approved 221–212, with 12 Republicans against and the 5 wayward Democrats in favor. Article Four, charging the President with abuse of high office, was rejected 148–285, with 81 Republicans against and 1 lone Democrat, Mississippi's Gene Taylor, in favor.

Earlier that morning Hillary had gone to Capitol Hill to meet with the House Democratic caucus. She was enormously popular with the members, in no small measure owing to the yeoman work she had done on their behalf in the fall campaign. She addressed them in a simple, straightforward fashion and thanked them for the support they had given the President and her. She made it abundantly clear that she loved her husband and wasn't abandoning him and that they shouldn't either.

The next step was for the Senate to hold a trial and then vote on whether or not to remove Clinton from office. Here again, the outcome was never in doubt. It takes a two-thirds majority—67 senators—to remove an impeached president. The Republicans held only a 55–45 edge, and at least 4 Republican senators were expected to vote in the President's favor. The trial began on January 7, 1999.

I watched much of the trial in The Hague, where I was advancing a trip for Hillary. The very sight of those sanctimonious Republican House impeachment managers made my blood boil. My country was being humiliated over our long-simmering culture war, and it was unfolding before the eyes of the entire world. I was hurt and embarrassed.

On February 12, 1999, the Senate voted to reject both articles of impeachment. The sorry spectacle was finally over. But I fear it will haunt American politics for many decades to come.

26

SUNRISE ON THE SAHARA

March–July 1999

THERE'S NOTHING LIKE SOME GOOD RUINS TO KEEP THINGS IN perspective. Sure, we were the world's only remaining superpower, but evidence of the fallibility of power literally lay in ruins at my feet.

I'd visited Mongolia, the homeland of Genghis Khan, Rome, and Athens, and now I was in Tunisia, which when it was known as Carthage had been a great and powerful nation. The remains of all these once-vast empires served as a reminder that a thousand years from now—if by some miracle our poor beleaguered planet still supports human life—some other nation will be top dog. Our tenure as leader of the pack will live on only in history courses and guidebooks and through our artifacts, admired in museums, and our ruins tramped over by tourists.

Hillary was coming to North Africa as part of her annual spring break pilgrimage with Chelsea. After the impeachment ordeal, the trip was bathed in a particularly sweet sense of relief. The Tunis we encountered a few miles from the Carthage ruins was a bustling modern city, more European in its influences than African. It had high-rise apartment buildings overlooking the seashore and a busy commercial center.

Tunisia, in North Africa across the Mediterranean from Italy, has a fascinating history. Carthage began as a Phoenician trading center around 1100 B.C. It flourished and soon developed an intense rivalry with Rome. The two fought several wars, and it was from Carthage that Hannibal set out across the Alps with his elephants. Rome ultimately proved more powerful, laying waste to Carthage, selling its people into slavery, and sprinkling the earth with salt, then reestablishing the place as an outpost of its own empire. Once the Romans left town Carthage was ruled in turn by the Vandals and the Byzantines before the coming of Islam in A.D. 698. Most of the ruins in the country today are Roman.

When we arrived in mid-March, it was the runup to Eid al-Adha, the Feast of Sacrifice, the conclusion of the Muslim hajj (the pilgrimage to Mecca), when every family must slaughter a sheep. Sheep were *everywhere:* tied to trees, riding in the back seats of Mercedeses, lashed to the balconies of high-rise apartments, grazing on lawns in the city's fanciest neighborhoods. One didn't need to travel far to realize that the transition from third world to first wasn't yet complete.

Preparations for Hillary's visit were going smoothly, so my team of seven took the weekend off and drove south to Remada, on the edge of the Sahara. There we rented camels, engaged a guide named Mohammed, and trekked out into the desert at sunset. We rode for about two hours and spent the night at a Bedouin camp not far from the Libyan border. The camp had a buffer of desert grass all along the perimeter to keep the wind down. Our accommodations consisted of three lean-to tents, each nothing more than a stretch of canvas tied to long, crooked sticks. "Bathroom" facilities were the nearest bush, a fact less than thrilling to the three females in our party. As soon as the sun went down, the temperature dropped, and we bundled up. I'd bought a furry Bedouin garment with a hood at one of the local markets and looked like an ewok from *Star Wars.* Hey, in the middle of the desert night it's definitely function over fashion. Dinner was a rather tasty lamb and vegetable stew served around a campfire. We had a great time singing Arabic songs Mohammed gamely tried to teach us.

It got dark out there. Really dark. No light for miles and miles except for a beautiful canopy of stars that appeared so close and bright you felt you could reach up and touch them. The quiet was different too. There was total silence, broken only by the occasional snort of a camel. It was as if someone had turned off all of life's background noises, the ones we urban dwellers are so used to that we forget they're there.

In the morning we were up, shivering and trying to breathe life back into our campfire, eager to see the sunrise over the Sahara. It was awe-inspiring, and I couldn't help musing on the many places life had taken me. As a kid I never in a million years imagined I'd one day be sitting on the sands of the Sahara watching the sun come up. The sands of Cape Cod, maybe.

Hillary arrived in fine fettle. She was rested and ready to explore. She was always happy to be out seeing the world with her daughter.

The state dinner the Tunisians threw was unique because only women were allowed to attend. Men were prohibited because of a fashion show that took place after dinner in which some of the models appeared without the veils of purdah and wore dresses that didn't cover their ankles. We males couldn't be trusted to control ourselves given such fleshy temptation. This seemed like a real anachronism since the women at our hotel pool went topless.

I was in Hillary's suite before the dinner, waiting for her to finish dressing. We were a few minutes late. My cell phone rang. It was our ambassador, a career appointee. "We can't be late for this dinner. You go in there and tell Hillary to leave right now!" she screamed.

"Ambassador, the First Lady will leave when she's ready to leave and not a moment sooner. Is that clear?"

"Don't you dare talk to me like that. I want you to hand your telephone to Hillary right now so I can talk to her myself."

"I'd suggest you stop screaming at me and call the presidential palace and figure out some way to take the blame for this yourself. You're a diplomat. You know the rules. One more thing: Don't forget which government you're working for."

The ambassador had been a pain all week, often seeming more concerned with protecting Tunisian interests than American ones. I was glad I had the chance to give her a little of her own back.

Huma Abedin, Hillary's personal assistant, who had been born in Saudi Arabia, took my place at the dinner, making sure all the arrangements were in order. She reported that the event went well, although there didn't seem to be any rush among the staff to buy the conservative clothing featured in the fashion show.

One of the places the Tunisians had been pushing for the First Lady to visit was a new village about forty miles outside Tunis with the catchy and evocative name of Village 2626. I checked it out and found that it lived up to its name. It amounted to a collection of tiny cement-block houses, all painted white with blue trim. Each house was about fifteen by fifteen feet, divided into a kitchen, bathroom, bedroom, and living room. The village had replaced a collection of shanty huts, and the administration of President Ben Ali considered it a symbol of its beneficence. I hardly thought the place would wow the First Lady, but our hosts were insistent, and I acquiesced.

So the following morning we left Tunis to show the First Lady Village 2626. As we approached, we heard ever-louder chants of "Hill-a-ry! Hill-a-ry!" No, wait. That wasn't "Hill-a-ry!" It was "Ben A-li!" When we reached the village, we found the streets lined with hundreds of near-hysterical Tunisians holding up large color posters of their autocratic president, General Zine al-Abidine Ben Ali, and shouting out his name *at the tops of their lungs.* "Ben A-li! Ben A-li!" The din was incredible, and it never let up. Not for one single second did it let up. At first it was odd. Then it was annoying. Then it was migraine inducing. It drove us all crazy! These folks were being given housing by Ben Ali, and they had been told they had to show their support for him in front of the American visitors. You got the distinct impression that the ones who yelled the loudest got first choice of houses. I won't say we rushed through the tour, but we sure didn't linger. The chant was still ringing in my ears an hour later.

On her final morning in Tunisia Hillary paid a visit to the American cemetery where five thousand U.S. troops who had lost their lives in World War II's North African campaign lay buried. One of the personnel from the American embassy, a stiff-backed army colonel of around sixty who sported a chestful of medals, was in charge of the wreath laying. The colonel was an odd sort; he sometimes got this faraway look in his eye and smiled when no one had said anything funny.

Before Hillary's arrival he and I had walked among the rows and rows of austere white crosses, stretching nearly as far as the eye could see. It was a bright, clear day and early enough that the desert heat hadn't yet descended. We walked among the graves, quiet and reflective, until the colonel broke the silence. "You know, Mr. Halley, I'm personal friends with many of the men buried here," he said.

"Oh," I answered noncommittally, my mind doing some quick arithmetic. The North African campaign had ended in 1945, fifty-four years earlier; the colonel was sixty-two tops. Hmm.

Just then the colonel stopped in front of a grave and spoke: "Good morning, Johnny, how are you today? . . . Are you? I'm so glad to hear that. It's a fine morning. Guess what, lad? The First Lady is coming to visit you. . . . I know, it is exciting."

I think I knew why the colonel was posted in Tunisia.

Later we toured the Roman ruins. Afterward I walked with Hillary, the ambassador, and A. T. Smith, the head of her Secret Service detail, back to the motorcade. Hillary turned to me. "I understand you've had a rough week of it putting this trip together."

"There've been a couple of rocky spots," I answered, not sure where she was going.

"It's too bad when our own people make it more difficult," Hillary said.

All blood drained from the ambassador's face, and she did her best to pretend not to hear a comment clearly directed at her. Smith, who was looking directly at the ambassador, said to me later: "She looked like the Big Girl (Hillary) had whacked her upside of the head with a two-by-four."

Hillary had spoken. And when Hillary speaks, people listen.

But it was Hillary who would soon be doing the listening. Rumors had begun to circulate that New York's venerable Senator Daniel Patrick Moynihan was going to retire in 2000 and that Hillary was considering a run for his seat. This was an intriguing prospect, and the more I thought about it, the more sense it made.

At first I was among those who counseled her against a run. Why not take a year off and get the hell away from Washington? Decompress a little and recharge her batteries. That would still leave her a year to campaign for the Senate seat in Illinois held by a Republican, and I thought she'd have a better shot as a native daughter than as a transplant to New York. She'd just endured seven years of investigations, innuendo, and scandal. Why jump right out of the frying pan into the inferno? But as she edged closer to a decision, I began to understand her thinking. She had finally hit her stride and learned to deal with all the pressures. She had expanded the role of first lady into a bully pulpit, and she was riding high in public opinion polls. Why stop, only to have to rebuild that kind of momentum after a year out of the public spotlight? She was ready, she and New York State were a good fit, and it would give her a chance to come into her own. I told her I'd support her in whatever decision she reached.

In May I once again had the pleasure of advancing a trip the First Lady was taking to Ireland, this time to the beautiful western part of the country. She had been invited to give the commencement address at the National University of Ireland at Galway, where she was to receive an honorary doctorate. I suppose it was officially work, but I considered it an all-expenses-paid vacation.

One tradition that's different in Ireland from in the United States is the wearing of academic robes. In our country a person wears the robes of her own school when visiting another. This leads to very colorful academic processions. In Ireland everyone wears the colors of the host school. Hillary had brought her Wellesley robe and mortarboard along and was somewhat disappointed that she wouldn't get the chance to wear them.

The school sent over a robe and about a dozen hats so that Hillary could pick her favorite. A small group of us were gathered in her hotel suite just after her arrival. "Oh, goodness, will you look at all these choices," she exclaimed. Then she grabbed one of the hats and stuck it on. It was way too small and perched precariously atop her head. She looked in the mirror and said, "I *don't* think so."

She then proceeded to give us an impromptu fashion show, complete with running commentary. A traditional mortarboard was dubbed "the nutty professor look," and a rounded hat was rejected because "the only thing that's missing is a propeller on top."

She finally settled on a floppy model. Then she tilted it at a rakish angle. "Zees iz ze Parisian loo-k," she said. Then she pulled it down over one eye and purred: "And this is Bacall." Then she squared it primly front and center. "And this is the schoolmarm."

She had us all in stitches.

This was a woman on the upswing. Her immediate future was coming into focus, and the lively, witty, rambunctious Hillary we knew and loved was back.

The next time I saw her was in Orlando, Florida, in early July. The talk of a possible Senate run was now public, with many prominent Democrats urging her to take the plunge. New York City's popular Republican mayor, Rudy Giuliani, was the likely GOP nominee, and the Democrats were desperate to come up with a marquee name to try to hold the seat. Hillary was edging close to a decision, but with her usual methodical preparation. She had announced she would embark on a listening tour across New York State to hear people's concerns and to get to know the turf.

Hillary was coming to Orlando for the National Education Association's annual convention, where she was going to speak and receive the NEA's Friend of Education Award. When she landed at the airport, I had barely started up the steps to her plane when she came bounding out. "Hello, Pat!" she said as she surveyed the hot, humid tarmac. "Why do you suppose the teachers chose Florida in July?"

"Probably for the good room rates. And we want them to save as much money as possible so they can contribute to your campaign, now, don't we?"

She broke into a big smile and stepped into the limousine.

Hillary's speech to the convention was preceded by a twenty-minute video that the union had produced. It was slick, impressive, and moving as it recounted all that she had done to promote education, as first lady both of Arkansas and of the nation. It was an adrenaline-producing introduction, and the crowd ate up her speech. When she finished, by some strange coincidence the song "New York New York" began to play, the crowd went wild, and she began to work the rope line, looking every inch the candidate.

Under the music, I was sure I heard sports announcer Michael Buffer intoning: "Ladies and gentlemen, leeettt's get ready to rummmmmble."

27

EMBRACEABLE YOU

November 1999–February 2000

IN POLITICS, YOU'VE GOT TO BE CAREFUL WHOM YOU HUG. IN THE Byzantine ethnic politics of New York, you've got to be *really* careful. It was early November, and Hillary's candidacy was all but official when she hugged the wrong person, and boy, did she suddenly get an earful.

I was advancing the Petra, Jordan, segment of a trip the First Lady was taking to the Middle East, including Israel. The timing was intentional. Jews are among New York State's most powerful voting blocs, and they were a group with which Hillary had a somewhat rocky relationship. A little more than a year earlier she had expressed the belief that sooner or later Palestine would have to be granted nationhood. The Republicans in New York had been repeating her remark ad nauseam, sensing an opportunity to weaken the support Democratic candidates traditionally enjoyed among Jewish voters. Unfortunately, on this trip she made their job a whole lot easier.

Advancing Hillary, the almost candidate, was tricky. Beyond the obvious complications of balancing her two roles, there were a host of legal and ethical questions. It was decided early on that she would continue to have Secret Service protection (she will be the last first lady to have it for her entire life; Congress passed a law that future first ladies will be protected only during their husbands' terms) and would use air force jets even for campaign stops. Mindful of the legal bills and damaged reputations Ken Starr had left in his wake, we all were anxious to make sure we operated well within the letter of the law. In my case, that meant that as a government employee I would work only on trips that were part of her official duties as first lady—ergo Petra.

The ancient rose-colored city of Petra is one of the most spectacular man-made sites in the world. It consists of ancient ruins of the empire of the Nabataean people's capital city and dates to around 1500 B.C. Petra was a hub for trade and commerce, a key metropolis of the ancient civilizations of Arabia and Mesopotamia. It thrived for more than a thousand years until protracted wars with first the Romans and then Muslim armies, invading as part of their religious crusade, caused it to falter. The city was largely abandoned and was "lost" to the Western world from 1189 until it was rediscovered by the Swiss-born explorer Johann Ludwig Burckhardt in 1812.

What remains are principally the elaborate tombs the Nabataeans carved into the red rocks of the surrounding cliffs. Building them would be an amazing engineering achievement today. It's incredible to think that these monuments were constructed more than a thousand years ago.

You enter Petra by hiking through the siq, a mile-long rock fissure with 100-foot walls that are just far enough apart to allow an oxcart to pass. The walls are so close together that you have to crane your neck up to see the sun. At the very end of the siq you turn a corner and emerge into a natural square that's dominated by an enormous tomb called the Treasury, a 130-foot-high structure with six Doric columns, carved into the red stone and topped with an urn believed to contain ancient treasure. It's a breathtaking sight. The Treasury was made famous when it appeared in the film *Indiana Jones and the Lost Crusade*.

As amazing as Petra was by day, it was even more spectacular at night. Our guides led us slowly through the siq, accompanied by eerie flute music. The only illumination was the flickering of candle-powered lanterns. We reached the end and turned into the large open square. The Treasury was bathed in soft light, and the cliffs rose around us, candles flickering in some of the high tombs. I felt goose bumps at the back of my neck and could imagine myself entering boisterous, magical Petra a thousand years ago. Now that's what I call a walk-through.

Two days later Hillary arrived aboard the king's helicopter, which he had graciously lent her for the day to spare her the long drive from Amman.

We had vehicles lined up to take her to the top of the siq to begin her tour, but she felt like stretching her legs and decided to walk the half mile. The minister of tourism, who was on hand as an official greeter, immediately dispatched an aide who caught up with us on the way down the trail with a string of horses.

"Pat, what are those horses for?" Hillary whispered to me, eyeing the approaching equines warily.

"They want you to ride them into the city. I don't recommend it since the sight of you on horseback with everyone else walking would be a little much."

"I agree. See if you can get rid of them without offending anyone."

The minister began a sales pitch. "It's hot, and these trails are tricky. The First Lady would be much better off on a horse. That way she won't twist her ankle."

"Oh, Minister, that's very kind of you," I said before lowering my voice. "Can I have a private word with you?"

"Certainly."

We stepped away.

"Look, I don't want this to get out because it could be somewhat embarrassing at home, but Mrs. Clinton is allergic to horses. If she gets on one, she'll be coughing and sneezing all day. We don't want that, do we?"

My little prevarication worked. He looked at me knowingly and winked. The horses disappeared.

Hillary and Chelsea were accompanied by Jordan's new queen, Her Majesty Queen Rania, and by the king's sister, Princess Aisha Bint Hussein. The press corps trailing us was acting particularly rambunctious, and I asked Marsha Berry, Hillary's communications director, what had put the bee in their bonnet.

"We had a little incident yesterday with Suha Arafat. They're dying to put Hillary on the spot. I suppose we'll have to make a statement at some point."

Marsha then explained that the day before, at a joint appearance in the West Bank with Suha Arafat, the wife of the Palestinian leader had caused quite a controversy when she said in the course of her lengthy remarks: "It is important to point out the severe damage caused by intensive daily use of poison gas by Israeli forces in past years has led to increased cancer rates among Palestinian women and children." It was one line in a broad-ranging speech, and it is suspected she meant to say "tear gas" instead of "poison gas," but the impact of accusing the Israelis of "poisoning" Palestinian women and children was outrage. When she concluded her remarks, Suha Arafat embraced Hillary, a not uncommon gesture in that part of the world. The hug from hell had been duly recorded by the assembled media. Already the *New York Post,* owned by the right-wing Rupert Murdoch, was trying to use the incident to the conservatives' advantage.

We made our way into the siq and began the long descent into Petra. Our Secret Service were out in front of us, and I sure hoped none of our agents or the Jordanians felt the need to fire his weapon, because one round let loose in that long stone corridor could kill a dozen people before it stopped ricocheting.

As we neared the dramatic turn into the square where the Treasury was located, I stopped the massive entourage and after no small amount of pleading, directing, and arm waving, convinced all but Hillary, Chelsea, the queen, and the princess to hold back so we could take a picture of their entering Petra. Afterward we left the square and passed a beautiful amphitheater.

"Pat, I'd like to get a picture of my whole traveling staff here," Hillary said, gesturing to the White House photographer.

We lined up on the old stones of the amphitheater. I looked around for someone to take a shot with my camera. Chelsea offered, a typical Chelsea thing to do, but we wanted her to be in the picture too. Princess Aisha, overhearing our conversation, graciously took my camera and did the honors.

It was a poignant moment because we realized that in all probability this was to be our last overseas trip together. Hillary's traveling circus was playing its last show, and the battle-tested team of people who supported her, from the White House, State, and the military, was taking its final bow. We'd been together from the frozen tundra of Russia and Norway to the jungles of Africa and the sands of the Sahara. Somehow, crisscrossing New York for the next year just didn't seem to have the same appeal. The world travel had been fun while it lasted and worth every day of jet lag and every linguistic and culinary challenge we'd had to overcome. This team had seen a lot of the world, and a lot of the world had been exposed to Hillary.

Our next stop was at the ruins of a Byzantine church where ancient scrolls had been found and were being translated. Hillary was to present a grant from the United States to help with the effort. We had the press assembled to cover the event, but the journalists had another topic on their minds, the already infamous hug.

"Mrs. Clinton, how could you embrace someone who made such derogatory remarks about Israel?" "How much damage do you think this is going to do to your Senate campaign?" "Are you going to apologize to America's Jews?"

Hillary listened with her face set. Then she said, "I was there in my capacity as first lady, not as a potential candidate for the Senate. Everyone who supports this effort toward resolving outstanding issues among the parties should refrain from inflammatory rhetoric and baseless accusations. We do not believe that any kind of public inflammatory statements or excessive rhetoric is helpful to the peace process."

The press wasn't buying it, and the rat-a-tat-tat barrage of shouted questions continued. We had to cut off the questioning and move Hillary out of there. The minefield of being both the first lady and a political candidate had just seen its first explosion.

She had made a political mistake, not a diplomatic one. The proper reaction of a first lady to Mrs. Arafat's remarks was clear: Be as demure as possible so as not to exacerbate an already difficult situation. The Arab-Israeli peace process was at a delicate stage. However, a political candidate would be expected to denounce the words and the speaker in the strongest possible terms.

The incident became a major embarrassment for the campaign. But if New York Republicans thought they could scare her out of the race, they were wrong. Ten weeks after we returned from Petra, I got a call to help organize Hillary's official announcement that she would be a candidate for the U.S. Senate from New York.

The level of expectations was unique for a first-time candidate. She was also by no means assured of victory. Rudy Giuliani was already attacking her positions and her "carpetbagger" status and was making not so oblique references to what he termed her ethical troubles. On the other hand, she was *Hillary,* hero to many. Plus she'd raised a prodigious amount of money, which never hurts. The race was drawing massive national and international coverage, and analysts had deemed it likely to be closer and more hotly contested than even the presidential race.

The announcement event was going to be held in a gym at State University of New York at Purchase, in suburban Westchester County, just north of the city. It would be a seminal occasion for Hillary. For the first time, after a long career of tirelessly supporting her husband and countless other candidates, she would be speaking on her own behalf. Having to shift gears like that isn't easy. You have to go from "we should elect" to "I want your support," and for the first time you speak to your audiences in the first person: "I will fight to ensure better education for your children." With so many people watching and so much at stake it was critical that the event run flawlessly.

I was doing the gig on vacation time, not wanting to generate any headlines about government employees helping the First Lady's bid. This restriction would severely limit the amount of time I could spend on the campaign trail for her, but it allowed me to participate at critical junctures. A large part of me wanted to play a more significant role, but I also understood that what she needed most were New Yorkers, who really knew the lay of the land, and not her Boston Boys.

Saturday morning, the day before the event, I was caught up in the whole thing, having a blast, running around the gym, making calls on my cell phone, worrying, triple-checking details, when it suddenly hit me: I was not doing this for Bill Clinton or some other candidate the First Lady was endorsing. I was doing it for Hillary herself. My gal was running for the United States Senate. It was another goose bump moment.

I couldn't help recalling my initial reluctance to work for Hillary, in part because she was a secondary, someone related to the candidate, rather than the candidate himself. Now she was the principal about to stand before the electorate and face its decision. I was immensely proud of her and knew that she'd knock them dead.

The day of the event dawned clear and very cold. As the press began to set up, a Billy Joel CD of "The Piano Man" was playing over and over and *over* again. I'd been at the gymnasium for about eight hours and thought I'd go crazy if I heard the song one more time. I told the soundman to change it. He pressed a button on his mixing board, and we were treated to Joel's "Captain Jack." No one paid any attention to the song; the doors wouldn't open for another ninety minutes; Hillary was still at her house in Chappaqua. I was shocked when Mayor Giuliani called a press conference the next day to denounce Hillary for playing "Captain Jack" at her announcement because the song, according to the mayor, aggrandized drug abuse. It was a totally bogus attack, but that was the tone the Republicans were determined to take.

The campaign's crowd-building efforts had paid off, and there were *a lot* of people. With every seat in the house filled we still had a long line pressing against the front door. The fire marshal was on hand with a clicker, and he informed me we had reached our limit.

I grabbed a bullhorn: "Ladies and gentlemen, the fire marshal has just informed me that the gymnasium has reached its legal capacity. If you'll be so kind as to go to the auditorium we've set aside across the campus, you'll get a terrific view of everything on closed-circuit TV. Thank you for your cooperation."

My thanks were premature. These were New Yorkers, used to (1) lines and (2) getting their way. They didn't budge, and it took me three or four increasingly desperate and pleading announcements before they began to accept the facts and reluctantly make their way to the overflow auditorium.

Hillary's speech went off without a hitch, and the event looked great on television. It was carried live on four channels, an unprecedented level of coverage. She acknowledged that it was likely to be a brutal campaign, with endless rehashes of the various scandals the Clinton enemies had investigated over the past eight years, but she made her point with humor. "I know it's not going to be an easy campaign, but hey, dis is New YAWK."

The crowd erupted into cheers and laughter.

28

PUSH COMES TO SHOVE

May 2000

BY MAY THE CAMPAIGN WAS IN FULL SWING, AND THE POLLS SHOWED A seesawing race between Hillary Clinton and Rudy Giuliani. One day Hillary would be up by three or four points; the next it would be the mayor by the same margin. As usual, the New York State electorate was breaking into three distinct groups. New York City was overwhelmingly for the First Lady, as was to be expected in that Democratic stronghold. The city's suburbs were solidly for Giuliani—again, no surprise. Where things were interesting was in the battle for the upstate vote. This massive region, which stretches from fifty miles north of Manhattan up to the Canadian border and west to Buffalo, is usually a slam dunk for the GOP. Not this time. Hillary had been courting it with a passion, visiting the small cities, towns, and villages and winning votes the old-fashioned way: shaking hands, attending county fairs, and dropping in at local coffee shops. In this respect she was borrowing a page from her husband's play-book. On more than one occasion, I'd heard the President repeat his maxim that a hand shaken is a vote won and quote county election results from his runs for governor in which he believed an extra hour spent greeting folks had provided the winning margin. Hillary's hard work was paying off. Political pros were amazed at how competitive the race was upstate.

I hadn't seen her since the announcement in February. I was thrilled when the campaign called and asked me to take some of my vacation time to run her operation at the State Democratic Convention in Albany.

There are certain mileposts in any candidacy, and officially securing the nomination for U.S. senator would be a big one for Hillary. How the convention played, in the media and among the Democratic faithful who would be in attendance, was critically important. There had been some halting moments early in her campaign, and she had been criticized for being disorganized or less than fully engaged. Most of these missteps were attributable to the fact that she was a first-time candidate, and despite her blue-chip backing from the President, it was her own political organization, not his, that was running her Senate bid. However, the campaign was coming together nicely by the beginning of May, and the convention was an opportunity for her organization to show its stuff. It wanted to turn the traditionally low-key event into a splashy show of support.

My main frame of reference for state Democratic conventions was Massachusetts, where I'd played a major role in over a dozen. In the Bay State these affairs were big, noisy, bare-knuckle blowouts with over five thousand delegates and another twenty-five hundred alternates. Candidates typically spent many months and a tremendous amount of money courting votes. During the convention each candidate set up a sophisticated whip system to monitor and influence floor votes, and the party's power blocs, such as labor and teachers, played major roles. The stakes were high because without 15 percent of the delegate vote a candidate couldn't get on the ballot. Moreover, because Massachusetts was such a heavily Democratic state, winning the primary was often tantamount to winning the election.

I assumed that New York, being a large, diverse, and sophisticated state, had conventions that were just as intense as Massachusetts. I was wrong. The only delegates were the three hundred members of the State Democratic Committee, and the last convention had been held in a hotel ballroom and had drawn about five hundred people. Hillary was about to change all that. The press corps alone had already reached three hundred, and the campaign was shooting for a crowd of ten thousand.

The convention was being held at the Pepsi Arena in downtown Albany, just across the highway from the Hudson River. Home to the city's professional basketball and arena football franchises, it seats about fifteen thousand and had room for maybe a thousand more on the arena floor. My thoughts quickly turned from the political skulduggery of a floor fight to the challenge of filling all those seats. I reviewed the state party's crowd-building efforts and called Hillary's campaign headquarters in Manhattan to see how many bodies it was planning to produce.

I quickly learned that Hillary enjoyed enthusiastic and unequivocal support of party leaders across the state. Folks were ecstatic she'd chosen New York as her new home. Judith Hope, the chairperson of the party, and her staff were working like demons to ensure the success of Hillary's candidacy. There was real electricity surrounding the campaign.

Reassured that there would be a large and friendly crowd, I turned my attention to producing the show, with the goal of creating maximum excitement in the hall. I chose the stirring theme from *The Natural* for Hillary's entrance. Then I worked with the lighting people. As soon as Hillary's name was announced, the hall would go dark and the music would start. Six spotlights would come up and begin sweeping the crowd as the music built. Fifteen seconds into the piece, the music takes a dramatic upbeat, and at that moment all six spots were to converge on the stage—and Hillary appears! I was sure the impact of the lights and music would be thrilling and the crowd would go wild. After her speech we'd bring up the *Chariots of Fire* theme music and let loose a massive balloon and confetti drop. With a campaign volunteer playing the part of the First Lady, we practiced the moves over and over until everyone had them down perfectly.

There were conflicting rumors about whether or not the President would be on hand. It didn't matter too much to me one way or the other; the evening was designed in such a way that we could easily accommodate him. The one downside of his coming was that everyone entering the arena would have to go through a metal detector, possibly extending the time it would take to fill all those seats, but even that was manageable. The night before the convention we got what was supposedly the final decision from the White House: The President would be staying in Washington. However, I'd been through such debates before and suspected it was his political advisers, not the President, who had made the call. The Bill Clinton I knew would never miss such an important moment in Hillary's life. So despite their statement that he wouldn't attend, I began to make plans for his appearance in Albany.

The convention was scheduled to start at five o'clock. About eleven that morning I got a panic-stricken call from Rob Rosen, the director of presidential advance. "He's coming to Albany," Rob said. "I'm sorry for the short notice, but he insisted. You've got to do whatever you can to make this work."

"Don't worry about a thing," I said. "Just get him to the arena. I'll handle everything else."

I left a short while later to meet Hillary at the airport. As she emerged from the plane, I said, "Hello, I'm Pat Halley, and I'll be your advance man today."

She laughed and gave me a big hug. "Pat, it's great to see you. I've missed you."

"I bet you say that to all the advance men."

I was thrilled to see that she was confident and relaxed, as wasn't always the case before a big speech. And this was a big speech. If she could fire up these folks, they'd go home to cities and towns all over the state, roll up their sleeves, and get to work for her candidacy. Sure, they all were Democrats to begin with, but in a close campaign, enthusiasm can provide the winning margin.

Our first event was the state's firefighters' union rally, held at a restaurant in Rockefeller Plaza, where she picked up their endorsement. The place was jam-packed, and Hillary got a thunderous ovation that further boosted her already high spirits. Then it was off to the convention for a reception hosted by Sheldon Silver, speaker of the state assembly. Hillary shook about three hundred hands. I was amazed at how much she'd loosened up as a campaigner and how she, like her husband, now seemed to feed off the energy of the people who came to see her.

While the reception was going on backstage, the crowd was entering the arena itself. The turnout was huge, and people were still waiting in line when the fire marshal cut us off. The count: fifteen thousand, exceeding all expectations. Once again Hillary had demonstrated her drawing power, even on a weeknight in an upstate city.

Hillary was rehearsing her speech in the holding room when the President arrived, and I led him from his motorcade through the backstage corridors to his wife. He was mobbed along the way by the movers and shakers of New York politics. I remember supermodel Christie Brinkley looking awestruck and beautiful.

The convention program got bogged down and ran longer than we'd expected. The wait in the holding room stretched to a couple of hours. My plan was to have the President enter first and take his seat on the stage so

Hillary could have her grand entrance all to herself. Then the Clintons decided they'd like to go on together. I said it was fine with me and asked the President if he wanted to be briefed on the stage directions. He was preoccupied reviewing Hillary's speech and said he would figure it out when he got there. This made me a little nervous because everything was timed to the second, but you don't argue with the President. At least I hadn't up until then. Ten minutes later that changed.

As Judith Hope wound up her introduction, I led the Clintons down the now-empty corridor to the backstage area. The stage had been designed with two tiers, and as we mounted the second tier, both Secret Service details dropped off and took positions about twenty feet away. The three of us were standing behind the curtain as Judith finished, bringing the crowd to their feet by announcing what everyone knew: Hillary had won the nomination. The lights went out; the crowd began to cheer wildly. The music swelled, and the spotlights swept the crowd.

Hillary knew the drill and was waiting patiently for my signal to enter. The President didn't know what was happening and began demanding to go on. "Let's go. You're waiting too long. We have to go out *now*," he growled.

"Not yet. Wait until I give you the signal!" I said, moving to block his way.

"Damn it, Pat! You're being too cute by half. We're losing them! *Let's go!*" he screamed over the roaring crowd. Then he shoved me, trying to push past me onto the stage.

I knew, as did Hillary, that if they went out at that point they'd be entering in the dark. It was critical that they wait for the music to peak and the spotlights to converge.

The President, who is a big man, shoved me again, one time too many. I was working for Hillary, and I wasn't going to let *anyone* screw up her entrance. I shoved him back. Hard. He shoved me. Hard. I shoved him. Harder. Both of us meant it. I was in a fight with the leader of the free world. The Secret Service watched in horror. Hillary hissed, "Stop it, boys!"

At that very moment the music hit the cue spot, and I pulled back the curtain. The President instantly regained his composure and escorted Hillary onto the stage to wave after wave of adulation from the crowd. I stood behind the curtain rubbing my burning shoulders.

After Hillary's speech and a boisterous demonstration the Clintons left the stage, and we headed back to the holding room. The President put his arm around me as we walked down the hall. "That was a great show, Pat. You did a magnificent job."

Believe me it took everything I had to hold my tongue, but I managed to keep it to a simple "Thank you, Mr. President."

I mean, can you believe this guy? One minute he's beating the shit out of me, and the next thing you know he's my best buddy. That's President Clinton in a nutshell.

Back in the holding room he was more excited than Hillary, who was clearly relieved to have the speech behind her and was relaxing quietly. He was holding court, telling stories about his exploits as a political organizer in Connecticut during the McGovern campaign.

We left the hall and drove to a nearby hotel, where Hillary was going to make brief remarks to a postconvention party. We entered through the loading dock where the trash was stored, and it stank. "There's that Secret Service smell again," the President said as we scurried up the stairs.

His agents, who rarely let him enter a building through the front door, were used to this line and took his good-natured ribbing in stride. It was impossible to stay mad at the guy—unless you were a right-wing politician who made a career out of it—and I'd already forgiven him for nearly messing up Hillary's big moment.

The ballroom was packed, hot, and sweaty. Hillary was onstage, joined by the President and just about every elected Democrat in the state. In the middle of all the sound and fury, I was struck by her poise and confidence. Even surrounded by all those heavyweights, it was Hillary whose star shone brightest.

I was immensely proud of her and marveled at how far she'd come from the day I first met her in Port Chester. The woman who had viewed the handshaking and the small talk as work was gone, replaced by a political dynamo. She'd always been able to win people over with her brainpower, but now she was attracting them with her gracious presence. She was finally comfortable letting people see the real Hillary, the complex, driven, and deeply humane woman I had come to respect and love.

29

DON'T STOP THINKING
ABOUT TOMORROW

November 2000

THERE ARE FEW THRILLS IN THE WORLD COMPARABLE TO THE LATE moments of a winning campaign. As the days grow shorter and the summer heat gives way to fall's crisp air, you can *feel* the attention of the electorate focusing on you. The excitement builds, and the adrenaline rush gets more and more intense. It's a good thing too. Because by that stage of the campaign the candidate and everyone around her have become numb. The only thing that keeps you going is the energy you take from your crowds. But the euphoric sense that the finish line is in sight, tantalizingly close, is tempered by a nagging urge to do that one more senior citizen event or shake the one last hand that could spell the difference between victory and defeat.

It had been a tumultuous six months. In May, Giuliani had dropped out of the race because he was battling prostate cancer. He had been replaced by a little-known Long Island congressman, Rick Lazio, who was boyish and appealing, but unseasoned and nowhere near as skilled as Giuliani. His campaign, which raised *fifty million* dollars, much it from out-of-state Hillary haters, consisted mostly of attacks on her and a focus on the fact that he'd had the good fortune to be born in New York. He made an enormous mistake in their first debate when, in clear violation of the rules, he crossed the stage, brandishing an agreement to forgo soft money, leaned in close to Hillary, and demanded that she sign it. He came across as belligerent and bullying.

Then there were the push polls. A push poll is a modern-day political dirty trick. A voter is called by a research firm hired by one campaign and asked a question about the opposing candidate that is phrased in a misleading or derogatory manner. The ostensible reason is to see if a voter's mind is changed after hearing the negative. In reality it's just a ruse to dish up dirt.

The push poll calls in Hillary's race were especially vicious. Newspapers reported that the Republican-sponsored research firm asked voters if they knew that "Hillary Clinton supports terrorist organizations, like the one that caused the death of the sailors on the USS *Cole*." It was a reference to the tragic attack on October 12, 2000, on a U.S. Navy ship anchored in Yemen that claimed the lives of nineteen sailors. To suggest Hillary had been complicit in a terrorist act was ludicrous and offensive. The remark was intended to have a second edge as well since the "terrorist organization" line was a reference to her observation a couple of years earlier that a Palestinian state in the Middle East seemed inevitable. Her opponents hoped to drive a wedge between her and New York's key Jewish constituency.

While the content of the push poll was inflammatory and offensive, the very fact the Republicans had stooped so low was encouraging; it was a sign they were desperate. Hillary's slight lead in the polls, steady throughout the long, hot summer, was holding. Now it was crunch time.

I had saved as much vacation time as possible and in late October presented myself to the campaign as available for the duration. Hillary was making a bus swing through key upstate cities, and I was asked to put on events in Albany and Schenectady.

I was reunited with the folks who had helped me put on the convention, and we went exploring for possible sites. We chose a delicatessen in Schenectady and then decided on a senior citizen event, followed by a college rally in Albany. The rally was going to be the last event of the cross-state tour, so we wanted it to be big.

I stood on the sidewalk outside Gershon's Deli and waited for Hillary's campaign bus. The last of fall's leaves were blowing across the streets of downtown Schenectady, it was overcast, and there was a definite chill in the air. When the bus arrived, I bounded aboard and greeted Hillary and Chelsea. I hadn't seen Hillary since the middle of July, and I was somewhat taken aback by how worn out she looked. Her face lacked its usual color, and sleep deprivation had left bags under her eyes. This was a woman who was pushing herself to the limits of physical endurance. But her spirit wasn't flagging, and she greeted me warmly. "Patti told me you're going to be around for the rest of the campaign, and I'm thrilled."

"Me too," I replied. "It hasn't been easy sitting on the sidelines in Boston while you're out here having all this fun."

"What have we got here?" she asked, gesturing to the deli and the crowd gathering on the sidewalk.

I immediately slipped into the familiar role of lead advance and began my briefing. It seemed like old times. A crowd. An event. A busy day of campaigning. And just enough energy to get through it all.

We had stacked a few people into Gershon's so the place wouldn't seem empty in the lull time between the breakfast and lunch rushes, and Hillary and Chelsea went from table to table shaking hands and sharing a few words. Word spread that she was in the neighborhood, and after she'd sampled some hot pastrami for the cameras, she emerged to a cheering throng. There were a couple of forlorn Lazio supporters at the edge of the crowd. The Hillary I'd worked with as first lady would have waved politely and retreated to her limousine. Hillary the Senate candidate waded into the crowd with gusto, shaking hands and posing for countless snapshots. Then she surveyed the street, suggested we visit some of the other merchants, and proceeded to go from store to store saying hello. When she reached the end of the block, she stopped and let the reporters gather around.

"I'm happy to be in Schenectady today, and I really appreciate the support the people here are showing for my campaign," she said. "I'd be happy to take any questions."

The knot of reporters inched closer, some trying to position their microphones near her mouth, others jostling to get the best picture. It was just the kind of encounter I'd spent eight years trying to avoid. Hillary hated being mobbed, and the press was the worst. Now she was inviting it. My, how things had changed.

I joined Hillary, Chelsea, Kelly Craighead, and the rest of the gang for the ride from Schenectady to Albany. It was a tired but happy group. Hillary closed her eyes and leaned back in her seat for a few minutes. When she awoke from her catnap, she asked Kelly to place a call to a newspaper editor she was courting for an endorsement. When Kelly got through, Hillary took the phone.

"I'm proud of the campaign we've run, and I'd really love to have your support," she said, gathering steam as she went. "There's a lot the next senator can do for New York, particularly upstate. I see so many opportunities to create jobs, promote economic activity, and improve education. I've learned a lot in the past few months about the incredible unfulfilled potential of this region, and I've tried to make that one of the central themes of my campaign."

She listened intently as the editor posed a question.

"I can't speak for my opponent or his supporters. I have no control over what they choose to do or not do. But I've spent my time trying to convince people that we can do better. That we should come together to build, not spend all our energy tearing each other apart. They can attack all they want, but in the end I think people want someone who's listening to them and will work on their behalf. Your paper has been particularly astute at picking up that difference between me and my opponent and pointing it out to your readers. I hope you'll take the next step now and give me your endorsement." She closed with some personal chitchat and hung up.

Our rally was at the College of St. Rose in Albany, a Catholic school with several thousand students. We held it in the gymnasium, the largest building on campus. It was packed to the rafters with over two thousand screaming supporters who had come to cheer the next senator from the great state of New York. Hillary was introduced by Mayor Gerald Jennings and came bounding up onto the stage to the strains of Tina Turner's "Simply the Best." The thundering ovation shook the building. I stood stage right and surveyed the crowd. College students. Senior citizens. Union members in windbreakers. Small children with their parents. White folks. Black folks. Latinos. A sprinkling of Asians. All screaming at the top of their lungs and waving Hillary signs or American flags. It was quite a sight, and it was all for her.

Hillary wrapped up her speech and came off the stage to "Happy Days Are Here Again," a song that had served another New Yorker, Franklin Delano Roosevelt, well in his campaigns sixty years earlier. The crowd surged forward to shake her hand.

A week to go, a lead in the polls, and support that was growing every day. It was beginning to look as if Hillary were going to make history. Again.

So it ended, roughly 350 miles from where it all began. After nine years of nearly nonstop travel with Hillary Rodham Clinton, thirty-six countries, twenty-five states, and close to a million miles, we stood at the finish line of the 2000 Senate race.

I couldn't help recalling the trepidation I'd felt when Steve Graham first recruited me to help advance the wife of our presidential nominee. Her media image and reputation among political operatives was less than stellar, and she was only the *wife* of the candidate, damn it, the little-known spouse of a governor from a small southern state, while I was someone who worked only for the main attraction and even then only when I felt like it.

We'd shared a lot in those intervening years. The incredible euphoria of winning the most powerful and coveted job in the world. The satisfaction of seeing Chelsea grow from an awkward child into a confident, graceful young lady. Travel to the most beautiful and exotic reaches of the globe. Close encounters with some of the most interesting and powerful people in the world. A best-selling book. A Grammy Award for the recorded version of *It Takes a Village*. A newspaper column read by millions. Scandal. Death. Betrayal. The loss of a parent. A vengeful prosecutor zealously seeking to destroy her.

Now she was a day away from winning a seat in the U.S. Senate representing the second-biggest state in the country. Exhausted and barely able to press on, she still exuded that magical aura that had captivated me in a church hall in Port Chester nine years earlier and never let me go.

Hillary spent her final day on the campaign trail flying around upstate before returning home for one last stop in Manhattan. She did events in Buffalo, Albany, Jamestown, and finally Rochester. Our event in Rochester was a rally at an elementary school in the city's Brighton neighborhood.

The French Road Elementary School was a model of what good public education was all about, the type of school Hillary loved to visit as first lady. It had an active student body, an engaged and committed group of parents, and an inspired principal in the person of Steven Schafheimer. The school's students tested well above the state average and had raised more money in the past two years for the American Heart Association than any other school in the country. It was located in one of those swing suburban areas that would decide the election, and it was anxious to host Hillary for her last upstate event.

The sun was just beginning to drop toward the horizon as Hillary's small air force jet rolled to a stop at the Rochester airport. It had been a warm day and looked as if it were going to be a crisp, clear night. If only the weather would hold for another twenty-four hours. Voters, particularly Democrats, like good weather.

I boarded and found a relaxed, upbeat, exhausted Hillary. She had Chelsea along, and that always lifted her spirits.

"Welcome to Rochester, the last stop on your magical mystery tour!" I said.

"Well, if it isn't Patrick Halley!" Hillary called out. "Fancy meeting you here."

"Hey, Hillary, I never miss Rochester in November."

By this stage of the campaign she'd asked the Secret Service to forgo the armored limousine and was traveling in a minivan. It was more spacious and comfortable, and her aides were able to ride with her.

It was a relatively short ride from the airport to the school. When we were about a mile away I noticed cars parked along the side of the road and people walking. Many were carrying Hillary for Senate signs, and most had small children with them. They turned and cheered as our little motorcade passed by.

The school had a massive front lawn, and it was jammed with thousands of people. We drove carefully through the path the local police had cleared and pulled up to the entrance. When the door to Hillary's van slid open, the crowd pressed forward, and a roaring cheer went up. A thousand points of light lit the gathering dusk as cameras flashed.

Hillary emerged and stood up tall. I could sense the gathering force of her energy, emotion, and focus. She began shaking hands. It was bedlam as people reached over one another from deep in the crowd, trying desperately to touch her. Mothers held up their small babies, and teenagers kept up an ear-piercing shriek. Whatever cobwebs of exhaustion remained were swept away as the crowd's energy pumped pure adrenaline to Hillary's heart.

The gymnasium was packed way beyond capacity, and the cafeteria, where we had set up a closed-circuit feed for the overflow, was full. The fire marshal, who had been as generous as he possibly could about letting people in, had finally shut the building, leaving close to a thousand people outside. This crowd was big. Really big.

Hillary took the stage to a rousing ovation and stood by as eleven-year-old Sean Beckett welcomed everyone and introduced Senator Chuck Schumer. The consummate pro, Schumer knew he wasn't the star attraction and kept his remarks brief. He closed with a warm introduction of the candidate. Hillary stepped to the podium and waited for the cheers to die down. Then she leaned slightly forward to the microphone. "I'd like everyone, particularly the young girls seated up front here on the floor, to notice something."

With a sweep of her arm she indicated the people sharing the stage with her: the local members of Congress, the president of the town council, the town supervisor, the town clerk, the chair of the school board, and the president of the teachers' union.

"With the exception of Senator Schumer, Principal Schafheimer, and Sean Beckett, whom I'd like to thank for that lovely introduction, we're all women. And that's all right," she said with a chuckle, "because we believe in affirmative action, and we *welcome* the men who join us on this stage today."

The crowd roared with laughter and burst into applause. She'd made a major point. Women had come a long way in politics and in society in general, and she'd played a part in that. She dived into her stump speech.

Afterward Hillary shook hands in the gymnasium, and then she went to the cafeteria to say a few words and shake even more hands. All told she took about forty-five minutes, so I was astounded when we exited the building to see a thousand or more people still waiting in the dark, hoping to catch a glimpse of her. They'd been there for more than two hours and hadn't even been able to hear what was going on inside. Hillary shook as many hands as she could, until I told her we were running late and gently insisted we really had to get back to the airport.

We stood on the tarmac at the steps to her plane as the staff boarded and the stewards retrieved her books and briefcase from the van. Chelsea said thanks and gave me a big hug before climbing aboard.

Then Hillary and I stood there alone, bathed in light from a streetlamp. "I've been around a lot of these, and I have a real good feeling about tomorrow," I said. "You're going to win, and I don't even think it's going to be close."

"Let's hope you're right. I've been feeling good about this the last few days too." She leaned forward and embraced me, looking right into my eyes. "God bless you, Pat. You've been here with me since the beginning. I'm so grateful."

My throat began to stick, and I could feel a lump in my chest. "I'm proud of you and appreciate your letting me be a small part of it."

She gave my hand a squeeze, walked up the steps, and turned and waved to the people watching through the windows of the terminal. The hatch was secured, and the plane taxied out to the runway. A few moments later I heard the roar of the jet engines as it came hurtling down the runway, lifted off, and began to gain altitude. I was just able to make out the wheels as the pilot brought them up into the body of the aircraft.

Hillary was on her way, and as far as I was concerned, that was a great thing for America.

〜

INDEX